LEARN
GERMAN
(DEUTSCH)
THE FAST AND FUN WAY

by Paul G. Graves, Ph.D.
University of Colorado

Heywood Wald, Coordinating Editor
Chairman, Department of Foreign Languages
Martin Van Buren High School, New York

To help you pace your learning, we've included
stopwatches *like the one above* throughout
the book to mark each 15-minute interval.
You can read one of these units each day
or pace yourself according to your needs.

BARRON'S

CONTENTS

All inquires should be addressed to:
Barron's Educational Series, Inc.
250 Wireless Boulevard
Hauppauge, New York 11788

Library of Congress Catalog Card No. 83-26643

International Standard Book No. 0-8120-2855-4

Library of Congress Cataloging-in-Publication Data
Graves, Paul G.
  Learn German the fast and fun way.

  1. German language—Conversation and phrase books—
English. I. Title.
PF3121.G72 1985 438.3'421 83-26643
ISBN 0-8120-2855-4

PRINTED IN THE UNITED STATES OF AMERICA

56   880   15 14

To my wife, Eva Alkalay Graves

Cover and Book Design   Milton Glaser, Inc.
Illustrations   Juan Suarez

Major Sites, Munich

Congratulations, dear friend! Buying this book was a splendid idea. You will enjoy learning a new and beautiful language.

Beautiful? Yes, I know; people have been made to believe that Italian is more melodious, French more elegant, Spanish more virile—but who wants to sing, wear tails or be macho all the time?

I have it on good authority (my own) that German is a down-to-earth, no-nonsense, yet at the same time surprisingly poetic language that you will love to learn.

Let's lay to rest some misconceptions.

No. **Donaudampfschiffahrtsgesellschafts-kapitänswitwe** (widow of a captain of the Danube steamship company) is not the longest word known. There is a place in Wales whose Welsh name is longer by a couple of inches.

No. Speaking German won't give you a sore throat. I've been practicing it for years and to no ill effect. Like the Scots and the Dutch, Germans cherish their gutturals.

No. It's not true that the average German male wears short leather pants, likes to yodel, and feeds on sausages, potatoes and sauerkraut.

On the other hand.

Yes. It's true that German is closely related to English, and that you will easily recognize hundreds of words.

Yes. It's true that Germans have a crush on their beer—but so will you, once you taste it. (Personally, I adore their wine, also.)

Yes. It's true that haggling in stores will get you nowhere, that service personnel are less tip-hungry than elsewhere, that hotel rooms are generally clean, and that trains run on time. True also that there's an abundance of theaters and opera houses, concerts and ballet.

Let's quickly talk about some of the major cities. Frankfurt is one of West Germany's foremost transportation hubs, and also its financial center. It is served by a major international airport.

In the fall you can enjoy merry-making at Munich's Oktoberfest. The city is famous also for its great theaters, fine concerts, and rich art galleries.

If you seek elegance, Düsseldorf, a metropolis of the Rhine valley, takes first place. It is the fashion capital of West Germany and one of its wealthiest cities as well.

Hamburg, the "Venice of the North," is one of the great seaports of the world. It is also an important cultural center noted especially for its major magazine and book publishing firms. The St. Pauli district in Hamburg is well known for its steamy nightlife.

Once the German capital, Berlin is now a special entity, technically not part of either West or East Germany. However, West Berlin has close economic and social ties with West Germany, and East Berlin serves as the East German capital. The divided city is located well within East Germany.

Bonn is now the West German capital. In the past it was a little university town famous as the birthplace of the composer Ludwig van Beethoven. It was raised to its present eminence by political intrigue. Berlin, itself out of the running, promoted Bonn, fearing that Frankfurt would get the prize and keep it permanently, even after the two Germanies might be reunited.

Away from the big, noisy cities, Germany's old-fashioned beauty is still intact. The enchanting valleys of the Rhine and the Mosel, the Neckar and the Danube, the vistas of the Black Forest and the Bavarian Alps, the ancient cathedrals, medieval towns, and legendary castles are wonders no tourist should miss.

West Germany is governed under a Grundgesetz (Basic Law), adopted in 1949 as a provisional constitution. This law guarantees rights to individuals and provides for a relatively decentralized form of government designed to prevent the emergence of a dictatorship like that of Adolf Hitler, who controlled Germany from 1933 to 1945. West Germany is divided into ten Länder (states) and has close ties with West Berlin. The head of state of West Germany is the Bundespräsident (Federal President). The head of government is the Bundeskanzler (Federal Chancellor), who is elected by the lower house of parliament, called the Bundestag. The upper house, the Bundesrat, represents the interests of the ten Länder.

Why study German, you might ask.

Let's look at the practical application of it. Today, German is spoken by close to ninety million people living in West Germany, East Germany, Austria, and the greater part of Switzerland. It is used and understood by millions elsewhere in Europe and around the world.

German is one of the great international languages, particularly valuable in the fields of science, technology, and commerce. And speaking of commerce, did you know that the Federal Republic of Germany is one of the leading economic powers, ranking second only to the United States among the world's trading nations? West Germany is particularly noted for manufacturing automobiles—such car-makers as Volkswagen, Mercedes-Benz, BMW, and Porsche are known around the globe. Other major products include industrial machinery, steel, chemicals, and electronic equipment.

You are now ready to set out on the exciting journey of learning a new language. This book is designed to make the learning process as easy, interesting, and convenient as possible. We have used verbs only in the present tense so that you can quickly gain a conversational knowledge of German. After you have mastered the level of language in this book, you will certainly want to learn the forms of the verbs in other tenses.

PRONUNCIATION

We have tried to make the phonetic transcriptions in the text as self-explanatory as possible so that you do not have to learn a complex phonetic alphabet to use this book. Please read the pronunciation guide *before* you begin using the text so that you will know what the few unusual symbols mean.

Accent

German words of more than one syllable are usually stressed on the first syllable. However, there are many exceptions, and in this book the accented syllable will be indicated by capital letters in the phonetic transcription of each word: Vater (FAH-teR) father.

Syllabification

German words are divided before single consonants and between double ones:

    sagen sa-gen (to say)
    kommen kom-men (to come)

The consonant combinations *sch*, *ch*, *ß* (ss), *ph*, are counted as single consonants. Compound words are divided into their individual parts:

    Flugnummer Flug-num-mer (flight number)

By and large, German syllabification presents no problems for English speakers learning German.

VOWELS

German has **long vowels**, **short vowels**, and **diphthongs**. A vowel is usually long when doubled (*Boot* [boht] boat), when followed by an *h* (*Fehler* [FAY-leR] mistake), or when followed by a single consonant (*rot* [roht] red). Vowels generally are short when followed by two or more consonants (*essen* [ES-en] to eat). Diphthongs may be divided into three groups: *ai, ay, ei, ey* (*eier* [EI-eR] eggs), *au* (*grau* [grow] gray), and *äu, eu* (*Beutel* [BOY-tel] bag).

The final *e* in German words is never silent as it is in such English words as *late* and *spoke*. It is always pronounced, and it sounds like the final *a* in the English *sofa*. To mark this unstressed mid-central vowel as different from a silent English *e* (and to remind you to pronounce this German sound!), we have given it the symbol *-eh*: *bitte* (BI-teh) please; *Wände* (VEN-deh) walls.

The German vowels also include three with an umlaut (¨). They are *ä*, *ö*, and *ü*. These vowels with umlauts can also be either long or short. The *ä* presents no problems. The short *ä* is always pronounced like short *e*. For all practical purposes, you can pronounce the long *ä* like the long *e*.

The umlauts *ö* and *ü* are not easy for speakers of English and require some practice. The short *ö* is something like the vowel sounds in the English word *fur*. Try to say a long German *e* and round your lips at the same time. This rounding of the lips has to be still more extreme to produce the long *ö*.

The German *ü* is like *u* in the French word *une*. Say the English vowel sound *ee* as in *seen*, keep your tongue in that position, then round your lips into the English *oo* position, as in *boot*. As with the long and short *ö*, so here the long *ü* is "pushed farther forward" and the lips rounded a little more than with the short *ü*.

In German the vowel *y* is pronounced like the long *ü*: *Symphonie* (zǖm-foh-NEE).

The German diphthongs are easy for speakers of English.

SHORT VOWELS	English Equivalent	Symbol	LONG VOWELS	English Equivalent	Symbol
b*i***tten** (to ask)	b*i*n	i	**b***ie***ten** (to offer)	b*ea*n	ee
Bett (bed)	b*e*t	e	**Beet** (flower bed)	b*ai*t	ay
St*a***dt** (city)	h*o*t	a	**St***aa***t** (state)	f*a*ther	ah
L*o***ch** (hole)	l*o*rry	o	**h***o***ch** (high)	l*oa*d	oh
Fl*u***ß** (river)	p*u*t	u	**F***u***ß** (foot)	b*oo*t	oo

SHORT UMLAUT	English Equivalent	Symbol	LONG UMLAUT	English Equivalent	Symbol
W*ä***nde** (walls)	b*e*t	e	**sp***ä***t** (late)	b*ai*t	ay
H*ö***lle** (hell)	k*er*nel	ö	**H***ö***hle** (cave)	[none]	ȫ
H*ü***tte** (hut)	[none]	ü	**H***ü***te** (hats)	[none]	ǖ

DIPHTHONGS		English Equivalent	Symbol
ai	**H***ai***n** (grove)	h*igh*	ei
ei	**m***ei***n** (my)	h*igh*	ei
äu	**H***äu***te** (skins)	j*oy*	oy
eu	**h***eu***te** (today)	j*oy*	oy
au	***au*f** (on)	c*ow*	ow

4

CONSONANTS

Most German consonant sounds have very near equivalents in English. The following German consonants are spelled and pronounced as they are in English:

f, h, k, l,
m, n, p, t

The only consonant sounds in German that are unfamiliar to English speakers are the two represented by *ch* in words like *ich* and *Buch*.

GERMAN LETTERS	Symbols	Pronunciation/Example
ch	ch	Pronounced like the *ch* in the Scottish word *loch*. Make it by saying an *h*, then cutting off the flow of air by raising the back of your tongue. Occurs only after the vowels *a*, *o*, and *u* and the diphthong *au*. Example: *Buch* (booch) book.
ch	ç	The closest sound English has to the *ch* in *ich* is a strongly aspirated and drawn out *h*, as in *Hugh* or *Hubert*. Say *Hugh*, giving the initial *h* a long duration and a lot of air, and you will be very close to the *ich* sound. Example: *ich* (iç) I.
chs	ks	Pronounced like the English letter *x*. Example: *Lachs* (laks) salmon.
c	ts k	*c* before *e, i, ä,* or *ö* is pronounced *ts*. Example: *Celsius*. *(TSEL-see-us)* Otherwise, it is pronounced like *k*. Example: *Café* (ka-FAY) coffee house.
b d g	p t k	The letters, *b, d, g* are pronounced as they are in English if they occur at the beginning of a syllable. Example: *gehen* (GAY-en). However, if they occur at the end of a syllable or before a *t*, they are pronounced like *p, t, k*. Examples:

> b lieb, liebt (leep, leept) dear, loves
> d Lied   (leet)   song
> g flog, fliegt (flohk, fleekt) flew, flies

Note, too, that the combination *-ig* at the end of a word or syllable is pronounced like *ich*. Example: *windig* (VIN-diç) windy.

Also, the second *g* in *Garage* (ga-RAH-žeh) is pronounced like that in the English word *garage*. The symbol for this kind of *g* is *ž*.

GERMAN LETTERS	Symbols	Pronunciation/Example
h	h	*h* is silent only when it indicates that a preceding vowel is long, as mentioned above. Example: *Stahl* (shtahl) steel. Otherwise, it is always pronounced as in English *house*. Example: *hoch* (hohch) high.
j	y	*j* is pronounced like English *y*. Example: *ja* (yah) yes.
kn	kn	In English, the *k* in *knee* is silent. In German, *both* the *k* and the *n* are sounded. Example: *Knie* (knee) knee.

GERMAN LETTERS	Symbols	Pronunciation/Example
ng	ng	Pronounced as in English *singer*, not as in *finger*. Example: *Ding* (ding) thing.
pf, ps	pf, ps	As in *kn*, both letters in the combinations *pf* and *ps* are pronounced in German. Examples: When you ask for pepper *(Pfeffer)* in German, don't ask for (FEF-eR) but for (PFEF-eR). And in *Psychologie*, the *p* is pronounced (psü-çoh-loh-GEE), not (sü-çoh-loh-GEE).
qu	kv	As in English, *q* in German is always followed by a *u*. However, this combination is pronounced *kv*. Example: *Qualität* (kvah-lee-TAYT) quality.
r	r	*R* not at the end of a word: You will not be misunderstood if you use an American *r*, but your German will sound much more authentic if you learn the German *r*. To make it, pronounce the back *ch* sound, then add voice to it. Some native speakers of German use a trilled, frontal *r* like the Spanish *r*. Example: *rot* (roht) red.
r	R	*R* at the end of a word (and in some other environments) is pronounced something like the final *r* in the British pronunciation of words like *mother* and *father* (mothah, fathah). Another similar sound is the Boston *r* as in *there* (''theyah''). Example: *Vater* (FAH-teR) father.
s	z	*S* can be pronounced in two ways. It is pronounced like *z* in *zoo* before and between vowels. Example: *sie* (zee) she. It is usually pronounced *sh* before *p* and *t*. Examples: *spät* (shpayt) late; *stehen* (SHTAY-en) to stand.
ß, ss	s	Both pronounced like English *s* in *soft*. Examples: *Maße* (MAHS-eh) measure; *Masse* (MAS-eh) mass. ß is a ligature of the letters *s* and *z*.
sch	sh	Pronounced like English *sh* in *shoot*. Example: schon (shohn) already.
tsch	tch	Pronounced like English *tch* in *itch*. Example: *deutsch* (doytch) German.
tz	ts	Prounounced like English *ts* in *hats*. Example: *Platz* (plats) place, square.
v	f	Pronounced like English *f* in *father*. Example: *Vater* (FAH-teR) father.
w	v	Pronounced like English *v* in *vine*. Example: *Wasser* (VAS-eR) water.
z	ts	Pronounced like English *ts* in *hats*. Examples: *geizig* (GEI-tsiç) greedy, stingy; *Kreuz* (kroyts) cross.

HOW ENGLISH AND GERMAN ARE SIMILAR

English is a Germanic language so you will find many similarities between English and German. Here are a few examples.

NOUNS		ADJECTIVES		VERBS	
Arm	arm	**blau**	blue	**backen**	to bake
Ball	ball	**blind**	blind	**beginnen**	to begin
Bier	beer	**frei**	free	**binden**	to bind
Buch	book	**gut**	good	**bringen**	to bring
Freund	friend	**hart**	hard	**fallen**	to fall
Garten	garden	**kalt**	cold	**finden**	to find
Land	land	**lang**	long	**füllen**	to fill
Preis	price	**leicht**	light	**helfen**	to help
Schiff	ship	**rot**	red	**rollen**	to roll
Vater	father	**warm**	warm	**senden**	to send

(bal)
der Ball
ball

(beeR)
das Bier
beer

(shif)
das Schiff
ship

(booch)
das Buch
book

(froynt)
der Freund
friend

(FAH-teR)
der Vater
father

(mohnt)
der Mond
moon

GETTING TO KNOW PEOPLE

(LOY-teh) *(KEN-en-lern-en)*
Leute kennenlernen

| **1** | *(ein)* *(ge-SHPRAYÇ)* *(AN-fang-en)*
 Ein Gespräch anfangen
 Starting a conversation |

Learning to greet people and to start a conversation is very important. Read over the following dialogue several times, pronouncing each line carefully. The dialogue contains basic words and expressions that you will find useful.

Mark and Mary Smith, their daughter Anne, and their son John have just arrived at Munich airport and are looking for their luggage. Mark approaches an airline employee:

	(GOO-ten) (tahk)	
MARK	**Guten Tag.**	Hello.
	(voh-MIT) (kan) (iç)	
CLERK	**Guten Tag. Womit kann ich**	Hello. What can I do for you? (*lit.* With what can
	(EEN-en) (DEEN-en)	
	Ihnen dienen?	I serve you?)
	(ZOO-cheh) (MEI-neh) (KOF-eR)	
MARK	**Ich suche meine Koffer.**	I'm looking for my suitcases.
	(eeR) (NAH-meh) (BIT-eh)	
CLERK	**Ah; Ihr Name, bitte?**	I see; your name, please?
	(ist)	
MARK	**Mein Name ist Mark Smith.**	My name is Mark Smith.
	(VO-heR) (KO-men) (zee)	
CLERK	**Woher kommen Sie?**	Where do you come from?

	(KO-meh) (ows)(dayn) (feR-EIN-ik-ten)	
MARK	**Ich komme aus den Vereinigten**	I come from the United States.
	(SHTAH-ten)	
	Staaten.	
	(EER-eh) (FLOOK-num-eR)	
CLERK	**Ihre Flugnummer?**	Your flight number?
	(DREI-hun-deRt-drei)	
MARK	**Dreihundertdrei aus New York.**	303 from New York.
	(EIN-en) (mo-MENT)	
CLERK	**Einen Moment, bitte.**	One moment, please.

As the clerk looks through some papers on his desk, Hans, a German business friend, runs into Mark.

	(vee) (gayts)	
HANS	**Tag, Mark. Wie geht's?**	Hi, Mark. How are you?
	(meeR) (unt) (deeR)	
MARK	**Hans! Mir geht's gut. Und dir?**	Hans! I'm O.K. And you?
	(zayR) (bist) (doo) (heeR) (owf)	
HANS	**Sehr gut. Bist du hier auf**	Very good. Are you here on a vacation?
	(FAYR-i-en)	
	Ferien?	
	(yah) (lǎs) (miç) (fa-MEE-li-e)	
MARK	**Ja. Laß mich dir meine Familie**	Yes. Let me introduce my family to you. My
	(FOHR-stel-en) (frow)	
	vorstellen. Meine Frau Mary, meine	wife Mary, my daughter Anne and my son John.
	(TOCH-teR) (zohn)	
	Tochter Anne, und mein Sohn John.	
	(net) (KEN-en) (tsoo) (LER-nen)	
HANS	**Nett, Sie kennen zu lernen.**	Nice to meet you.
	(ent-SHUL-dig-en)	
CLERK	**Entschuldigen Sie, mein Herr,**	Excuse me, sir, the suitcases come with the next
	(dee) (mit) (dayr)	
	die Koffer kommen mit der	airplane.
	(NAYÇ-sten) (MAH-shee-neh)	
	nächsten Maschine.	
	(tsum) (TOI-fel)	
MARK	**Zum Teufel!**	Heck! (*lit.* To the devil!)
	(ge-DULT)	
HANS	**Geduld, Mark!**	Patience, Mark!
	(das) (zoh) (ET-vas) (pas-EERT)	
MARK	**Daß so etwas passiert!**	That something like that happens.
	(DAN-keh)	
	(to the clerk) **Danke.**	Thanks.
CLERK	**Bitte.**	You're welcome.
	(owf) (VEE-deR-zay-en)	
MARK (to Hans)	**Auf Wiedersehen!**	So long.

HANS	**Auf Wiedersehen, alle.**	See you, all.

(AL-eh)

ALL	**Auf Wiedersehen.**	See you.

Now here is your first exercise, based on the dialogue you have just studied. Try to fill in the missing words without looking at the dialogue. To help refresh your memory, the first letter of each missing word is given.

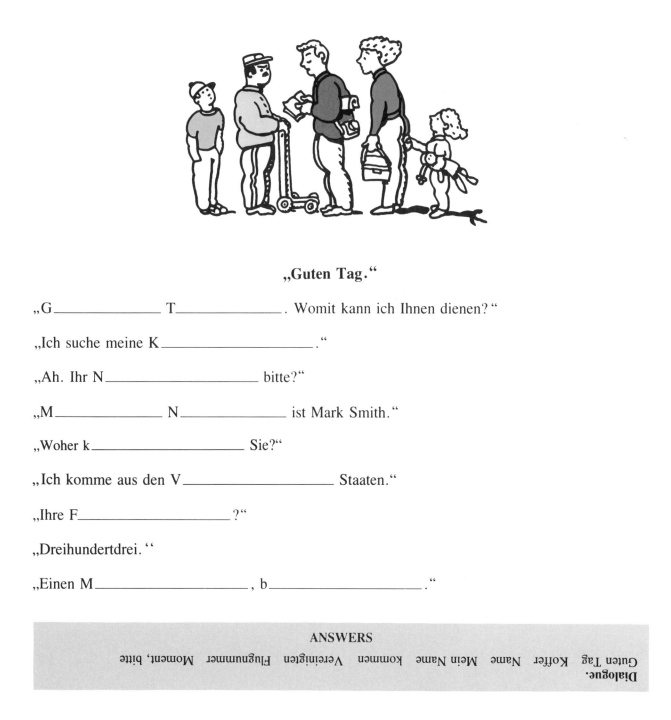

„Guten Tag.“

„G_____ T_____ . Womit kann ich Ihnen dienen? “

„Ich suche meine K_____ .“

„Ah. Ihr N_____ bitte?“

„M_____ N_____ ist Mark Smith.“

„Woher k_____ Sie?“

„Ich komme aus den V_____ Staaten.“

„Ihre F_____ ?“

„Dreihundertdrei. ‘‘

„Einen M_____ , b_____ .“

10

Here is another exercise, which you may find more difficult. Try to rearrange the following groups of words to form sentences that are in the dialogue. Don't be discouraged if you can't make the words fit together properly. You're just beginning to learn a new language. Soon an exercise like this will be easy.

1. dir, meine, vorstellen, mich, laß, Familie

2. kommen, die, mit, Koffer, Maschine, nächsten, der

3. alle, Wiedersehen, auf

(LOY-teh)   *(unt)*   *(DING-eh)*
LEUTE UND DINGE
People and Things

One of the first things you will need to know in German is how to name people and things. This, of course, is the function of the noun. German nouns are divided into three genders. The gender of a word can be indicated by the definite article. The German singular noun is preceded by the definite article *der* if it is masculine, by *die* if it is feminine, or by *das* if it is neuter. *Die* is used with all plural nouns. In English, as you know, *the* performs all these functions. In German, nouns are always capitalized, no matter where they occur in the sentence. In English the plural is formed by adding an -s (dog, dogs, right?). In German there are a variety of plural endings. And some words add an umlaut in the plural.

As you learn each new noun, it is important that you

1. Always learn the definite article.

2. Always learn the plural.

Singular and Plural

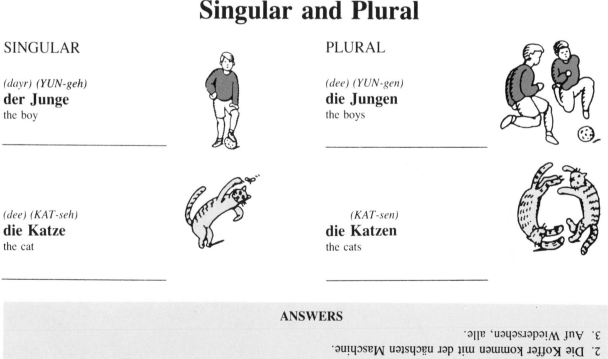

SINGULAR

(dayr) (YUN-geh)
der Junge
the boy

_____

(dee) (KAT-seh)
die Katze
the cat

_____

PLURAL

(dee) (YUN-gen)
die Jungen
the boys

_____

(KAT-sen)
die Katzen
the cats

_____

SINGULAR	PLURAL

SINGULAR

(foos)
der Fuß
the foot

PLURAL

(FǕ-seh)
die Füße
the feet

_____

_____

(BLOO-meh)
die Blume
the flower

(BLOO-men)
die Blumen
the flowers

_____

_____

(hows)
das Haus
the house

(HOY-zeR)
die Häuser
the houses

_____

_____

(AP-fel)
der Apfel
the apple

(EP-fel)
die Äpfel
the apples

_____

_____

(OW-toh)
das Auto
the car

(OW-tohs)
die Autos
the cars

_____

_____

(MUT-eR)
die Mutter
the mother

(MÜT-eR)
die Mütter
the mothers

_____

_____

(AR-beits-heft)
das Arbeitsheft
the workbook

(AR-beits-hef-teh)
die Arbeitshefte
the workbooks

_____

_____

SINGULAR	PLURAL

(KOO-gel-shrei-beR)
der Kugelschreiber
the ballpoint pen

die Kugelschreiber
the ballpoint pens

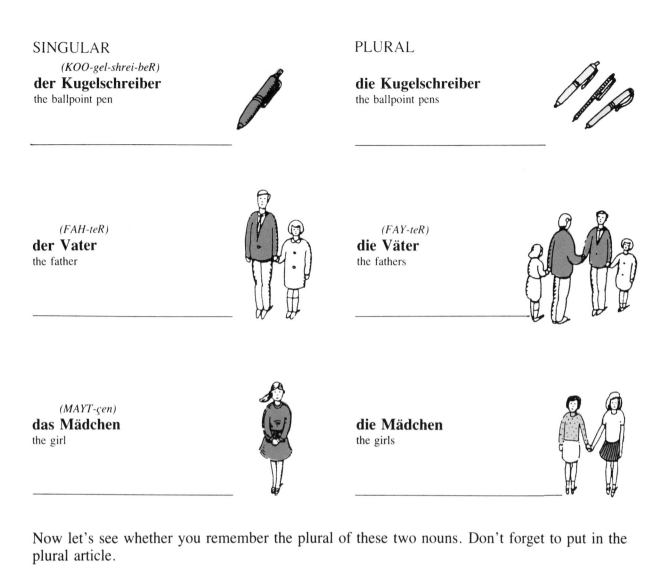

_____

_____

(FAH-teR)
der Vater
the father

(FAY-teR)
die Väter
the fathers

_____

_____

(MAYT-çen)
das Mädchen
the girl

die Mädchen
the girls

_____

_____

Now let's see whether you remember the plural of these two nouns. Don't forget to put in the plural article.

die Mutter
the mother

_____
the mothers

der Junge
the boy

_____
the boys

ANSWERS

die Mutter   die Jungen

13

(ein) *(EIN-eh)* *(ein)*

Ein, eine, ein

"A" and "An"

Now we come to the indefinite articles (in English *a* as in "a book," or *an* as in "an apple"). Again, there are three genders in German—*ein* is used with a masculine noun, *eine* with a feminine noun, and *ein* with a neuter noun. (Notice that the indefinite article can be the same for masculine and neuter nouns.)

Here are two feminine nouns:

(EIN-eh)
eine Mutter
a mother

(EIN-eh) *(FROYN-din)*
eine Freundin
a girlfriend

Here are two neuter nouns:

(ein)
ein Auto
an automobile

(ein)
ein Mädchen
a girl

Here are six masculine nouns:

(ein) *(ON-kel)*
ein Onkel
an uncle

(ein) *(froynt)*
ein Freund
a friend

(ein) *(shtoo-DENT)*
ein Student
a student

(ein) *(bowm)*
ein Baum
a tree

ein Junge
a boy

ein Vater
a father

14

Got it? Now test yourself by putting the appropriate indefinite article in front of the following nouns:

1. _____ Katze

2. _____ Baum

3. _____ Freundin

4. _____ Freund

5. _____ Mädchen

6. _____ Junge

7. _____ *(TAN-teh)* Tante
   aunt

8. _____ Onkel

9. _____ *(SHPEE-gel)* Spiegel
   (masculine) mirror

10. _____ Apfel

Here is another exercise. It may be difficult, but give it a try. Identify each picture by writing in the German word for it along with the proper indefinite article.

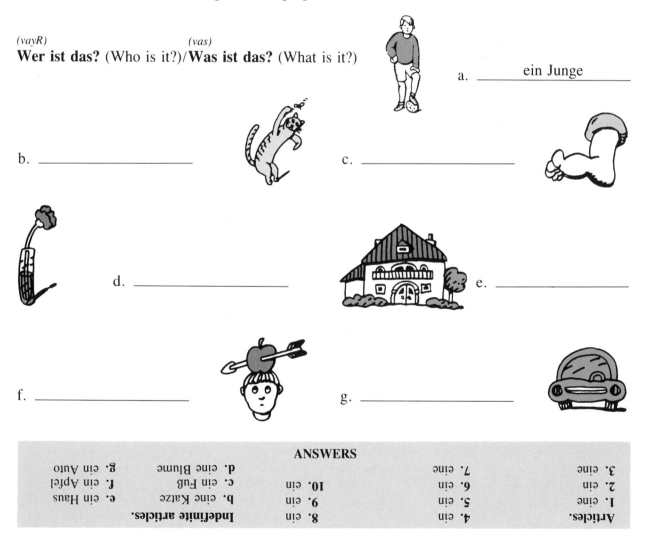

(vayR)   *(vas)*
Wer ist das? (Who is it?)/**Was ist das?** (What is it?)

a. _____ ein Junge

b. _____

c. _____

d. _____

e. _____

f. _____

g. _____

h. _____

i. _____

j. _____

k. _____

l. _____

(iç)   *(unt)*   *(doo)*   *(eeR)*   *(unt)*   *(zee)*

„Ich" und „Du," „Ihr," und „Sie"
"I" and "you"

It is very important to know how to say "I" and "You" in your new language.

"I" IS SIMPLY ICH

"YOU" IS GIVEN IN TWO WAYS
(a casual or familiar form and a polite form)

CASUAL		
DU *(doo)*	when addressing a family member or a friend	**Singular**
IHR *(eeR)*	when addressing family members or friends	**Plural**
POLITE		
SIE *(zee)*	when addressing strangers, superiors, etc.	**Singular** and **Plural**

In English, "I" is always capitalized. In German, *ich, du,* and *ihr* are not capitalized except at the start of a sentence while *Sie* is always capitalized.

ANSWERS

h. ein Kugelschreiber   **i.** ein Arbeitsheft   **j.** ein Onkel   **k.** eine Tante   **l.** ein Spiegel

VON VERWANDTEN REDEN
(fon) (feR-VAN-ten) (RAY-den)

Talking About Relatives

This is Hans' family tree. Note the word for each of the relatives.

(HIL-deh)
Hilde
(GROHS-mut-eR)
die **Großmutter**
grandmother

(LUT-viç)
Ludwig
(GROHS-fah-teR)
der **Großvater**
grandfather

(ZEEK-freet)
Siegfried
(FAH-teR)
der **Vater**
father

(BAYR-ta)
Berta
(MUT-eR)
die **Mutter**
mother

(klows)
Klaus
(ON-kel)
der **Onkel**
uncle

(LOT-eh)
Lotte
(TON-teh)
die **Tante**
aunt

(hans)
Hans
(zohn)
der **Sohn**
son
(BROO-deR)
der **Bruder**
brother

(GEE-se-la)
Gisela
(TOCH-teR)
die **Tochter**
daughter
(SHVES-teR)
die **Schwester**
sister

(PAY-teR)
Peter
(FET-eR)
der **Vetter**
or
(koo-ZAN)
der **Cousin**
cousin

(mah-REE)
Marie
(koo-ZEEN-eh)
die **Kusine**
cousin

Hans

17

Look carefully at the family tree and then try to answer the following questions about the relationships. Don't forget to use the correct form of the article: *der*, *die*, or *das*.

1. Peter ist _____der Vetter_____ von Hans.
   of

2. Lotte ist _____ von Peter.

3. Gisela ist _____ von Hans.

4. Lotte ist _____ von Hans.

5. Hans ist _____ von Gisela.

6. Marie ist _____ von Hans.

7. Hans ist _____ von Siegfried.

8. Berta ist _____ von Marie.

9. Ludwig ist _____ von Gisela.

10. Hilde ist _____ von Peter.

Now here is an exercise that should be fun. Write in the plurals of the following words and find them in the word-search puzzle.

Haus _____

Arbeitsheft _____

Apfel _____

Kugelschreiber _____

Mutter _____

Mädchen _____

Vater _____

```
H Ä U S E R D T M Ä D C H E N P W E D R
P O I T O A R B E I T S H E F T E N V X
M Ü T T E R Q S T I Ä P F E L O J H G F
P I G F H K U G E L S C H R E I B E R D
W Y D V Ä T E R L I A U T O M O B I L E
```

Let's try another quick exercise. Fill in the blanks with German words so that the sentences make sense: Here are the words you can choose from: *Großmutter, Onkel, Bruder, Mutter, Tochter, Kusine, Sohn, Vetter.*

1. I am the son of my _____ .

2. My father has an only _____ .

3. The brother of my father is my _____ .

4. The son of my mother is my _____ .

5. The mother of my father is my _____ .

6. My sister is our mother's _____ .

7. The son of my uncle is my _____

8. The daughter of my aunt is my _____ .

It's time to return to the Smiths, just beginning their trip to Germany. Test your readiness too by trying to understand the following short paragraph. Read the selection and then answer the questions that follow.

Herr Mark Smith wohnt in Chicago.

(ayR) *(ZEI-neh)* *(fa-MEEL-i-eh)* *(zint)* *(yetst)* *(DOYTCH-lant)*
Er und seine Familie sind jetzt in Deutschland.
he   family

(zooçt)
Er sucht seine Koffer. Er, seine Frau,
looks for his

seine Tochter und sein Sohn sind auf Ferien.

(zahkt) *(tsoo)*
Er sagt zu Hans: „Laß mich dir meine
says to

Familie vorstellen."

TRUE or FALSE Please mark the following statements with T or F.

1. Herr Smith wohnt in Chicago. _____

2. Er und seine Kusine sind auf Ferien. _____

3. Er ist jetzt in Deutschland. _____

4. Er sagt zu Hans: „Laß mich dir meine Familie vorstellen." _____

5. Herr Smith sucht sein Auto. _____

6. Herr Smith und seine Familie sind auf Ferien. _____

19

Here are the German words for parts of a house. Study them and say them aloud.

(hows)
EIN HAUS
a house

(VASH-be-ken)
das Waschbecken
sink

(KÜL-shrank)
der Kühlschrank
refrigerator

(toy-LE-teh)
die Toilette
toilet

(KÜ-çeh)
die Küche
kitchen

(hayrt)
der Herd
stove

(TREP-eh)
die Treppe
stairway

(BAH-deh-van-eh)
die Badewanne
bathtub

(BAH-deh-tsim-eR)
das Badezimmer
bathroom

(VOHN-tsim-eR)
das Wohnzimmer
living room

(VANT-shrank)
der Wandschrank
closet

(SHLAHF-tsim-eR)
das Schlafzimmer
bedroom

(ZOH-fa)
das Sofa
sofa

(bet)
das Bett
bed

(FEN-steR)
das Fenster
window

(GAR-ten)
der Garten
garden

(tish)
der Tisch
table

und
and

(SHTÜ-leh)
die Stühle
chairs

(tühR)
die Tür
door

(flur)
der Flur
hallway

20

ARRIVAL
(AN-kunft)
Ankunft

(UN-teR-kunft)   *(FIN-den)*
Unterkunft finden
Finding a place to spend the night

You'll probably book your hotel room from home—at least for your first night in Germany. But whether you have a reservation or not, you'll want to know some basic words that describe the services and facilities you expect to find at your hotel. Learn these words first, and notice how they are used in the dialogue you will read later.

(hoh-TEL)
das Hotel
hotel

(TSIM-eR)
das Zimmer
room

(preis)
der Preis
price

(BAH-deh-tsim-eR)
das Badezimmer
bathroom

(re-zer-VEER-ung)
die Reservierung
reservation

(re-zer-VEE-ren)
reservieren
to reserve

(tühR)
die Tür
door

(AN-ge-shtel-teh)
die Angestellte
clerk

(TSIM-eR-mayt-çen)
das Zimmermädchen
maid

(pas)
der Paß
passport

(FEN-steR)
das Fenster
window

(SHTUN-deh)
die Stunde
hour

Singular and Plural

We already learned quite a bit about forming the plural in German. Here are a few more forms . . . and then an easy quiz.

SINGULAR	PLURAL
der Freund	die Freunde
die Freundin	die Freundinnen
der Paß	die Pässe
der Spiegel	die Spiegel
die Großmutter	die Großmütter
der Großvater	die Großväter
der Sohn	die Söhne
die Tochter	die Töchter
der Bruder	die Brüder
die Schwester	die Schwestern
der Vetter	die Vettern
die Kusine	die Kusinen
das Hotel	die Hotels
das Zimmer	die Zimmer
der Baum	die Bäume

Now let's see whether you remember:

SINGULAR   PLURAL

eine _____   *(tsvei)*
                                      zwei _____
                                      two

ein _____   zwei _____

ein _____   zwei _____

eine _____   zwei _____

ein _____   zwei _____

ein _____   zwei _____

SINGULAR		PLURAL
eine	_____	zwei _____
ein	_____	zwei _____
ein	_____	zwei _____
ein	_____	zwei _____
ein	_____	zwei _____
ein	_____	zwei _____

(ven)   *(zee)*   *(EI-neh)*   *(FRAH-geh)*   *(SHTEL-en)*   *(VOL-en)*

WENN SIE EINE FRAGE STELLEN WOLLEN...
If you want to ask a question. . .

When you're traveling, you'll need to ask a lot of questions. It's very important to learn the following words so you can form questions in German.

(vas) was	what	*(vee)* wie	how
(vayR) wer	who	*(vee-FEEL)* wieviel	how much

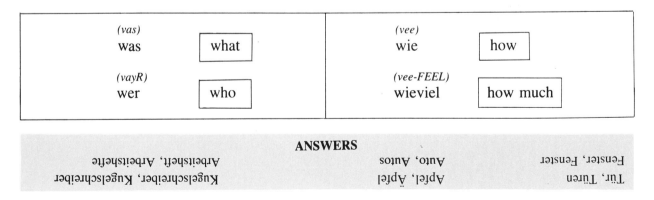

ANSWERS

Arbeitsheft, Arbeitshefte	Auto, Autos	Fenster, Fenster
Kugelschreiber, Kugelschreiber	Apfel, Äpfel	Tür, Türen

24

(van) **wann**	when
(voh) **wo**	where
(va-RUM) **warum**	why

(vee-FEEL) (gelt)
Wieviel Geld?
how much money

(broht)
Wieviel Brot?
how much bread

In the plural we add an -e to *wieviel*.

(vee-FEE-leh)
Wieviele Jungen?

Wieviele Mädchen?

To form a question, you simply reverse the word order:

(ist)
Der Junge ißt Brot.
eats

Ißt der Junge Brot?

In the question, the verb comes first, followed by the subject.

Now try to match up each question with its answer.

1. Was ißt Mary?
2. Wann kommen die Koffer?
3. Wo sind Mark und Marie?
4. Wer ist hier?
5. Wie ist das Wetter?
   weather   *(VET-eR)*
6. Wieviel kostet das?
   costs that   *(KOST-et) (das)*
7. Ißt das Mädchen jetzt?

(zee)
A. Sie sind in Deutschland.
   they
B. Mary ißt Brot.
C. Hans ist hier.
D. Das kostet zwei Mark.
E. Die Koffer kommen morgen.
   tomorrow   *(MOR-gen)*
F. Ja, das Mädchen ißt.
G. Das Wetter ist gut.
   good   *(goot)*

25

In the following dialogue you will learn some words and expressions that might come in handy when looking for a room to stay. Always read each dialogue line carefully and out loud.

MARK (to hotel employee) **Entschuldigen**
(re-zer-VEER-ung)
Sie, bitte. Ich habe eine Reservierung

für zwei Zimmer für heute nacht.

Ich heiße Mark Smith.

Excuse me, please. I have a reservation for two

rooms for tonight.

My name is Mark Smith.

ANGESTELLTER **Guten Morgen**, Herr

Smith. Ja, ich habe Ihre Reservierung
(baht)
für zwei Zimmer mit Bad. Aber wir
(pro-BLAYM)
stehen vor einem Problem.

Good morning, Mr. Smith. Yes, I do have your

reservation for two rooms with bath. But we are

faced with a problem.

MARK **Was ist los?**

What's the matter?

ANGESTELLTER **Die Dusche in einem der**
(DU-sheh)

Zimmer ist kaputt.

The shower in one of

the rooms is broken.

MARK **Das macht nichts.** Wir können die

That doesn't matter.

(VAN-eh)
Wanne benutzen.

We can use the bathtub.

ANGESTELLTER **Noch eine**
(SHVEE-riç-keit)
Schwierigkeit, Herr Smith. In einem

der Zimmer kann man das Fenster
(ÖF-nen)
nicht öffnen.

(There's) another difficulty, Mr. Smith. In one

of the rooms the window cannot be opened.

MARK (to his wife Mary) **Was sollen wir**

tun? Zimmer sind unmöglich zu

bekommen. Die Stadt ist von
(tu-RI-sten) *(ü-beR-SHVEMT)*
Touristen überschwemmt.

(dah)
MARY **Bleiben wir da. Ich bin viel zu**
(MÜ-deh) *(TSIM-er-zoo-cheh)*
müde, um jetzt auf Zimmersuche zu

gehen.

What are we going to do? It's impossible to get

any rooms. The city is

flooded with tourists.

Let's stay here.

I am much too tired to

go room-hunting now.

ANGESTELLTER **Sehr gut. Das kommt auf**
(TSVEI-hun-deRt)
200 Mark pro Tag.

Very good. That amounts to 200 marks per day.

(IN-kloo-zee-veh)
MARK **Ist das inklusive Frühstück?**

Does this include breakfast?

(ya-VOHL)
ANGESTELLTER **Jawohl.**

Yes, sir.

MARK **Also gut. Hier sind unsere**
(REI-zeh-pes-eh)
Reisepässe.

Well then. Here are our passports.

ANGESTELLTER **Wollen Sie bitte dieses**
(for-mu-LAHR)
Formular ausfüllen? Hier sind die

Schlüssel. Die Zimmer sind im dritten
(shtok)
Stock.

Would you please fill out this form? Here are

the keys. The rooms are on the fourth floor.*

(OWF-tsook)
MARK **Haben Sie einen Aufzug?**

Is there an elevator?

(na-TÜR-liç)
ANGESTELLTER **Natürlich. Dort drüben.**

Of course. Over there.

MARK **Danke schön.**

Thank you.

ANGESTELLTER **Bitte sehr. Ich hoffe,**

unsere Stadt gefällt Ihnen.

You're welcome. I hope you enjoy our city.

---

*Note that Germans designate floors in a building differently than Americans. In Germany, the street-level floor is called *das*
(ERT-ge-shos)
Erdgeschoß, not the first floor. The German first floor is above *das Erdgeschoß* and is the same as the American
second floor. Thus, when the German hotel clerk in our dialogue speaks of the third floor *(dritten Stock)*, he is referring to
what is known as the fourth floor in America.

Did you understand the German dialogue?   Try to fill in the missing words from memory:

1. Ich habe eine _____ für zwei Zimmer.

2. Wir stehen vor einem _____.

3. Wir können die Wanne _____.

4. Im anderen Zimmer kann man das _____ nicht öffnen.

5. Die Stadt ist von _____ überschwemmt.

6. Ist das inklusive _____?

7. Wollen Sie bitte dieses _____ ausfüllen?

8. Die Zimmer sind im dritten _____.

9. Der _____ ist dort drüben.

Can you make sentences out of these scrambled words?
1. kaputt, ist, Dusche, die   2. sollen, was, wir, machen   3. Schlüssel, hier, die, sind

(kom-OWD-eh)
die Kommode
chest of drawers

(SHPEE-gel)
der Spiegel
mirror

(LAM-peh)
die Lampe
lamp

(OWS-goos)
der Ausguß
sink

(HANT-tooch)
das Handtuch
towel

(DOO-sheh)
die Dusche
shower

(bet)
das Bett
bed

(BAH-deh-van-eh)
die Badewanne
bathtub

(KI-sen)
das Kissen
pillow

(ZOH-fa)
das Sofa
sofa

(tühR)
die Tür
door

(toy-LE-teh)
die Toilette
toilet

Pronomen und Verben

(proh-NOH-men)   *(unt)*   *(VAYR-ben)*

Pronouns and Verbs

You've already learned how to say "I" and "you" in German. Now it's time to move on to other pronouns—the words for "he," "she," "it," "we," and "they."

PRONOUNS	
SINGULAR	**PLURAL**
ich I	*(veeR)* **wir** we
(doo) **du** you (familiar) **Sie** you (polite)	*(eeR)* **ihr** you (familiar) **Sie** you (polite)
(ayR) **er** he **sie** she **es** it	**sie** they

It's pretty difficult to get along without verbs. Verbs are words that often express action—like talking, singing, or arriving (in Germany!). You can't get too far without first learning the different forms a verb can take. Now let's conjugate the verb *sagen* (to say). The *-en* denotes the infinitive. This is the verb form that you find listed in the dictionary.

(ZAH-gen)

SAGEN		
to say		
SINGULAR		
1st person:	**ich** **sag*e*** *(ZAH-geh)*	I say I am saying I do say
2nd person: (familiar form)	**du** **sag*st*** *(zahkst)*	you say you are saying you do say
3rd person:	**er** **sie** } **sag*t*** **es** *(zahkt)*	he/she/it says he/she/it is saying he/she/it does say

PLURAL		
1st person:	**wir sag**en	we say we are saying we do say
2nd person: (familiar form)	**ihr sag**t	you say you are saying you do say
3rd person:	**sie sag**en	they say they are saying they say
POLITE FORM: Singular and Plural		
2nd person:	**Sie sag**en	you say you are saying you do say

VERB ENDINGS
Present Tense

ich	_____ (verb)	-e		wir	_____	-en
du	_____	-st		ihr	_____	-t
er sie es	_____	-t		sie	_____	-en

	Sie	_____	-en

(ET-vas)
Der Junge sagt etwas.
The boy says something.

Die Jungen sagen etwas.
The boys say something.

Now try to put on the right endings.

(ZING-en)
singen
to sing

ich sing _____   wir sing _____

du sing _____   ihr sing _____

er sing _____   sie sing _____

Sie sing _____

(KOM-en)
kommen
to come

ich komm _____   wir komm _____

du komm _____   ihr komm _____

er komm _____   sie komm _____

Sie komm _____

Now put on the right endings according to each sentence.

Das Mädchen sag_____ etwas.   Du komm_____ und ich sing_____.

Die Onkel komm_____ morgen.   Wir sing_____ und ihr sing_____.

Mary sing_____ sehr gut.

To put any action in the negative just put *nicht* after the verb:

Affirmative	**Negative**
Ich singe. I sing.	**Ich komme nicht.** I don't come.
Wir singen. We sing.	**Sie kommen nicht.** They don't come.

Here is an easy review—you should be able to do it quickly. Fill in vertically the German equivalent of the words listed on the left.

```
      1.  2.  3.  4.  5.  6.
      S   I   N   G   E   N
```

1. to say
2. in
3. number
4. to give
5. he
6. name

31

Now try to put the correct article form in front of these plural nouns.

7. _____ Fenster   8. _____ Türen   9. _____ Hotels

10. _____ Zimmer   11. _____ Freundinnen   12. _____ Freunde

13. _____ Spiegel   14. _____ Onkel   15. _____ Pässe

16. _____ Badezimmer.

Are you surprised by the answers?

The following brief passage lets you test your comprehension of what you have learned in this unit about requesting a room in a hotel.

(KEI-neh) (SHÖ-nen)

Herr Jones hat keine Reservierung im Hotel. Sie haben keine schönen Zimmer mehr. Frau

(Mü-deh)   no   nice

Jones sagt dem Angestellten: „Wir sind sehr müde." Der Angestellte sagt: „Es tut mir leid.

(noor)   tired

Ich habe nur ein kleines Zimmer im dritten Stock. Das Zimmer hat kein Bad und

only

kostet 60 Mark. "

Did you understand the passage? Try answering the following multiple-choice questions. Circle the correct answer.

1. Was hat Herr Jones nicht?

   a. Brot   b. einen Schlüssel   c. eine Reservierung.

2. Das Zimmer im dritten Stock ist

   a. klein   b. groß   c. schön

3. Herr Jones spricht mit

   a. Paul   b. Peter   c. dem Angestellten

4. Frau Jones sagt, wir sind sehr

   a. Deutsche   b. müde   c. Engländer

5. Der Angestellte sagt:

   a. „Ich habe ein schönes Zimmer."   b. „Wir sind arm."   c. „Es tut mir leid."

6. Das Zimmer kostet

   a. 70 Mark   b. 60 Mark   c. 50 Mark

ANSWERS

Reading.
1. c 2. a 3. c 4. b 5. c 6. b

Articles.
7. die 8. die 9. die 10. die 11. die 12. die 13. die 14. die 15. die 16. die

32

SEEING THE SIGHTS

(ZAY-ens-vür-diç-kei-ten)   *(be-ZIÇ-ti-gen)*
Sehenswürdigkeiten besichtigen

3	*(tsu-REÇt-fin-den)* *(tsu)* *(foos)* **Zurechtfinden zu Fuß** Finding your way on foot

---

(vee)   *(KOM-eh)*   *(iç)*   *(tsum)*

Wie komme ich zum . . . ?
How Do I Get to . . . ?

"How do I get to. . . ?" "Where is the nearest subway?" "Is the museum straight ahead?" You'll be asking directions and getting answers wherever you travel. In the following dialogue John and Anne are trying to find a museum. Acquaint yourself with the words and phrases that will make getting around easier. Don't forget to read each line out loud several times to practice your pronunciation, and act out each part to be certain you understand the new words.

(FRAH-gen)   *(dayn)*   *(po-lee-TSIST-en)*

ANNE **John, fragen wir den Polizisten**
(man)   *(moo-ZAY-um)*
wie man das Museum findet.

John, let's ask the policeman how one finds

the museum.

(ent-SHUL-di-gen)

JOHN (to the policeman) **Entschuldigen**

Sie bitte, können Sie mir sagen,

wie ich das Museum finde?

Excuse me please, can you

tell me how to find

the museum?

(ge-VIS) *(GAY-en)* *(ge-RAH-deh-OWS)*

POLIZIST **Gewiß. Gehen Sie geradeaus**
(tsooR) *(Shıler-SHTRAH-seh)* *(dan)* *(reçts)*
zur Schillerstraße, dann rechts in die
(HEI-neh)
Heinestraße und dann rechts in die
(MOH-tsaRt)   *(FeR-KAYRS-am-peln)*
Mozartstraße, wo die Verkehrsampeln
sind.

Certainly. Go straight ahead to Schillerstraße, then

right into Heinestraße, then right into

Mozartstraße, where there are traffic lights.

Zwei *(SHTRAH-sen-tsü-geh)* **Straßenzüge** *(nach)* **nach den Verkehrsampeln finden Sie das Museum.**

Two blocks after the traffic lights you'll find the museum.

JOHN **Vielen Dank.**

Thanks a lot.

POLIZIST **Bitte sehr.** *(zayR)*

You're very welcome.

(After having followed the directions)

ANNE **Das ist nicht das Museum.**

That isn't the museum.

Es ist das Postamt. *(POS-tamt)*

It's the post office.

JOHN **Geduld, Anne.** *(ge-DULT)* **Es ist spät.**

Patience, Anne. It's late.

Gehen wir zum Hotel zurück. *(tsoo-RÜK)*

Let's go back to the hotel.

Fill in the missing dialogue parts:

1. „Fragen wir den P_____, wie man das M_____ findet."

2. „Entschuldigen Sie, bitte, können Sie mir sagen, wie ich das Museum

   f_____?"

3. „Gewiß. Geradeaus zur Schillerstraße, dann r_____ in die Heinestraße,

   dann r_____ in die Mozartstraße. Zwei Straßenzüge nach den

   V_____ finden Sie das M_____."

4. „Vielen _____."

Nützliche kleine Wörter
(NÜTS-li-çeh) *(KLEI-neh)* *(VÖR-teR)*

Helpful little words

in
in

Herr Smith wohnt *in* Amerika.

aus *(ows)*
from

Er kommt *aus* A_____

34

mit
with

1. Er kommt *mit* der F_____

(OH-neh)
ohne
without

2. Er kommt *ohne* K_____

(führ)
für
for

3. Wir brauchen das Zimmer *für* eine W_____

(fohR)
vor
in front of

4. Marks Katze ist *vor* dem H_____

(HIN-teR)
hinter
behind

5. Die Katze ist *hinter* dem H_____

(links)
links
left

6. Die Katze ist *links* vom H _____

rechts
right

7. Die Katze ist *rechts* vom H_____

(TSVI-shen)
zwischen
between

8. Die Katze ist *zwischen* H_____ #1

und H_____ #2

(UN-teR)
unter
under

9. Die Katze ist *unter* dem S_____

ANSWERS

1. Freundin 2. Koffer 3. Woche 4. Haus 5. Haus 6. Haus 7. Haus 8. Haus, Haus 9. Stuhl

35

(Ü-beR)
über
over

(shprinkt)
10. Die Katze springt *über* den M_____
jumps   moon

(noch)   *(EIN-mal)*   *(VAYR-ben)*
Noch einmal Verben
Verbs again

In the previous unit we conjugated the verb *sagen* (to say). Now you will learn to conjugate verbs that differ a little from *sagen*.

(SHPRE-çen) **SPRECHEN** to speak		SINGULAR AND PLURAL POLITE
SINGULAR	PLURAL	
1st person: *(SHPRE-çeh)* **ich spreche**	**wir sprechen**	**Sie sprechen**
2nd person: *(shpriçst)* **du sprichst**	*(shpreçt)* **ihr sprecht**	
3rd person: **er** **sie** **es** } *(shpriçt)* **spricht**	**sie sprechen**	

The endings are the same as in *sagen* or *singen* or *kommen*. But the vowel *e* changes to *i* in the second and third person singular.

(ZAY-en) **SEHEN** to see		SINGULAR AND PLURAL POLITE
SINGULAR	PLURAL	
1st person: *(ZAY-eh)* **ich sehe**	**wir sehen**	**Sie sehen**
2nd person: *(zeest)* **du siehst**	*(zayt)* **ihr seht**	
3rd person: **er** **sie** **es** } *(zeet)* **sieht**	**sie sehen**	

Here, the *i* in the second person singular becomes an *ie* which makes it a long *i* (ee).

Do you remember how to form the negative? Review the following examples.

Ich spreche nicht.   I do not speak.   **Er sieht nicht.**   He does not see.

ANSWERS

Endings. 10. Mond

36

Can you add the correct endings to the following verbs? The only two verbs used are *sprechen* and *sehen*.

a. Der Angestellte sprich_____.

b. Das Mädchen sieh_____.

c. Ich seh_____ nicht.

d. Ich sprech_____.

e. Die Katzen seh_____ nicht.

f. Die Jungen seh_____
   die Apotheke nicht.

g. Wir sprech_____.

h. Ihr seh_____.

i. Du sprich_____.

(EI-nig-eh) *(NÜTS-li-çeh)* *(VÖR-teR)*

Einige nützliche Wörter
Some useful words

(KEE-noh)
das Kino
movie theater

(ge-SHEFT)
das Geschäft
store

(LAY-bens-mi-tel-ge-sheft)
das Lebensmittelgeschäft
grocery store

(bank)
die Bank
bank

(a-poh-TAY-keh)
die Apotheke
pharmacy

(GAY-shteik)
der Gehsteig
sidewalk

(SHTRAH-seh)
die Straße
street

(EIN-kowf-en) *(GAY-en)*
einkaufen gehen
to go shopping

(vee) *(man)* *(owf)* *(ET-vas)* *(tseikt)*

Wie man auf etwas zeigt
How to point out something

Words like "this" and "these" are important to know, particularly when you go shopping. The German forms are easy to learn. They vary just a little depending on whether the noun is masculine, feminine, or neuter and whether it is singular or plural. Nouns of all three genders form the plural in the same way.

ANSWERS
a. spricht b. sieht c. sehe d. spreche e. sehen f. sehen g. sprechen h. seht i. sprichst

„DIES" UND „DIESE"

''This'' and ''These''

One (singular)		More than one (plural)
(DEE-zeR) **dies*er* Onkel**		**dies*e* Onkel**
(DEE-zeh) **dies*e* Mutter**		**dies*e* Mütter**
(DEE-zes) **dies*es* Mädchen**		**dies*e* Mädchen**

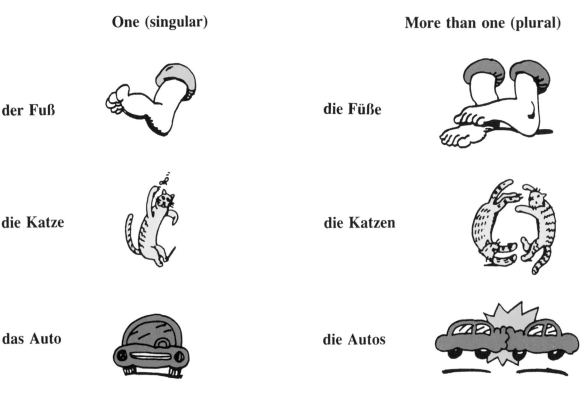

Instead of using *dieser, diese, dieses* we can also use the definite article *der, die, das* if we want to point out something:

One (singular)	More than one (plural)
der Fuß	**die Füße**
die Katze	**die Katzen**
das Auto	**die Autos**

Now let's try the following exercise. Put the appropriate form in each slot:

SINGULAR		PLURAL	
This: dieser, diese, dieses *or* der, die, das		**These:** diese *or* die	
dieser Fuß	der Fuß	diese Füße	die Füße

Here's a chance to test your knowledge of the verbs and prepositions you've learned up to now.

Fill in the blanks with the appropriate endings:

1. Marie sieh_____ Karl nicht.

2. Wir seh_____ das Haus.

3. Ihr seh_____ Marys* Haus.

4. Die Jungen seh_____ die Blumen.

5. Ich seh_____ Mary nicht.

6. Du sieh_____ Marks* Onkel.

*The s in **Marys** or **Marks** is the same as is used in English: "Mary's" or "Mark's" (the house of Mary; the uncle of Mark). But in German the apostrophe is not used.

ANSWERS

Endings.
1. sieht 2. sehen 3. seht 4. sehen 5. sehe 6. siehst

This and these.

SINGULAR	PLURAL	SINGULAR	PLURAL
dieses Auto, das Auto	diese Autos, die Autos	dieses Haus, das Haus	diese Häuser, die Häuser
dieser Onkel, der Onkel	diese Onkel, die Onkel	diese Katze, die Katze	diese Katzen, die Katzen

Fill in the blanks with the appropriate words:

1. Mark kommt _____ Amerika.
   (from)

2. Er kommt _____ Koffer.
   (without)

3. Er kommt _____ Frau Smith.
   (with)

4. Wir brauchen das Zimmer _____ eine Woche.
   (for)

5. Die Katze ist _____ dem Haus.
   (in front of)

6. Die Katze ist _____ vom Haus.
   (left)

7. Die Katze ist _____ vom Haus.
   (right)

8. Die Katze ist _____ Haus #1 und Haus #2.
   (between)

9. Die Katze ist _____ dem Haus.
   (under)

10. Die Katze springt _____ den Mond.
    (over)

11. Die Katze ist _____ dem Haus.
    (behind)

Fill in vertically the German equivalent of the words listed on the left.

1. from
2. passports
3. uncle
4. doors
5. houses
6. a (feminine article)
7. movie theater
8. it

| | 1. | 2. | 3. | 4. | 5. | 6. | 7. | 8. |
| | A | P | O | T | H | E | K | E |

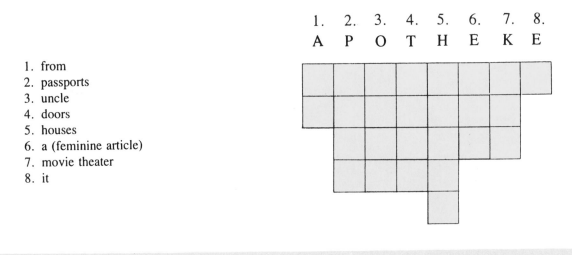

What's Mary doing? Read this passage to review German words for directions. Then try to answer the questions that follow.

Mary fragt den Polizisten: „Wo ist die Bank?" Der Polizist sagt ihr: „Gehen Sie rechts und dann links." Mary kommt zu den Verkehrsampeln und sieht die Bank nicht. Aber sie sieht das Postamt. Dann geht sie zum Hotel zurück.

Now try to answer the following questions:

1. Wer fragt den Polizisten, wo die Bank ist?

_____

2. Was sagt der Polizist?

_____

(voh-HIN)
3. Wohin (to where) kommt sie?

_____

4. Was sieht sie?

_____

5. Wohin geht sie zurück?

_____

ANSWERS

Questions.
1. Mary fragt den Polizisten. 2. Gehen Sie rechts und dann links. 3. Sie kommt zu den Verkehrsampeln.
4. Sie sieht die Bank. 5. Sie geht zum Hotel zurück.

41

1 Frauenkirche
2 Neues Rathaus
3 Peterskirche
4 Residenz
5 Nationaltheater
6 Theatinerkirche
7 Karlstor
8 Propyläen
9 Lenbachhaus
10 Alte Pinakothek
11 Neue Pinakothek
12 Universität
13 Siegestor
14 Monopteros

15 Haus der Kunst
16 Nationalmuseum
17 Friedensengel
18 Maximilianeum
19 Völkerkundemuseum
20 Isartor
21 Deutsches Museum
22 Maria-Hilf-Kirche
23 Gärtnerplatztheater
24 Sendlinger Tor
25 Paulskirche
26 Circus Krone
27 Olympiastadion
28 Olympiaturm

Munich

(Courtesy of Munich Tourist Office)

The following dialogue contains some useful words and expressions that you might find helpful when using public transportation. Always read the dialogue of a unit several times out loud.

MARY	*(SOL-en)* *(TAK-si)* *(tsoom)* *(NAY-men)* **Sollen wir ein Taxi zum Kino nehmen?**	Shall we take a taxi to the movie theater?
MARK	*(KOST-et)* *(tsoo-FEEL)* **Nein. Das kostet zuviel.**	No. It costs too much.
MARY	*(OO-bahn)* **Dann nehmen wir die U-Bahn.**	Then let's take the subway.
MARK	**Nein. Dann kann ich die** *(shtat)* **Stadt nicht sehen.**	No. then I can't see the city.
MARK	*(RIÇ-tik)* **Richtig. Wir nehmen** *(BE-seR)* *(bus)* **besser den Bus.**	Right. It's better if we take the bus.
MARK	*(goot)* **Gut.**	Good.
	(They get on a bus) **Entschuldigen Sie,** *(FAHR-kar-teh)* **bitte, wieviel kostet eine Fahrkarte?**	Excuse me, please, how much is a ticket?*
FAHRER driver	*(FAHR-eR)* **Eine Mark.**	One mark.
MARK	*(SHTEI-gen)* *(beim)* **Wir steigen beim Kino in der** **Schillerstraße aus.**	We are getting off at the movie theater on the Schillerstraße.
FAHRER	**Gut, mein Herr.**	All right, sir.
MARK	*(HÖHF-liç)* *(DOY-tchen)* **Wie höflich die Deutschen sind!**	How polite the Germans are!

Did you read the dialogue several times? Out loud? Test your understanding by filling in the missing dialogue parts in the following sentences.

„Nehmen wir ein T_____ zum Kino?"

„Nein. Das kostet z_____ ."

„Dann nehmen wir die U-_____ ."

*In many German cities bus and subway tickets must be purchased in advance. Tickets often are not collected, but nonuniformed personnel make spot-checks, and people without proper tickets must pay a substantial fine. You should always find out about the system used in the city you're visiting.

„Nein. Dann kann ich die S_____ nicht sehen."

„Richtig. Wir nehmen besser den B_____."

„Gut!"

„Entschuldigen Sie, bitte, wieviel kostet eine _____?"

„Eine Mark."

„Wir s_____ beim Kino in der Schillerstraße aus."

„Gut, mein Herr."

„Wie h_____ die Deutschen sind!"

Was ist das?

a. _____

c. _____

b. _____

d. _____

Mehr Verben

More Action Words

In the previous dialogue we had the verb *nehmen* (to take) and the verb *kosten* (to taste, to cost). Both are conjugated somewhat irregularly:

NEHMEN to take	KOSTEN to taste, to cost	
ich nehm*e*	ich kost*e*	Singular
du *nimmst*	du kost*est*	
er sie } *nimmt* es	er sie } kost*et* es	
wir nehm*en*	wir kost*en*	Plural
ihr nehm*t*	ihr kost*et*	
sie nehm*en*	sie kost*en*	
Sie nehm*en*	Sie kost*en*	Polite, Singular and Plural

Other verbs that take an *e* between stem and ending are *arbeiten* (AR-bei-ten) (to work), *antworten* (AN-tvor-ten) (to answer), *bitten* (BIT-en) (to ask), *finden* (FIN-den) (to find), *senden* (ZEN-den) (to send), and *reden* (RAY-den) (to talk).

Many German verbs have a vowel change in the second and third person singular. Such verbs include *schlafen* (SCHLAH-fen) (to sleep) and *fahren* (FAH-ren) (to go, travel, ride, drive).

SCHLAFEN to sleep	FAHREN to go	
(SCHLAH-feh) ich schlafe	(FAH-reh) ich fahre	Singular
(schlayfst) du schl*ä*fst	(fayRst) du f*ä*hrst	
er sie } schl*ä*ft es	er sie } f*ä*hrt es	
wir schlafen	wir fahren	Plural
ihr schlaft	ihr fahrt	
sie schlafen	sie fahren	
Sie schlafen	Sie fahren	Polite, Singular and Plural

45

Other verbs having a vowel change in the second and third person singular are

(FAL-en)
fallen (to fall)

(FAN-gen)
fangen (to catch)

(TRAH-gen)
tragen (to carry)

(VAK-sen)
wachsen (to grow)

(VA-shen)
waschen (to wash)

(SHAF-neR)
WAS MAN DEM SCHAFFNER SAGT
What to Say to the Conductor

Eine Karte, bitte.   One ticket please.

(EIN-shteig-en)
einsteigen   to get on

(OWS-shteig-en)
aussteigen   to get off

(UM-shteig-en)
umsteigen   to transfer

(AN-hal-ten)
anhalten   to stop

(HALT-eh-shtel-eh)
die Haltestelle   the stop

(SHTAY-en-bleib-en)
stehenbleiben   to remain standing (not move)

PLEASE NOTE: All five of the above-mentioned verbs have separable prefixes. That means that the two parts they consist of have to be separated in certain sentence patterns. Mark says „Wir *steigen* beim Kino *aus*." (''We get off at the movie theater''). Most of the time this kind of verb combines a preposition (*aus, ein, um*) with a verb (*steigen*). Sometimes two verbs are combined in one word (*stehen* and *bleiben*). If a conjugated form of the verb is used, the first part always stands at the end of the sentence: Ich steige ein; er steigt aus; wir steigen aus; sie steigen aus; der Autobus bleibt stehen.

(HOWPT-vör-tern)   *(ar-TEE-keln)*
Von Hauptwörtern und Artikeln
On Nouns and Articles

Let's backtrack a little. We have learned all about articles, and we know that in German there is *der*, *die*, *das*, whereas in English we are much more stingy. All we use is the word *the*. In English we do not divide nouns into genders.

German also is a little more complicated in identifying the function of a noun in a sentence. The function is shown by the noun's *case*. As you'll see on the accompanying tables, there are four cases in German. The case is indicated by the article and in some instances by the spelling of the noun. Let's look at cases involving masculine, feminine, and neuter nouns.

MASCULINE NOUNS

		Function in Sentence	
		English	German
The man is nice. **Der Mann ist nett.**		**subject**	*(NOH-mi-na-teef)* **Nominativ**
I like *the man*. *(mahk)* **Ich mag *den Mann*.**		**direct object**	*(A-ku-za-teef)* **Akkusativ**
I send the letters *to the man*. *(ZEN-deh)* *(BREE-feh)* **Ich sende *dem Mann* die Briefe.**		**indirect object**	*(DAH-teef)* **Dativ**
I like the hair *of the man*. *(hahr)* **Ich mag das Haar *des Mannes*.**		**possessive**	*(GAY-ni-teef)* **Genitiv**

The table below shows the four cases, **in the singular**, of the masculine word *Mann*:

der Mann	den Mann	dem Mann	des Mannes
subject	direct object	indirect object	possessive

In the plural the forms are:

die Männer	die Männer	den Männer*n*	der Männer

FEMININE NOUNS

		Function in Sentence	
		English	German
The woman is pretty. *(hüpsh)* **Die Frau ist hübsch.**		**subject**	**Nominativ**
I like *the woman*. **Ich mag *die Frau*.**		**direct object**	**Akkusativ**

47

FEMININE NOUNS

	Function in Sentence	
	English	German

| I send flowers *to the woman.*
Ich sende *der Frau* Blumen | indirect object | **Dativ** |
| I like the face *of the woman.*
(ge-ZIÇT)
Ich mag das Gesicht *der Frau*. | possessive | **Genitiv** |

Again we have four cases, this time the **singular** of a feminine noun:

die Frau	die Frau	der Frau	der Frau
subject	direct object	indirect object	possessive

In the plural, the forms are:

die Frauen	die Frauen	den Frauen	der Frauen

NEUTER NOUNS

	Function in Sentence	
	English	German

The girl is sweet. *(süs)* *Das Mädchen* ist süß.	subject	**Nominativ**
I love *the girl.* *(LEE-beh)* **Ich liebe *das Mädchen*.**	direct object	**Akkusativ**
I give a kiss *to the girl.* *(kus)* **Ich gebe *dem Mädchen* einen Kuß.**	indirect object	**Dativ**
I love the mouth *of the girl.* *(munt)* **Ich liebe den Mund *des Mädchens*.**	possessive	**Genitiv**

And here we have the four cases of a neuter noun:

das Mädchen	das Mädchen	dem Mädchen	des Mädchens
subject	direct object	indirect object	possessive

Of course, other nouns (and adjectives) have other endings. Watch out for those endings in the dialogues. In the dialogues you learn the language as it is actually spoken.

SUMMARY						
ARTICLES*						
	Singular			Plural		
	M	F	N	M	F	N
Subject	der	die	das	die	die	die
Direct Object	den	die	das	die	die	die
Indirect Object	dem	der	dem	den	den	den
Possessive	des	der	des	der	der	der

*M = masculine; F = feminine; N = neuter.

Did you notice? All nouns use the same articles in the plural. The plural of the noun itself can be formed in several ways. As a rule, nouns add an -n in the dative (indirect object) plural (den Männern) unless the plural form already has a final -n (den Frauen).

Here are two very important irregular verbs you should learn. They are *sein* (to be) and *haben* (to have).

(zein)
SEIN
to be

GERMAN	ENGLISH	EXAMPLE		
(bin)				
ich bin	I am	**Ich bin ein** _____.	(man)	
(bist)				
du bist	you are	**Du bist eine** _____.	(woman)	
er, sie,	he, she,			
(ist)				
es ist	it is	**Er ist ein** _____.	(boy)	
(zint)				
wir sind	we are	**Wir sind** _____.	(2 girls)	
(zeit)				
ihr seid	you are	**Ihr seid** _____.	(2 girls)	
sie sind	they are	**Sie sind** _____.	(2 girls)	
Sie sind	you are (polite)	**Sie sind** _____.	(professor)	

ANSWERS

Sein. Mann Frau Junge zwei Mädchen zwei Mädchen zwei Mädchen ein Professor

(HAH-ben)
HABEN
to have

GERMAN	ENGLISH	EXAMPLE		
(HAH-beh) **ich habe**	I have	**Ich habe einen** _____.	(key)	
(hast) **du hast**	you have	**Du hast einen** _____.	(suitcase)	
(hat) **er, sie, es hat**	he, she, it has	**Er hat ein** _____.	(book)	
(HAH-ben) **wir haben**	we have	**Wir haben** _____.	(flowers)	
(hapt) **ihr habt**	you have	**Ihr habt** _____.	(cats)	
sie haben	they have	**Sie haben** _____.	(cars)	
Sie haben	you have (polite)	**Sie haben** _____.	(sons)	

(fer-SHTAN-den)
Verstanden? (Did you understand?) Now here's a change of pace. A little puzzle that should be easy. Just fill in the correct German words vertically:

1. questions
2. right
3. all
4. and
5. he
6. no

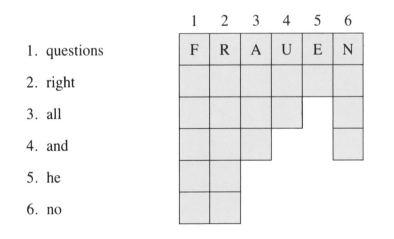

	1	2	3	4	5	6
	F	R	A	U	E	N

50

In English we frequently use contractions—for instance, "do not" is shortened to "don't." Contractions are common in German, too. For example, a preposition and an article are frequently combined and shortened. *Bei dem* (near the) becomes *beim*, *in dem* (in the) becomes *im*. But not all combinations of a preposition and an article are shortened to form a contraction. Thus, *in der* (in the) is never shortened, nor is *auf dem* (on the). Study the following table of frequently used German contractions of a preposition and an article.

(kon-trak-tsee-OH-nen)

Einige Kontraktionen
Some Contractions

Preposition and Article	Contraction	Example
an dem	= **am**	he stands *at the* bed: *am* Bett
auf das	= **aufs**	he puts the paper *on the* sofa: *aufs* Sofa *(ZÓH-fa)*
bei dem	= **beim**	they arrive *near the* market: *beim* Markt
hinter das	= **hinters**	the cat goes *behind the* house: *hinters* Haus
in dem	= **im**	the dog is *in the* house: *im* Haus
in das	= **ins**	the man goes *into the* house: *ins* Haus
über das	= **übers**	the mouse jumps *over the* girl: *übers* Mädchen
von dem	= **vom**	he comes *from the* movie theater: *vom* Kino
vor das	= **vors**	the boy runs *in front of the* girl: *vors* Mädchen
zu dem	= **zum** *(tsum)* (masc.)	the dog walks *to the* man: *zum* Mann
zu der	= **zur** *(tsooR)* (fem.)	the cat walks *to the* mother: *zur* Mutter

Got the idea? Contractions aren't very hard to learn. Let's practice a few:

1. Der _____Hund_____ ist _____ .

2. Der _____ geht _____ .

3. Die _____ springt _____ .

4. Der _____ geht _____ .

51

The following brief passage will allow you to test your comprehension of what you have learned in this unit about transportation.

                                                    (nahch)

Herr Schmidt und seine Frau nehmen den Bus. Nach zwei Haltestellen nehmen sie die
                                                        After

U-Bahn.

Sie steigen bei der Schillerstraße aus. Sie kommen am Markt an und kaufen
     (MEN-geh)
eine Menge.
   lot

Now try to answer the following questions:

1. Was nehmen Herr Schmidt und seine Frau?

_____

2. Was nehmen sie nach zwei Haltestellen?

_____

3. Wo kommen sie an?

_____

4. Was kaufen sie auf dem Markt?

_____

WIEVIEL UHR IST ES?
(ooR)

What time is it?

Es ist acht Uhr.

Es ist ein Uhr.

Es ist drei Uhr.

Es ist neun Uhr.

German indicates "A.M." by adding **morgens** to the time: *zwei Uhr morgens*. **Vormittags**
(MOHR-gens) — in the morning *(FOHR-mi-taks)*

indicates the later morning hours "before midday." **Mittags** means "in the period around

midday." **Nachmittags**, "after midday," indicates P.M. hours, as does **abends**, "in the
(NACH-mi-taks) *(AH-bents)*

evening:" **sieben Uhr abends** (seven in the evening).

WIR ZÄHLEN AUF DEUTSCH

(TSAY-len)

We count in German

Die Grundzahlen 1–1.000.000

(GRUNT-tsah-len)

Cardinal Numbers 1–1,000,000

0	1	2	3	4	5	6
(nul)	*(eins)*	*(tsvei)*	*(drei)*	*(feeR)*	*(fünf)*	*(zeks)*
null	**eins**	**zwei**	**drei**	**vier**	**fünf**	**sechs**

7	8	9	10
(ZEE-ben)	*(acht)*	*(noyn)*	*(tsayn)*
sieben	**acht**	**neun**	**zehn**

11	12	13	14	15	16
(elf)	*(tsvölf)*	*(DREI-tsayn)*	*(FEER-tsayn)*	*(FÜNF-tsayn)*	*(ZEÇ-tsayn)*
elf	**zwölf**	**dreizehn**	**vierzehn**	**fünfzehn**	**sechzehn**

17	18	19	20	21
(ZEEP-tsayn)	*(ACHT-tsayn)*	*(NOYN-tsayn)*	*(TSVAN-tsiç)*	*(EIN-unt-tsvan-tsiç)*
siebzehn	**achtzehn**	**neunzehn**	**zwanzig**	**einundzwanzig,** etc.

30	40	50	60	70
(DREI-siç)	*(FEER-tsiç)*	*(FÜNF-tsiç)*	*(ZEÇ-tsiç)*	*(ZEEP-tsiç)*
dreißig	**vierzig**	**fünfzig**	**sechzig**	**siebzig**

80	90	100	101	200
(ACHT-tsiç)	*(NOYN-tsiç)*	*(HUN-deRt)*	*(HUN-dert-eins)*	*(ZWEI-hun-dert)*
achtzig	**neunzig**	**hundert**	**hunderteins**	**zweihundert,** etc.

1000	1.000.000
(TOW-zent)	*(mil-YOHN)*
tausend	**eine Million**

Die Ordnungszahlen 1–10

(ORD-nungs-tsah-len)

Ordinal Numbers 1–10

1st	2nd	3rd	4th	5th
(AYRS-teh)	*(TSVEI-teh)*	*(DRIT-teh)*	*(FEER-teh)*	*(FÜNF-teh)*
der Erste	**der Zweite**	**der Dritte**	**der Vierte**	**der Fünfte**

6th	7th	8th	9th	10th
(ZEÇS-teh)	*(ZEE-ben-teh)*	*(ACH-teh)*	*(NOYN-teh)*	*(TSAYN-teh)*
der Sechste	**der Siebente**	**der Achte**	**der Neunte**	**der Zehnte**

Now you are ready to learn more about telling time. You will note that a particular time can be expressed in more than one way in German.

Es ist sechs Uhr zehn.
six o'clock and ten (minutes)

(mi-NOO-ten)
Es ist zehn Minuten nach sechs.
ten minutes after six

(fünf) *(feeR-unt-FÜNF-tsiç)*
Es ist fünf Uhr vierundfünfzig.
five fifty-four

Es ist sechs Minuten vor sechs.
six minutes before six

Es ist zwei Uhr dreißig.
two thirty

(halp)
Es ist halb drei.
half before three

Es ist ein Uhr fünfzehn.
one fifteen

(FEER-tel)
Es ist ein Viertel nach eins.
quarter after one

Es ist Viertel zwei.
quarter of the way to two

Es ist zwei Uhr fünfundvierzig.
two forty-five

Es ist ein Viertel vor drei.
a quarter of three

Es ist dreiviertel drei.
three quarters of the way to three

The twenty-four hour system is being used more and more, not only in Germany but all over Europe. It is more practical because it makes the German equivalents of A.M. and P.M. unnecessary.

(tsook) *(FEER-tsayn)*
Der Zug kommt um 14 Uhr (vierzehn Uhr) an.   The train arrives at 2 P.M.
(ZEÇ-tsayn)
Er fährt um 16.30 (sechzehn Uhr dreißig) ab.   It leaves at 4:30 P.M.

1 P.M. = 13 — dreizehn Uhr.

2 P.M. = 14 — vierzehn Uhr.

8 P.M. = 20 — zwanzig Uhr.

To understand the 24-hour system, just deduct 12 from any number of 12 hours or later. Thus, 13.25 is equivalent to 1:25 P.M., 19.27 equals 7:27 P.M., and 0.37 is the same as 12:37 A.M.

Now test yourself on telling time. Remember, there is more than one way of expressing time.

Wieviel Uhr ist es?

a. 2:24   Es ist zwei Uhr vierundzwanzig. _____

b. 6:15 _____

c. 7:30 _____

d. 9:40 _____

e. _____   f. _____   g. _____

(FAHR-plan) **FAHRPLAN** Timetable	(BRÜ-sel) **Brüssel** Brussels	(veen) **—Wien** Vienna		
7.00	**ab**	**Brüssel**	**an**	20.00
13.30	**an**	**Frankfurt**	**ab**	15.00
15.00	**ab**	**Frankfurt**	**an**	13.30
20.15	**an**	(MÜN-çen) **München**	**ab**	8.30
8.30	**ab**	**München**	**an**	20.00
10.30	**an**	(ZALTS-burk) **Salzburg**	**ab**	18.00
10.45	**ab**	**Salzburg**	**an**	17.45
12.00	**an**	(lints) **Linz**	**ab**	16.00
12.30	**ab**	**Linz**	**an**	15.30
15.00	**an**	**Wien**	**ab**	13.00

ab = departs
an = arrives

Referring to the timetable, complete the following sentences:

(fayr-LEST)
1. Der Zug nach Wien verläßt Brüssel um _____ und kommt in Wien
   leaves

um _____ an.

2. Wie lange braucht der Zug von Wien nach Salzburg? _____ .

3. Der Zug verläßt München um _____ und kommt in Brüssel um

_____ an.

Now let's look at numbers in a different context—shopping.

Mr. Smith goes to a department store in Munich.

Er kauft:

(hoot)
einen Hut (dreißig Mark),
   hat
(hemt)
ein Hemd (siebenundzwanzig Mark),
   shirt
(SHOO-eh)
Schuhe (neunzig Mark).
shoes

(irt)   *(nooR)*
Aber der Angestellte irrt sich und sagt: „Es tut mir leid, das Hemd kostet nur zweiundzwanzig
   makes a mistake   only

(tsahlt)
Mark." Wieviel zahlt Herr Smith?
   pays

4. DM _____

The following dialogue contains some expressions useful in telling time.

Read it aloud a few times.

MARK **Entschuldigen Sie, bitte, wieviel**   Excuse me, please, what time is it?

Uhr ist es?

(MIT-eR-nacht)
EIN MANN **Es ist Mitternacht.**   It is midnight.

(sein)   *(noch)*
MARK **Wie kann das sein? Es ist noch**   How can it be? It is still daytime.
(IM-eR)
immer Tag.

EIN MANN	**Entschuldigen Sie, dann ist es**	Excuse me, then it is noon.
	Mittag.	
	(SHPAH-sen)	
MARK	**Spaßen Sie?**	Are you joking?
EIN MANN	**Nein. Ich habe keine Uhr. Sind**	No. I don't have a watch.
	(too-RIST)	
	Sie ein Tourist?	Are you a tourist?
MARK	**Ja.**	Yes.
	(VO-len) (KOW-fen)	
EIN MANN	**Wollen Sie eine Uhr kaufen?**	Do you want to buy
	Zwanzig Mark.	a watch? 20 marks.
MARK	**Aber Sie sagen, daß Sie keine Uhr**	But you say that you don't have a watch.
	haben.	
EIN MANN	**Fünfzehn Mark.**	Fifteen marks.
MARK	**Nein, danke.**	No, thank you.
EIN MANN	**Hier ist Ihre Uhr. Ich bin ein**	Here is your watch. I am an honest pickpocket.
	(AYR-li-çR) (TASH-en-deep)	
	ehrlicher Taschendieb.	

See if you remember the dialogue by filling in the blanks:

1. „Entschuldigen Sie, mein Herr, wieviel _____ ist es?"

2. „Es ist _____ ."

3. „Wie kann das sein, es ist noch immer _____ ."

4. „Entschuldigen Sie, dann ist es _____ ."

5. „_____ Sie?"

6. „Nein. Ich habe keine _____ . Sind sie ein _____ ?"
   „Ja."

7. „Wollen sie eine Uhr _____ ? _____ Mark."

58

8. „Aber Sie _____, daß Sie keine Uhr haben."

9. „Fünfzehn _____."

10. „Nein, _____."

(UN-zeR-eh)   (REI-ze-play-neh)

Unsere Reisepläne
Our Travel Plans

(HOY-teh)
heute, München
today, Munich

(GES-teRn)
gestern, Bonn
yesterday, Bonn

morgen, Wien
tomorrow, Vienna

Some words come up often as you travel. You've already been introduced to quite a few. Here are some more German words frequently used by tourists.

German	English

(VE-teR)
immer gutes Wetter

always good weather

(VEE-deR)
wieder in Deutschland

again in Germany

(owch)   (ÖS-te-reiç)
auch in Österreich

also in Austria

ANSWERS

8. sagen 9. Mark 10. danke

59

German	English
(shohn) *(FRANK-furt)* **schon in Frankfurt**	*already* in Frankfurt
(dort) *(varm)* **dort ist es warm**	*there* it is warm
(heeR) *(kalt)* **hier ist es kalt**	*here* it is cold
(gelt) **ich brauche *viel* Geld**	I need *much, a lot of* money
(VAY-niç) *(HAH-reh)* **er hat *wenig* Haare**	he has *little* hair
(yetst) ***jetzt* gehe ich schlafen**	*now* I go to bed
***jetzt* schlafe ich**	*now* I go to sleep
***gut,* ich auch**	*good*, *okay*, me too
(BES-seR) **dieses Bier ist *besser***	this beer is *better*
(dan) ***dann* ins Kino**	*then* to the movies
(SHTROO-del) ***zuviel* Strudel!**	*too much* strudel!
(gern) **ich komme *gern***	I come *gladly*
(nee) ***nie(mals)* wieder!**	*never* again!
(niçts) *(tsoo)* ***nichts* zu <u>se</u>hen**	*nothing* to see
(NEE-mant) ***niemand* dort**	*nobody* there

Here's a little exercise. See if you can remember the meaning of the underlined words. Match the German sentences with their English equivalents.

1. <u>Heute</u> sind wir in Wien.
2. Er ist <u>schon</u> in München.
3. <u>Morgen</u> sind wir in Linz.
   (TSEI-tiç)
4. Wir essen <u>immer</u> zeitig.
   early
5. <u>Jetzt</u> kommt der Bus.
6. Er hat <u>wenig</u> Geld.
7. Sie ist <u>nie</u> dort.
8. <u>Dann</u> fahren wir nach Bonn.
9. Das kostet <u>zuviel</u>.

a. The bus is coming <u>now</u>.
b. <u>Tomorrow</u> we are in Linz.
c. <u>Today</u> we are in Vienna.

d. He is <u>already</u> in Munich.

e. We <u>always</u> eat early.
f. She is <u>never</u> there.
g. That costs <u>too much</u>.
h. He has <u>little</u> money.
i. <u>Then</u> we will go to Bonn.

Verben

Action words

Tun (to do) and *wissen* (to know) are two more irregular verbs that you should learn.

(toon) **Tun** to do		*(VIS-en)* **Wissen** to know	
(TOO-eh)		*(veis)*	
ich tue	I do	ich weiß	I know
(toost)		*(veist)*	
du tust	you do	du weißt	you know
er tut	he does	er weiß	he knows
wir tun	we do	wir wissen	we know
		(vist)	
ihr tut	you do	ihr wißt	you know
sie tun	they do	sie wissen	they know
Sie tun	you do (polite)	Sie wissen	you know (polite)

Now let's review some of the verb forms we have learned lately:

ich _____
am

wir _____
are

ich _____
have

wir _____
have

du _____
sleep

du _____
eat

ihr _____
do

ich _____
know

du _____
are

ihr _____
are

du _____
have

ihr _____
have

er _____
takes

er _____
sees

du _____
do

du _____
know

er _____
is

Sie _____
are

er _____
has

sie _____
have

er _____
works

wir _____
do

er _____
does

er _____
knows

Mein und Dein
Mine and Yours

Here you have a short summary of the possessive adjectives, words that tell you what belongs to you and what belongs to him or her. They always precede the noun, and their endings reflect the *gender* and *case* of the nouns they modify. In the singular, the endings are the same as those for the indefinite article *ein*.

John ist *mein* Mann.
masculine

Mary ist *meine* Frau.
feminine

Das ist *mein* Buch.
neuter

ANSWERS		
er weiß	du weißt	ich weiß
er tut	du tust	ihr tut
wir tun	er sieht	du ißt
er arbeitet	er nimmt	du schläfst
sie haben	ihr habt	wir haben
er hat	du hast	ich habe
Sie sind	ihr seid	wir sind
er ist	du bist	**Verbs.** ich bin

62

Here is a list of the possessive adjectives. The forms shown here are in the nominative case.

POSSESSIVE ADJECTIVES—NOMINATIVE CASE			
possessive adjective in English	with masculine nouns	with feminine nouns	with neuter nouns
my	mein Sohn	meine Tochter	mein Zimmer
your	dein Vater	deine Mutter	dein Haus
his	sein Freund	seine Schwester	sein Bild
her	ihr Freund	ihre Schwester	ihr Bild
our	unser Baum	unsere Katze	unser Kino
your	euer Vetter	eure Tür	euer Postamt
their	ihr Spiegel	ihre Straße	ihr Bier
your (polite)	Ihr Onkel	Ihre Bank	Ihr Auto

The possessive adjectives all take the same ending in the **plural** for all three genders. For example,

mein*e* Söhne, mein*e* Freundinnen, mein*e* Zimmer (nominative)
mein*er* Söhne, mein*er* Freundinnen, mein*er* Zimmer (genitive)

In the **singular**, the endings vary according to gender and case.

Examples:
Genitive: das Buch mein*es* Mannes my husband's book
Dative: Sie gibt ihr*em* Mann ein Buch. She gives her husband a book.
Accusative: Sie liebt ihr*en* Mann. She loves her husband.

Genitive: das Buch mein*er* Frau my wife's book
Dative: Er gibt sein*er* Frau ein Buch. He gives his wife a book.
Accusative: Er liebt sein*e* Frau. He loves his wife.

(ka-PEERT)
Kapiert? Did you get it? Try to apply your new knowledge of German possessive adjectives to the following little exercise.

SINGULAR

1. _____ Blume
        my
2. _____ Haus
        your   (familiar)
3. _____ Freund
        his
4. _____ Freundin
        her

PLURAL

_____ Blumen
        my
_____ Häuser
        your   (familiar)
_____ Freunde
        his
_____ Freundinnen
        her

ANSWERS
Possessives.
1. meine, meine 2. dein, deine *or* euer, eure 3. sein, seine 4. ihre, ihre

	SINGULAR			PLURAL

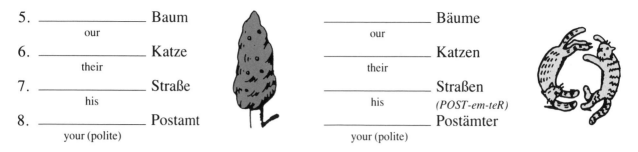

5. _____ Baum
      our

_____ Bäume
      our

6. _____ Katze
      their

_____ Katzen
      their

7. _____ Straße
      his

_____ Straßen
      his
      (POST-em-teR)

8. _____ Postamt
      your (polite)

_____ Postämter
      your (polite)

Uhrzeit. The following brief passage will test your comprehension of what you have learned in this unit about telling time.

„**Wieviel Uhr ist es?**" fragt der Vater seine Tochter.
„**Drei Uhr,**" sagt die Tochter.
      (fleekst)
„**Um wieviel Uhr fliegst du nach Deutschland?**"
      (ANT-vor-tet)
„**Um fünf Uhr zwanzig,**" antwortet die Tochter.
„**Auf Wiedersehen und gute Reise!**"
      (FAH-tee)
„**Auf Wiedersehen, Vati.**"

Now try to answer the following questions:

1. Was fragt der Vater seine Tochter?

_____

2. Was sagt die Tochter?

_____

3. Um wieviel Uhr fliegt die Tochter nach Deutschland?

_____

True or False?

4. Die Mutter spricht mit ihrer Tochter. _____

5. Sie fliegt nach England. _____

6. Es ist jetzt sieben Uhr. _____

ANSWERS

Dialogue.
1. Wieviel Uhr ist es? 2. Drei Uhr. 3. Um fünf Uhr zwanzig 4. F 5. F 6. F

5. unser, unsere 6. ihre, ihre 7. seine, seine 8. Ihr, Ihre

Trains are a very important form of transportation in West Germany, for people as well as freight. You'll probably take a train when in Germany, so the following dialogue should prove very useful. Be sure to read it aloud.

(Al-es) (EIN-shtei-gen)
Alles einsteigen!
All   aboard!

MARY **Also das ist der Bahnhof.** *(AL-zoh) (BAHN-hohf)*

Well, this is the train station.

ANNE **Vati, nehmen wir den Schnellzug** *(SCHNEL-tsook)*

nach Hamburg? *(HAM-burk)*

Dad, do we take the express train to Hamburg?

MARK **Nein, der kostet zu viel.**

No, that costs too much.

ANNE **Nehmen wir den Eilzug?** *(EIL-tsook)*

Do we take the limited-stop train?

MARK **Ja.** (to a ticket clerk) **Entschuldigen**

Sie, bitte, wieviel kostet eine

Rückfahrkarte für vier Personen nach *(RÜK-fahR-kar-teh)   (peR-ZOH-nen)*

Hamburg?

Yes. Excuse me, please, how much is a return ticket for four persons to Hamburg?

(SHAL-ter-be-amter)
SCHALTERBEAMTER **Eilzug?**
ticket clerk

Limited-stop train?

MARK **Ja.**

Yes.

65

SCHALTERBEAMTER **Zweihundert Mark.**	200 marks. Here are the tickets.

Hier sind die Fahrkarten.

(NIÇT-row-cheR)

MARK **Vielen Dank. Gibt es Nichtraucher** Many thanks. Are there nonsmoking sections?

(AP-tei-leh)
Abteile?

SCHALTERBEAMTER **Ja. Der Zug hat** Yes. The train has smoking and nonsmoking

(ROW-cheR)
Raucher und Nichtraucher Abteile. sections.

Now fill in the missing dialogue parts:

1. „Also das ist der B_____.“

2. „Vati, nehmen wir den S_____ nach Hamburg?“

3. „Nein, das k_____ zu viel.“

4. „Nehmen wir den E_____?“

   „Ja.“

5. „Entschuldigen Sie, wieviel k_____ eine R_____ für

   vier P_____ nach Hamburg?“

   „Eilzug?“

   „Ja.“

6. „Zweihundert Mark. Hier sind die F_____.“

There are various types of trains, the fastest being the *TEE-Zug* (Trans-Europe-Express). Also fast is the *IC-Zug* (Intercity-Zug). Less expensive is the *D-Zug* or *Schnellzug*, but this train is less speedy and makes more stops. The *Eilzug* is somewhat slower than the *D-Zug*. The *Personenzug* is the cheapest and slowest. It stops at all stations. Freight is transported by the *Güterzug*.

Tickets can be purchased beforehand from a travel agent or at the railroad station. There usually is no problem getting a seat. There are a number of reduced-fare plans.

Here is a train schedule from Köln (Cologne) to several other European cities. For example, if you want to go to København (Copenhagen) from Köln, there are six trains possible. If you leave Köln at 10 A.M., you will arrive in København at 7:45 P.M. (remember, the train schedules in Europe use the 24-hour system).

Köln

ar an	Observations Bemerkungen		ar an	Observations Bemerkungen
Genova			**Innsbruck**	
6 57	20 07	IC ✕ ✕ Milano	7 57	16 38	IC ✕
15 20	8 06	✕ Milano C Ⓢ	Ⓒ 8 57	17 26	IC ✕ ✕ München TEE ✕
18 46	9 07¹⁾	↝ ↤	9 03	18 36	IC ✕ ✕ München
¹⁾ Ⓦ ar/an 9 56			10 03	19 00	IC ✕
			15 57	1 30	IC ✕ ✕ München Ⓡ
Hamburg Hbf			23 28	9 50	↝ ↤ ✕ München Ⓡ ✕
Ⓒ 5 32	9 48	IC ✕	Ⓒ ①–⑥		
7 00	11 14	IC ✕			
Ⓒ 8 03	12 14	IC ✕	**København**	
9 00	13 14	IC ✕	3 28	14 09	✕ Hamburg
10 00	14 14	IC ✕	7 00	16 29	IC ✕ ✕ Hamburg
10 08	14 57		10 00	19 45	IC ✕
Ⓒ 11 00	15 14	IC ✕	13 00	22 45	IC ✕ ✕ Hamburg
12 03	16 14	IC ✕	Ⓑ 19 00	6 45	IC ✕ ✕ Hamburg ↝ ↤
13 00	17 16	IC ✕	22 39	9 09	↝
14 00	18 14	IC ✕	Ⓑ ①–⑥, ⑦		
15 00	19 14	IC ✕			
Ⓑ 16 03	20 16	IC ✕	**Koblenz**	
17 00	21 14	IC ✕	5 36	6 37	✕
18 00	22 16	IC ✕	Ⓒ 5 57	6 49	IC ✕
Ⓑ 19 00	23 16	IC ✕	6 57	7 49	IC ✕
20 03	0 16	IC ✕	7 00	13 55	⊿
Ⓓ 23 26	5 44	↝ ↤	7 38	8 38	✕
Ⓑ ①–⑥, ⑦			7 57	8 49	IC ✕
Ⓒ ①–⑥			8 24	9 23	✕
Ⓓ Ⓢ; Ⓦ: ①–⑥, ⑦			9 03	9 55	IC ✕
			9 20	10 24	✕
Hannover			9 57	10 49	IC ✕
5 50	9 13		10 49	11 40	TEE ✕
6 14	9 51	✕	10 57	11 49	IC ✕
Ⓒ 7 03	9 59	IC ✕	11 57	12 49	IC ✕
Ⓒ 8 02	10 58	IC ✕	12 32	13 33	
9 03	11 57	IC ✕	12 57	13 49	IC ✕
Ⓓ 10 03	12 57	IC ✕	13 57	14 49	IC ✕
Ⓓ 11 03	13 57	IC ✕	14 14	15 20	
12 02	14 57	IC ✕	14 57	15 49	IC ✕
13 03	15 57	IC ✕	15 20	16 21	
13 25	16 46	✕	15 57	16 49	IC ✕
Ⓐ 14 03	16 57	IC ✕	16 22	17 28	
15 03	17 57	IC ✕	16 57	17 49	IC ✕
Ⓑ 16 02	18 58	IC ✕	17 17	18 21	
Ⓑ 17 03	19 59	IC ✕	17 57	18 49	IC ✕
18 03	20 57	IC ✕	18 46	19 45	
19 03	22 00	IC ✕	Ⓓ 18 57	19 49	IC ✕
20 02	23 00	IC ✕	19 57	20 49	IC ✕
Ⓐ ①–⑥			20 47	21 43	
Ⓑ ①–⑥, ⑦			Ⓓ 21 03	21 55	IC ✕
Ⓒ ①–⑥, except/sauf/ohne 18 VI, 26 XII, 21, 23 IV			21 35	22 32	
Ⓓ ①–⑥			22 36	23 43	
			23 28	0 31	
Heidelberg			Ⓒ ①–⑥, except/sauf/ohne 18 VI, 26–31 XII, 21, 23 IV		
Ⓒ 5 57	8 39	IC ✕	Ⓓ ①–⑥, ⑦, except/sauf/ohne 17 VI, 25 XII, 20, 22 IV		
6 57	9 39	IC ✕ ✕ Mannheim IC ✕			
7 38	10 29	✕	**Liège**	
7 57	10 39	IC ✕	4 47	6 39	
8 24	11 24	✕	7 05	8 41	
Ⓒ 8 57	11 39	IC ✕	Ⓒ 8 09	9 27	IC ✕
Ⓒ 9 57	12 39	IC ✕ ✕ Mannheim IC ✕	8 21	10 07	
10 57	13 39	IC ✕	9 07	10 41	
11 57	14 39	IC ✕	11 12	12 37	
12 57	15 39	IC ✕	13 20	14 48	IC ✕
13 57	16 39	IC ✕	15 08	16 34	
14 57	17 39	IC ✕	16 35	18 10	IC ✕
15 57	18 39	IC ✕	17 06	18 43	✕
16 57	19 39	IC ✕ ✕ Mannheim IC ✕	18 18	19 45	✕
17 57	20 39	IC ✕	20 20	21 51	
Ⓑ 18 57	21 39	IC ✕	23 37	1 14	
19 57	22 42	IC ✕ ✕ Mannheim IC ✕	Ⓒ 29 V–19 XI, 12 XII–7 I, 5 III–2 VI;		
Ⓑ ①–⑥, ⑦			①–⑥ 21 XI–10 XII, 9 I–3 III		
Ⓒ ①–⑥					

Now use the schedule to complete the following questions:

Leave Köln at 3:08 P.M. Arrive in Liège at _____.

Leave Köln at _____ and arrive in Heidelberg at 4:39 P.M.

Leave Köln at 8:47 P.M. and arrive in Koblenz at _____.

(Vee)   *(man)*   *(um)*   *(ET-vas)*   *(BIT-et)*

Wie man um etwas bittet
Asking for something

There are two ways you can say "I want" in German. The second way is more polite.

(vil)
ICH WILL

Ich will ein Glas Bier.   I want a glass of beer.

du willst, er will—

but watch out for the plural:
     (VOL-en)   *(volt)*
wir wollen, ihr wollt, sie wollen

(möç-teh)
ICH MÖCHTE

A little more polite:

Ich möchte ein Glas Bier.   I would like a glass of beer.

du möchtest, er möchte

wir möchten, ihr möchtet, sie möchten

Sie möchten

See if you can match up the verb forms with their meanings in English:

1. ich will	A. they want
2. er möchte	B. she wants
3. sie wollen	C. I want
4. sie will	D. he would like
5. ihr wollt	E. they would like
6. sie möchten	F. you want

ANSWERS

1. C 2. D 3. A 4. B 5. F 6. E

Matching.

4:34 P.M., 1:57 P.M., 9:43 P.M.

68

Here's a further exercise. Fill in the missing word.

(ES-en)

1. Er _____ jetzt essen.
      wants (to eat)

2. Sie _____ ins Kino gehen.
         they would like (to go)

3. Wir _____ zum Bahnhof fahren.
          want (to drive)

4. Sie _____ den D-Zug nehmen.
         she wants (to take)

5. _____ Blumen?
    would you (familiar) like

6. Er _____ ein Glas Milch.
         would like   milk

You got them all correct?

(zahR) (goot)
Sehr gut!
Very   good!

ALLES EINSTEIGEN!

reisen
to travel

(tsook)
der Zug
train

(sich NEE-der-zets-en)
sich niedersetzen
to sit down

(AP-teil)
das Abteil
compartment

(SHLEES-fach)
das Schließfach
locker

(FAHR-gast)
der Fahrgast
passenger

ANSWERS
Fill-ins.
1. will 2. möchten 3. wollen 4. will 5. Möchtest du 6. möchte

(ge-PEK-an-nah-meh-shte-leh)
die Gepäckannahmestelle
baggage checking counter

(ge-PEK-ap-fer-ti-gung)
die Gepäckabfertigung
baggage dispatch

(VAR-teh-zahl)
der Wartesaal
waiting room

(KOW-fen)
Fahrkarten kaufen
to purchase tickets

(FAHR-plahn)
der Fahrplan
train schedule

(BAHN-shteik)
der Bahnsteig
railway platform

(KOF-eR-koo-lee)
der Koffer-Kuli
luggage cart

(ge-PEK-tray-geR)
der Gepäckträger
porter

WORD HUNT
**Can you find these eight words in German that are
hidden away in this puzzle?**

1. to travel
2. train schedule
3. waiting room
4. compartment
5. we
6. movie theater
7. to fall
8. all

N	Z	L	W	I	R	G	K	A
R	I	N	A	M	P	F	I	B
F	A	H	R	P	L	A	N	G
E	A	B	T	E	I	L	O	E
S	B	O	E	B	P	L	L	I
R	E	I	S	E	N	E	B	Z
N	Z	N	A	F	O	N	C	I
O	L	Z	A	R	L	M	G	G
E	D	R	L	G	N	A	A	L

Reflexivpronomen
Reflexive Pronouns

A reflexive verb refers or "reflects" the action back to the subject of a sentence. This is done by means of reflexive pronouns, such as "myself" and "yourself." Here are the reflexive pronouns in German.

Example:

(VA-sheh)

ich	wasche	mich
subject	verb	object
I	wash	myself

ich wasche mich	I wash myself
(vesht)	
du wäscht dich	you wash yourself
(vesht) *(ziç)*	
er, sie, es wäscht sich	he, she, it washes himself, herself, itself
(VA-shen)	
wir waschen uns	we wash ourselves
(vasht)	
ihr wascht euch	you wash yourselves
sie waschen sich	they wash themselves
Sie waschen sich (polite)	you wash yourself, yourselves

There are no special words for the reflexive pronouns in the first and second persons; we use the personal pronouns *mich, dich, uns, euch.* The reflexive pronoun for all three genders in the third person singular is *sich,* and *sich* is also the reflexive pronoun for the third person plural and for the formal *Sie* (you).

SUMMARY		
Subject	Verb	Reflexive Pronoun (object)
ich	_____	mich
du	_____	dich
er, sie, es	_____	sich
wir	_____	uns
ihr	_____	euch
sie	_____	sich
Sie	_____	sich

Let's practice using reflexive pronouns with the verb *amüsieren* (*a-mü-ZEE-ren*), which in its reflexive form is *sich amüsieren*, which means—you guessed it—to amuse oneself, to enjoy oneself.

ich amüsiere _____   du amüsierst _____

er amüsiert _____   wir amüsieren _____

ihr amüsiert _____   sie amüsieren _____

Here are some more reflexive verbs. Study them and then complete the short exercise that follows. It should be easy. You're well into your new language.

sich rasieren: (*rah-ZEE-ren*)   to shave oneself

sich entschuldigen: to excuse oneself, to apologize

sich erinnern: (*eR-IN-ern*)   to remember

1. Wann rasiert er _____?

2. Entschuldigst du _____?

3. Ihr erinnert _____.

4. Wir rasieren _____.

5. Sie amüsiert _____.

6. Erinnert sie _____?

7. Ich entschuldige _____.

8. Amüsierst du _____?

(iç) *(bin)*

Ich bin . . .
I Am . . .

As you travel, you'll meet people from a variety of countries. Here are some ways nationality is identified in German.

(a-may-ree-KAH-neR)

Ich bin Amerikaner.
I am American.

(ÖS-teR-rei-çeR)

Ich bin Österreicher.
Austrian

(ows-TRAH-lee-eR)

Ich bin Australier.
Australian

(BEL-gee-eR)

Ich bin Belgier.
Belgian

(ENG-len-deR)

Ich bin Engländer.
English

(ka-NAH-dee-eR)

Ich bin Kanadier.
Canadian

(çi-NAY-zeh)

Ich bin Chinese.
Chinese

(DAY-neh)

Ich bin Däne.
Danish

(HOL-en-deR)

Ich bin Holländer.
Dutch

(fran-TSOH-zeh)

Ich bin Franzose.
French

(DOY-tcheR)

Ich bin Deutscher.
German

(i-ta-lee-AY-ner)

Ich bin Italiener.
Italian

(ya-PAH-neR)

Ich bin Japaner.
Japanese

(mek-si-KAH-neR)

Ich bin Mexikaner.
Mexican

(NOHR-vay-geR)

Ich bin Norweger.
Norwegian

(POH-leh)

Ich bin Pole.
Polish

(RUS-eh)

Ich bin Russe.
Russian

(SHPAHN-ee-eR)

Ich bin Spanier.
Spanish

(SHVAY-deh)

Ich bin Schwede.
Swedish

(SHVEI-tseR)

Ich bin Schweizer.
Swiss

(TÜR-keh)

Ich bin Türke.
Turkish

In the preceding examples nationality was given in the masculine form. The feminine form usually, but

(a-may-ree-KAH-ner-in)

not always, ends with *-in.* For instance, a woman would say „Ich bin Amerikanerin" or „Ich bin

(çi-NAY-zin)   *(DOY-tcheh)*

Chinesin" or „Ich bin Deutsche."

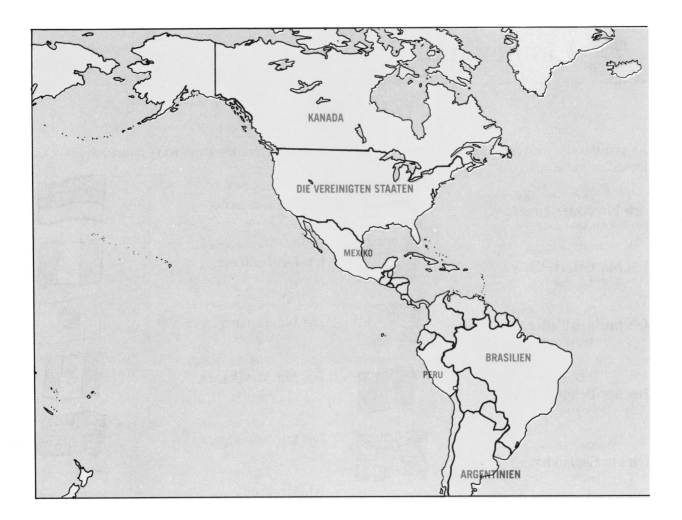

All of the following countries except two are classified as neuter. The definite or indefinite article is hardly ever used with the "neuter" countries. The article is used, however, with the "feminine" countries (die Schweiz, for instance) and the "plural" countries (die Vereinigten Staaten, for example).

(OWS-tral-ee-en)
Australien   Australia

(ÇEE-na)
China   China

(DOYTCH-lant)
Deutschland   Germany

(i-TAL-i-en)
Italien   Italy

(MEKS-ee-ko)
Mexiko   Mexico

(SHPAHN-i-en)
Spanien   Spain

(feR-EI-niç-ten) (SHTAH-ten)
die Vereinigten Staaten
(a-MAY-ree-kah)
von Amerika   U.S.A.
   or
(oo-es-ah)
die U.S.A.

(shveits)
die Schweiz   Switzerland

(KA-na-da)
Kanada   Canada

(FRANK-reiç)
Frankreich   France

(GROHS-bri-tah-ni-en)
Großbritannien Great Britain

(ÖS-teR-reiç)
Österreich   Austria

(YAH-pan)
Japan   Japan

(RUS-lant)
Rußland   Russia

(ma-ROK-oh)
Marokko   Morocco

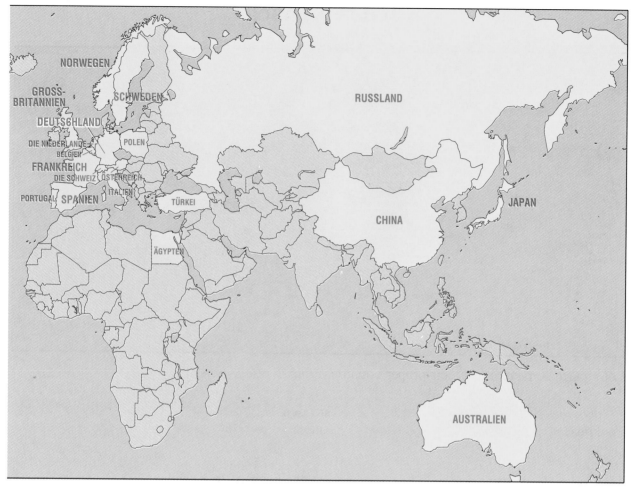

(iç)   (SHPRE-çeh)

Ich spreche
I speak . . .

Let's learn to say the names of some languages. As in English, the name of the language is often very similar to the name of the country.

(Eng-lish)
Ich spreche Englisch.

(RU-sish)
Ich spreche Russisch.

(doytch)
Ich spreche Deutsch.

(çi-NAY-zish)
Ich spreche Chinesisch.

(fran-TSÖ-zish)
Ich spreche Französisch.

(yo-PAH-nish)
Ich spreche Japanisch.

(SHPAH-nish)
Ich spreche Spanisch.

75

Ich reise nach

I am traveling to . . .

Let's place some cities in their proper countries. *Auf Deutsch, bitte.*

(FRAH-geh)	(ANT-vort)
Frage	**Antwort**
question	answer

1. Wo ist Vancouver?   Vancouver ist in Kanada.

2. Wo ist Los Angeles? _____

3. Wo ist Stockholm? _____

    (pa-REES)

4. Wo ist Paris? _____

5. Wo ist Madrid? _____

6. Wo ist London? _____

    (rohm)

7. Wo ist Rom? _____

8. Wo ist Casablanca? _____

(feR-LOHR-en)   *(OO-bahn)*

Verloren in der U-Bahn

Lost in the Subway

Knowing the frustrations of not being understood, can you imagine how Anne felt when she lost her purse?

BERLIN (Bus and Subway System)

From Berliner Verkehrs-Betriebe (BVG). Reprinted by permission.

ANNE (to policeman at desk in police station)

Entschuldigen Sie bitte, sprechen Sie Englisch?	Excuse me, please, do you speak English?
(VAY-niç)	
POLIZIST **Ein wenig. Womit kann ich**	A little. How can I help you?
(be-HILF-liç)	
Ihnen behilflich sein?	
ANNE **My purse—**	
(HANT-ta-sheh)	
POLIZIST **Ihre Handtasche?**	Your purse?
(vek)	
ANNE **Ja. Die ist weg! In der U-Bahn . . . .**	Yes. It is gone. In the subway . . . .

77

POLIZIST	*(leit)* *(BAHR-gelt)* **Das tut mir leid. Viel Bargeld?** **Cash?**
	I am sorry. Much cash?
ANNE	**Cash—nur ein paar Mark. Aber** **tausend Mark in—in—**
	Only a few marks. But 1,000 marks in—in—
POLIZIST	*(REI-zeh-sheks)* **Reiseschecks? Traveler's** **checks?**
ANNE	*(kre-DIT-kar-ten)* **Ja. Auch Kreditkarten und mein** *(REI- zeh-pas)* **Reisepaß. Was soll ich tun?**
	Yes. Also credit cards and my passport. What shall I do?
POLIZIST	**Haben Sie die Nummern der** **Reiseschecks?**
	Do you have the numbers of the traveler's checks?
ANNE	**O ja.**
	Oh yes.

POLIZIST	*(bü-ROH)* *(gleiç)* **Gut. Ein Büro ist gleich hier** *(er-ZETST)* **um die Ecke. Dort ersetzt man** *(HO-fent-liç)* **hoffentlich die Reiseschecks.**
	Good. An office is right around the corner. There they can hopefully replace the travelers checks.
ANNE	**Ersetzt?**
	Replace them?
POLIZIST	**Ja. Und dort kann man Ihnen** *(FEE-leiçt)* **vielleicht auch mit den Kreditkarten** **helfen.**
	Yes. And there they can possibly also help you with the credit cards.

ANNE	**Und mein Reisepaß?**
	And my passport?
POLIZIST	**Da müssen Sie zum** *(kon-zu-LAT)* **amerikanischen Konsulat. Möchten** *(FOR-moo-lar)* **Sie bitte dieses Formular ausfüllen?** *(HIN-zets-en)* **Sie können sich dort hinsetzen.**
	With this you have to go to the American consulate. Would you please fill out this form? You can sit there.
ANNE	**Vielen Dank.**
	Many thanks.
POLIZIST	*(ge-SHAY-en)* **Gern geschehen. Und es tut** *(VIRK-liç)* **mir wirklich leid.**
	Don't mention it. And I am truly sorry.

Autos und Kleinbusse
Cars and Vans

(SHTRAH-sen-shil-deR)

Straßenschilder
Road Signs

(bei) *(dayR)* *(OW-toh-feR-mee-tung)*

BEI DER AUTOVERMIETUNG
At the Car Rental Office

Read the following dialogue closely. It should prove useful if you want to rent a car — perhaps to see the many sights of Vienna (Wien). As always, say each German line out loud several times.

MARK	**Guten Morgen. Ich möchte einen** *(MEE-ten)* **Wagen mieten.**	Good morning. I would like to rent a car.
ANGESTELLTER	*(LAN-geh)* **Für wie lange?**	For how long?''
MARK	**Zwei Wochen.**	Two weeks.
	(VAR-ten)	
ANGESTELLTER	**, Warten Sie mal . . . wir** *(OH-pel)* *(FOLKS-vah-gen)* **haben einen Opel und einen Volkswagen.** *(KLEIN-eR)* **Der Volkswagen ist kleiner.**	Let's see . . . we have an Opel and a Volkswagen. The Volkswagen is smaller.
MARK	**Ich nehme den Volkswagen. Ist der** *(UN-be-shrenk-teR)* **Preis mit unbeschränkter** *(KEE-loh-may-teR-tsahl)* **Kilometerzahl?**	I'll take the Volkswagen. Is the mileage (number of kilometers) included in the price?
ANGESTELLTER	**Ja, aber Sie zahlen für** *(ben-TSEEN)* *(FÜ-reR-shein)* **das Benzin. Ihr Führerschein und eine** **Kreditkarte, bitte.**	Yes, but you pay for the gas. Your driver's license and a credit card, please.
MARK	*(TSEI-gen)* **Können Sie mir zeigen, wie die** *(SHAL-tung)* **Schaltung und die Lichter** *(funk-tsee-oh-NEE-ren)* **funktionieren?**	Can you show me how the gear shift and the lights work?
ANGESTELLTER	*(na-TÜR-liç)* **Natürlich. Hier ist der** *(SHLÜS-el)* *(OW-toh-pah-pee-reh)* **Schlüssel und die Autopapiere. Ich** **komme mit Ihnen.**	Of course. Here is the key and the car papers. I am coming with you.
MARK	*(OW-toh-mah-ti-sheh)* **Das Auto hat automatische** **Schaltung, nicht wahr?**	The car has automatic transmission, right?
ANGESTELLTER	**Nein, das Auto hat** *(GANG-shal-tung)* **Gangschaltung.**	No, the car has manual shift.
MARK	*(HIM-mel)* **Ach du lieber Himmel, ich kann** **nur automatische Schaltung fahren!**	Oh my heavens, I can only drive an automatic!

Wichtiges für den Autofahrer

(VIÇ-ti-ges) *(füR)* *(dayn)* *(OW-toh-fah-reR)*

Essential Phrases for Drivers

(feR-IRT) **Ich habe mich verirrt.**	I am lost.
(ga-RAH-žeh) *(NAY-eh)* **Gibt es* eine Garage in der Nähe?**	Is there a garage nearby?
Was ist los?	What's the matter?
(ge-RAH-deh-ows) *(VEI-teR)* **Fahren Sie geradeaus weiter.**	Continue straight ahead.
Fahren Sie hier links, dann rechts.	Turn left here, then right.
(feR-KAYR) *(shlim)* **Der Verkehr ist schlimm.**	The traffic is bad.
Sie haben recht.	You are right.
(UN-reçt) **Sie haben unrecht.**	You are wrong.
der Schlüssel	key
die Autopapiere	car papers
der Führerschein	driver's license
das Benzin	gasoline
(veit) *(NAH-eh)* **weit, nahe**	far, near
(dort) *(DRÜ-ben)* **dort drüben**	over there
an der Ecke von	at the corner of
(NOR-den) *(ZÜ-den)* *(OS-ten)* *(VES-ten)* **der Norden, Süden, Osten, Westen**	north, south, east, west
die Kreditkarte	credit card
die Verkehrsampel	traffic light
bis	until, till

---

*Es gibt (literally: "it gives") is the equivalent of "there is" or "there are" in English.

(SHTRAH-sen-shil-deR)

STRASSENSCHILDER
Road Signs

If you're planning to drive while you're abroad, spend some time remembering the meanings of these signs.

Dangerous intersection

Danger!

Stop

Speed limit (in km/hr)

Minimum speed

End of limited speed

No entry

Yield right-of-way

Two-way traffic

Dangerous curve

Entrance to Autobahn

End of Autobahn

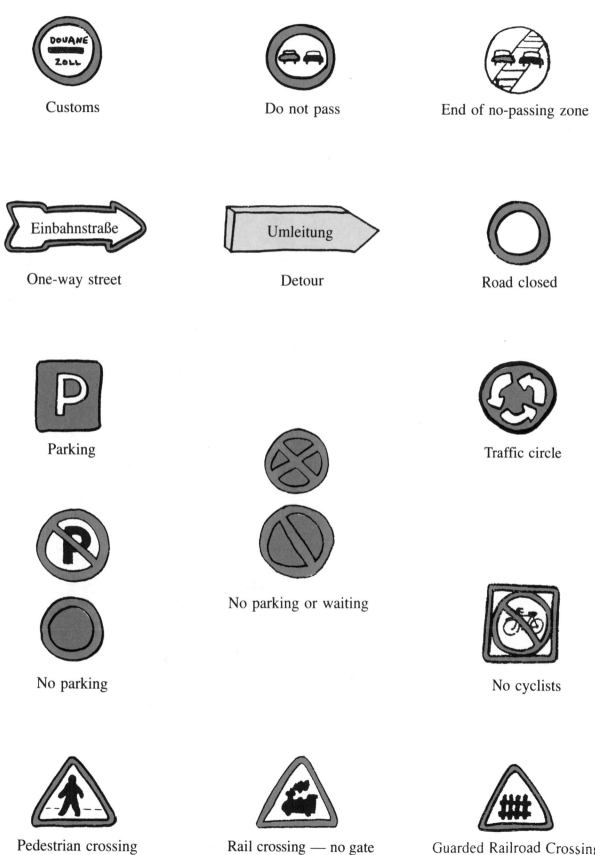

Customs

Do not pass

End of no-passing zone

One-way street

Detour

Road closed

Parking

Traffic circle

No parking or waiting

No parking

No cyclists

Pedestrian crossing

Rail crossing — no gate

Guarded Railroad Crossing

BEI DER TANKSTELLE
(TANK-shtel-eh)

At the Service Station

Hamburg

(Courtesy of Hamburg Tourist Office)

KUNDE *(KUN-deh)*
customer

Volltanken, bitte! *(FOL-tan-ken)*

Fill it up, please!

TANKWART *(TANK-vart)*
attendant

Normal oder super? *(nor-MAHL)* **Bleifrei?** *(ZOO-peR) (BLEI-frei)*

Regular or super? Leadfree?

KUNDE **Normal, bleifrei. Und sehen Sie** (op) (REI-fen) (ge-NOOK) **nach, ob die Reifen genug** (LUFT-druk) (öl) **Luftdruck haben, auch das Öl und** **das Wasser.**	Regular, unleaded. And check the air pressure in the tires, the oil and the water too.
TANKWART **Alles ist in Ordnung.** (be-ZOOCHT) **Haben Sie Hamburg besucht?**	Everything is okay. Did you visit Hamburg?
KUNDE **Ja, zum ersten Mal.**	Yes, for the first time.
TANKWART **Wie hat Ihnen die Stadt** **gefallen?**	How did you like the city?
KUNDE **Prima. Die St. Michaelis** (sankt) (mi-ça-AY-lis) (KIR-çeh) **Kirche—**	Super. St. Michael's Church—
TANKWART **Ah—der große Michel, das** (MI-çel) (VAHR-tsei-çen) **Wahrzeichen Hamburgs—**	Ah—the great Michel, the symbol of Hamburg—
KUNDE **das Rathaus, die Universität,** (RAT-hows) (u-ni-ver-zi-TAYT) **die Kunsthalle—**	the Town Hall, the University, the Art Museum—
TANKWART **Interessant, nicht wahr?** (in-ter-es-ANT)	Interesting, right?
KUNDE **Sehr. Ich fahre nach Kiel. Was ist** (keel) (KÜR-tse-steh) (SHTRE-keh) **die kürzeste Strecke?**	Very. I'm driving to Kiel. What is the shortest route?
TANKWART **Von hier geradeaus, bis Sie** (ge-rah-deh-OWS) **zur Autobahn kommen. Die geht** **direkt nach Kiel.**	From here straight ahead until you get to the Autobahn. It goes directly to Kiel.
KUNDE **Ist der Verkehr schlimm?**	Is the traffic bad?
TANKWART **Um diese Zeit gibt es vielleicht** (feR-KAYRS-shtow-ung-en) (an-ZONS-ten, **einige Verkehrsstauungen, ansonsten** **ist die Strecke gut.**	At this time, there may be some traffic jams; otherwise, the road is good.

DAS AUTO
The Car

(HOO-peh)
die Hupe
horn

(ar-ma-TOOR-en-bret)
das Armaturenbrett
dashboard

(VINT-shuts-sheib-eh)
die Windschutzscheibe
windshield

(LENK-raht)
das Lenkrad
steering wheel

(SHEIB-en-vish-eR)
die Scheibenwischer
windshield wipers

(KUP-lung)
die Kupplung
clutch

(GAS-pe-dahl)
das Gaspedal
accelerator

(BREM-zeh)
die Bremse
brake

(SHAL-tung)
die Schaltung
gear shift

(RÜK-shpee-gel)
der Rückspiegel
rear-view mirror

(MOH-tohr)
der Motor
motor

(dach)
das Dach
roof

(ba-teh-REE)
die Batterie
battery

(moh-TOHR-howb-eh)
die Motorhaube
hood

der Kühler
radiator

die Tür
door

(KÜL-eR-gril)
der Kühlergrill
radiator grill

(SHEIN-verf-eR)
der Scheinwerfer
headlight

(KO-feR-rowm)
der Kofferraum
trunk

(NUM-ern-shilt)
das Nummernschild
license plate

(ben-TSEEN-pum-peh)
die Benzinpumpe
gas pump

(FEN-steR)
das Fenster
window

(VAH-gen-tüR)
die Wagentür
car door

(ben-TSEEN-tank)
der Benzintank
gas tank

(TÜR-grif)
der Türgriff
door handle

(ca-roh-seh-REE)
die Karosserie
body (of car)

(KOHT-flü-gel)
der Kotflügel
fender

(REIF-en)
der Reifen
tire

(SHTOHS-shtang-eh)
die Stoßstange
bumper

86

Wichtige Ausdrücke übers Auto

(VIÇ-ti-geh) (OWS-drü-keh) (OW-toh)

Essential Expressions about Your Car

(REI-fen-pan-eh) **Ich habe eine Reifenpanne.**	I have a flat tire.
(shpringt) **Mein Wagen springt nicht an.**	My car does not start.
Meine Bremsen funktionieren nicht.	My brakes don't work.
Ich brauche Benzin.	I need gas.
(SHMEE-rung) **Der Wagen braucht Schmierung.**	The car needs grease.
(TSÜNT-kert-sen) **Sehen Sie sich die Zündkerzen an.**	Check the sparkplugs.
Waschen Sie den Wagen, bitte.	Wash the car, please.
Eine Straßenkarte, bitte.	A road map, please.
(me-ÇAH-ni-keR) **Ich brauche einen Mechaniker.**	I need a mechanic.
(AP-shlep-vah-gen) **Ich brauche einen Abschleppwagen.**	I need a tow truck.
Der Motor geht aus.	The car stalls.
Das Auto bleibt stehen.	The car doesn't move.
(lek) **Der Kühler hat ein Leck.**	The radiator has a leak.
(KLEE-ma-an-lah-geh) (HEITS-ung) **Die Klimaanlage　(Heizung) geht nicht.**	The air-conditioning (heater) doesn't work.
(ka-PUT) **Die Batterie ist kaputt.**	The battery is dead.

Now fill in the names for the following auto parts.

_____　　_____　　_____

_____　　_____　　_____

(IM-per-a-teef)

Der Imperativ
The imperative

In order to have people do things for you, you need to know how to use verbs in a "command" or "imperative" way. In German, the imperative can be formed by using the infinitive of a verb

(LAY-sen)

plus "Sie"—for instance, *Essen Sie!* (Eat!), *Lesen Sie das Buch!* (Read the book!)

There is also a familiar form of the imperative used among friends and family members. In this form a verb without a personal pronoun is used; the verb is a shortened form of the infinitive.

(balt)   *(FOHR-siçt)*

Examples of the familiar imperative are *Antworte bald!* (Answer soon!), *Fahre mit Vorsicht!* (Drive carefully!)

Here are some more examples of the familiar imperative.

For the following type of verb simply chop the ending *-en* off the infinitive to form the familiar imperative:

Stem-ending	Example	English
kommen	**Komm her!**	Come here!
holen	**Hol das Buch!**	Get the book!
gehen	**Geh ins Haus!**	Go into the house!
bleiben	**Bleib hier!**	Stay here!

88

If the stem of the verb ends in *-t, -fn* or *-ig* an *-e* is added:

Stem-ending	Example	English
antworten	**Antworte mir!**	Answer me!
öffnen	**Öffne die Tür!**	Open the door!
entschuldigen	**Entschuldige, bitte!**	Excuse me, please!

Remember the verbs that take an *i* or *ie* in the second person singular? They also change the *e* to *i* or *ie* in the imperative: *Gib! Sprich! Nimm!* As always there are exceptions, such as: *Sei gut, Seien Sie gut* (be good).

(UN-fall)

EIN UNFALL
An Accident

(HIM-els)   *(VIL-en)*

ERSTER FAHRER   **Um Himmels willen! Können**   For heaven's sake! Can't you be careful? Can't

(FOHR-ziçtiç)

Sie nicht vorsichtig sein? Können Sie   you read? Can't you see? *I* have the right-of-way!

(LAY-zen)

nicht lesen? Können Sie nicht sehen?

(FOHR-fahRt)

Ich habe Vorfahrt!

ZWEITER FAHRER **Ich weiß. Aber Sie**	I know. But you drive 150 kilometers per hour.
(ge-SHVIN-dik-keits-gren-tseh)	
fahren 150. Die Geschwindigkeitsgrenze	The speed limit is 60 kilometers.
ist 60.	
(HEL-fen)	
DRITTER FAHRER **Kann ich Ihnen helfen?**	Can I help you?
(HOH-len)	
ERSTER FAHRER **Ja. Holen Sie den**	Yes. Get the policeman over there. Let him
(po-li-TSIS-ten)	
Polizisten dort drüben. Er soll sich den	look at the damage.
(SHAH-den) (AN-zay-en)	
Schaden ansehen.	

POLIZIST **Was ist los?**	What's the matter?
(i-di-OHT) (dah)	
ERSTER FAHRER **Dieser Idiot da fährt in**	This idiot runs into my car. *His* fault.
(rein) *(shult)*	
meinen Wagen rein. *Seine* Schuld.	
(vahR) *(kerl)*	
ZWEITER FAHRER **Das ist nicht wahr. Der Kerl**	That is not true. The guy drives like a madman.
(feR-RÜK-teR) *(rahst)*	
fährt wie ein Verrückter. Er rast.	He speeds.
(NEE-mant) *(feR-LETST)*	
POLIZIST **Niemand ist verletzt? Gut.**	Nobody is hurt? Good. Your driver's licenses,
(in-fohr-MEE-ren)	
Ihre Führerscheine, bitte. Informieren	please. Inform your insurance companies.
(feR-ZIÇ-e-rungs-ge-zel-shaf-ten)	
Sie Ihre Versicherungsgesellschaften.	
Dort drüben an der Ecke ist eine Garage.	Over there at the corner is a garage.

IN DER GARAGE
At the garage

ZWEITER FAHRER (to a mechanic at the garage):	
(rash)	
Können Sie meinen Wagen rasch	Can you repair my car quickly?
(re-pa-REE-ren)	
reparieren?	
(me-ÇAH-ni-ker)	
MECHANIKER **Sie haben Glück. Das rechte**	You are lucky. The rear right wheel is bent, and
(HIN-teR-raht) *(fer-BOH-gen)*	
Hinterrad ist verbogen und der	the fender is dented. That's all. Telephone me
(EIN-ge-drükt)	
Kotflügel ist eingedrückt. Das ist alles.	tomorrow afternoon.
Rufen Sie mich morgen nachmittag an.	

Modalverben: müssen, können, dürfen

(moh-DAHL-ver-ben)   *(MÜS-en)*   *(KÖN-en)*   *(DÜR-fen)*

Modal Verbs: must   can   may

These are three important modal verbs. We use them all the time in German.

For example: *Ich **muß** jetzt gehen.*
I must go now.
*Ich **kann** Deutsch sprechen.*
I can speak German.
*Ich **darf** rauchen.*
I may smoke.

MÜSSEN must	KÖNNEN can	DÜRFEN may
(mus) **ich muß**	*(kan)* **ich kann**	*(darf)* **ich darf**
(must) **du mußt**	*(kanst)* **du kannst**	*(darfst)* **du darfst**
er **sie** } **muß** **es**	**er** **sie** } **kann** **es**	**er** **sie** } **darf** **es**
wir müssen	**wir können**	**wir dürfen**
(müst) **ihr müßt**	**ihr könnt**	*(dürft)* **ihr dürft**
sie müssen	**sie können**	**sie dürfen**
Sie müssen	**Sie können**	**Sie dürfen**

The modal verbs, sometimes called auxiliaries of mood, are rather easy to learn. You probably noticed that they are used with the infinitive of the verb.

Let's practice them:

1. _____ lesen?
   Can't you (plural polite)   *(ROW-chen)*

2. _____ sehen?
   Can't you (plural polite)

3. _____ rauchen.
   I am not allowed to   smoke

4. _____ hier bleiben.
   We must

5. _____ studieren?
   Do you have to (polite)

6. _____ es tun.
   She can

ANSWERS

1. Können Sie nicht **2.** Können Sie nicht **3.** Ich darf nicht **4.** Wir müssen **5.** Müssen Sie **6.** Sie kann

91

Here's another little exercise.

Put the words into the correct order so they form sentences. Note that you can make a statement of fact (declarative sentence) or a question out of each group of words. It all depends on the word order.

1. gut/er/singen/kann _____

2. kommen/Mark/heute/darf _____

3. du/das/kannst/machen? _____

4. essen/müssen/wir _____

AUSRÜSTUNG
(OWS-rüs-tung)

Equipment

The following are German words for items you may want to bring along if you go camping—and Germany has many lovely camping spots. You can buy camping gear in most cities as well as in many resort villages.

(tselt)
das Zelt
tent

(SHLAHF-zak)
der Schlafsack
sleeping bag

(KLEI-dungs-shtü-keh)
die Kleidungsstücke
articles of clothing

(PAD-el)
das Paddel
paddle

(DE-keh)
die Decke
blanket

(TASH-en-lam-peh)
die Taschenlampe
flashlight

(TAYR-mos-fla-sheh)
die Thermosflasche
thermos

(korp)
der Korb
basket

(PAD-el-boht)
das Paddelboot
canoe

(SHTEE-fel)
die Stiefel
boots

(AN-gel-roo-teh)
die Angelrute
fishing pole

(DOH-zen)
die Dosen
cans (of food)

(KOCH-ge-shir)
das Kochgeschirr
cooking utensils

(toy-LE-ten-ar-tee-kel)
die Toilettenartikel
toilet articles

(KOF-eR-rah-dee-o)
das Kofferradio
portable radio

(SHTREIÇ-höl-tseR)
die Streichhölzer
matches

(LUFT-ma-tra-tseh)
die Luftmatratze
air mattress

(EI-meR)
der Eimer
bucket

(KOR-ken-tsœ-eR)
der Korkenzieher
corkscrew

(SHACH-tel)
die Schachtel,

(be-HEL-teR)
der Behälter
box

Zum Campingplatz

(tsum) *(KEM-ping-plats)*

To the Campground

MARK	**Entschuldigen Sie. Gibt es einen Campingplatz hier in der Nähe?**	Excuse me. Is there a campground in the vicinity?

MARK **Entschuldigen Sie. Gibt es einen Campingplatz hier in der Nähe?**

Excuse me. Is there a campground in the vicinity?

JOHANN **Ja, etwa 20 Kilometer von hier.**
(TSEI-çen)
Sehen Sie diese Zeichen mit dem Zelt?
(FOL-gen)
Folgen Sie ihnen.

Yes, about 20 kilometers from here. Do you see these signs with a tent? Follow them.

MARK **Wissen Sie, ob es dort Toiletten**
(TRINK-vas-eR) *(DOO-shen)*
und Trinkwasser gibt? Und Duschen?
(e-LEK-tri-sheh)
Kann man dort elektrische Geräte
(AN-shlees-sen)
anschließen? Und wieviel kostet das?

Do you know whether there are toilets and drinking water there? And showers? Can you plug in electrical appliances there? And how much does it cost?

JOHANN **Ich weiß nicht. Halten Sie am**
(geRn)
Campingplatz. Die geben Ihnen gern
(OWS-kunft)
Auskunft.

I don't know. Stop at the camp ground. They'll gladly give you information.

Word Hunt: Can you find the German equivalent of these six terms in this puzzle?

1. tent

2. blanket

3. sleeping bag

4. fishing pole

5. boots

6. cans

D	O	R	Z	N	G	A	S	T	P
O	P	D	E	C	K	E	L	M	R
S	C	H	L	A	F	S	A	C	K
E	G	L	T	K	P	R	U	E	Ü
N	D	B	C	A	L	M	R	S	B
L	A	N	G	E	L	R	U	T	E
M	N	O	S	T	I	E	F	E	L

ANSWERS

Word Hunt.
1. Zelt 2. Decke 3. Schlafsack 4. Angelrute 5. Stiefel 6. Dosen

94

(LAY-bens-mit-el-ge-sheft)

Im Lebensmittelgeschäft

At the Grocery Store

ANNE *(HAL-bes)* **Guten Morgen. Ich möchte ein halbes**	Good morning. I would like half a kilo of
(NOO-deln) *(BUT-eR)* **Kilo Nudeln, 100 Gramm Butter, vier**	noodles, 100 grams of butter,
(LEE-teR) **Scheiben Schinken, einen Liter Milch,**	four slices of ham, a liter of milk,
(zalts) *(FLA-sheh)* **Salz, und eine Flasche Wein.**	salt, and a bottle of wine.
(SHACH-tel) **Auch eine Schachtel Streichhölzer.**	Also a box of matches.
(LAH-den-be-sits-eR) *(TSEL-ten)* **LADENBESITZER** **Zelten Sie hier?** Storekeeper	Are you camping here? Do you come here every
(hayr) **Kommen Sie jedes Jahr hier her?**	year?
ANNE **Ja, aber nicht nächstes Jahr.**	Yes, but not next year. Next year I will travel
Nächstes Jahr reise ich nach	to Norway. How much are the apples?
Norwegen. Wieviel kosten die Äpfel?	
LADENBESITZER **Achtzig Pfennig per Stück.**	Eighty pfennigs a piece.
ANNE **Soviel? Ich nehme einen.**	So much? I'll take one.
(TOY-eR) **LADENBESITZER** **Ja, die Äpfel sind teuer.**	Yes, the apples are expensive. Ten eggs cost
Zehn Eier kosten zwei Mark.	two Marks.
ANNE **Zwei Mark für zehn Eier?**	Two marks for ten eggs?
Sind die nicht zu klein?	Aren't they too small?
(BOW-eR) **LADENBESITZER** **Ja; der Bauer, der mir sie**	Yes; the farmer who is bringing them always
bringt, nimmt sie immer aus dem Nest	takes them out of the nest too early.
zu früh heraus.	

95

Can you remember these basics? Try writing the following expressions in German.

1. I need a box of matches. _____

2. I know. _____

3. I don't know. _____

4. Is there a camping ground near here? _____

5. Is there a service station near here? _____

6. Is there a hotel near here? _____

7. Excuse me. _____

(mayR) *(VIÇ-ti-geh)*
Mehr wichtige Verben
More important verbs

INFINITIVE	EXAMPLE	
(LAY-gen)		
legen—to put, lay	**Ich lege es auf den Tisch.**	I put it on the table.
sich legen—to lie down	**Ich lege mich aufs Sofa.**	I lie down on the sofa.
(LEE-gen)		
liegen—to lie	**Sie liegt im Bett.**	She lies (is lying) in bed.
(ZIT-sen)		
sitzen—to sit	**Warum sitzt du hier?**	Why are you sitting here?
sich setzen—to sit down	**Setz dich!**	Sit down!
(SHTAY-en)		
stehen—to stand	**Er steht im Zimmer.**	He is standing in the room.

Now let's try to use the new verbs in sentences. Fill in the blanks below.

1. Sie _____ auf dem Sofa.
   lies

2. Er _____ vor dem Spiegel.
   stands

3. Bitte _____!
   sit down (formal)

4. Wir _____.
   sit down

5. Er _____ das Buch auf den Stuhl.
   puts

6. _____!
   stand there! (familiar)

ANSWERS

Verbs.
1. liegt 2. steht 3. setzen Sie sich 4. setzen uns 5. legt 6. Steh dort

Can you remember?
1. Ich brauche eine Schachtel Streichhölzer. 2. Ich weiß. 3. Ich weiß nicht. 4. Gibt es einen Campingplatz hier in der Nähe? 5. Gibt es eine Tankstelle hier in der Nähe? 6. Gibt es ein Hotel hier in der Nähe? 7. Entschuldigen Sie.

96

Wie sagt man . . .
How do you say . . .

Here are some everyday expressions.

(kalt)
Mir ist kalt.
I am cold.

(heis)
Ihr ist heiß.
She is hot.

(FÜRÇ-ten)
Sie fürchten sich.
They are afraid.

(zoh-unt-zoh) *(SHLAYF-riç)*
Herr So-und-so ist schläfrig.
Mr. So-and-so is sleepy.

(shaymt)
Frau So-und-so schämt sich.
Mrs. So-and-so is ashamed.

Peter braucht etwas Brot.
Peter needs some bread.

Let's try an exercise based on the camping vocabulary you learned in this unit. Write in the proper words from the ones listed here:

Stiefel, Zelt, Schlafsack, Korkenzieher, Streichhölzer, Korb, Kofferradio, Angelrute

1. Wir brauchen einen _____ für die Weinflasche.

2. Er fischt mit der _____ .

3. Wir alle liegen unter einem _____ .

4. Das Brot ist in einem _____ .

5. Jeder schläft in einem _____ .

6. Zum Feueranmachen brauchen wir _____ .

7. An den Füßen haben wir gute _____ .

8. Aus unserem _____ kommt schöne Musik.

ANSWERS
1. Korkenzieher 2. Angelrute 3. Zelt 4. Korb 5. Schlafsack 6. Streichhölzer 7. Stiefel 8. Kofferradio

97

This is a similar fill-in-the-blank exercise. Now use the words:

kalt, heiß, schläfrig

1. Mir ist _____. Ich brauche einen Pullover.

2. Ihm ist _____. Er liegt in der Sonne.
   (SON-eh)
   sun

3. Ihr ist _____. Sie braucht keinen Pullover.

4. Sie ist _____. Sie geht schlafen.

Let's practice some of our irregular verbs again. Fill in the proper German forms.
Example: I am American.—Ich bin Amerikaner.

1. You (polite form) are American.—Sie sind Amerikaner.

   He _____   You (familiar, singular) _____

   She _____ (watch this!)   They _____

   We _____

2. I do not know.—Ich weiß nicht.

   You (polite form) _____   You (familiar, plural) _____

   We _____   He _____

3. I can go (I am able to go).—Ich kann gehen.

   He _____   You (polite) _____

   We _____   You (familiar, singular) _____

4. Ich habe ein Auto.—I have a car.

   You (familiar, singular) _____   We _____

   He _____   You (polite) _____

Januar · Februar · März · April · Mai · Juni · Juli · August · September · Oktober · November · Dezember

Did you notice that the German names for the months are almost the same as the English names? There also are similarities in the names of the seasons and in expressions about the weather.

(FRÜ-ling) **Es ist Frühling.**	It's spring.	*(DO-nert)* **Es donnert**	There's thunder
(kül) **Es ist kühl.**	It's cool.	*(blitst)* **und blitzt.**	and lightning.
(ZON-iç) **Es ist sonnig.**	It's sunny.	*(herpst)* **Es ist Herbst.**	It's fall.
(ZOM-eR) **Es ist Sommer.**	It's summer.	*(geest)* *(SHTRÖ-men)* **Es gießt in Strömen.**	It's raining cats and dogs.
Es ist heiß.	It's hot.	*(VIN-diç)* **Es ist windig.**	It's windy.
Es ist ein schöner Tag.	It's a beautiful day.	*(NAYB-liç)* **Es ist neblig.**	It's foggy.
(foyçt) **Es ist feucht.**	It's humid.	*(VIN-teR)* **Es ist Winter.**	It's winter.
(shvül) **Es ist schwül.**	It's muggy.	*(kalt)* **Es ist kalt.**	It's cold.
(SHTÜR-mish) **Es ist stürmisch.**	It's stormy.	*(BAY-ren-kel-teh)* **Es ist eine Bärenkälte.**	It's fiercely cold.
(RAY-gne-rish) **Es ist regnerisch.**	It's rainy.	*(schneit)* **Es schneit.**	It's snowing.

WIE IST DAS WETTER?

How is the Weather?

Das Wetter ist schön.

The weather is beautiful.

Das Wetter ist gut.

The weather is good.

(HER-liç)
Das Wetter ist herrlich.

The weather is superb.

(GROHS-ar-tiç)
Das Wetter ist großartig.

The weather is splendid.

(PREÇ-tiç)
Das Wetter ist prächtig.

The weather is magnificent.

Das Wetter ist kalt.

The weather is cold.

Das Wetter ist warm.

The weather is warm.

(shleçt)
Das Wetter ist schlecht.

The weather is bad.

(FURÇT-baR)
Das Wetter ist furchtbar.

The weather is awful.

(SHREK-liç)
Das Wetter ist schrecklich.

The weather is horrible.

(ad-yek-TEE-veh)
Adjektive
Adjectives

An adjective is a word used to modify a noun or pronoun. You've already been introduced to many adjectives in this book. Here are a few more. Remember to read them out loud.

(DUN-kel)
dunkel   dark   **Das Zimmer ist dunkel.**   The room is dark.

(hel)
hell   light   **Das Zimmer ist hell.**   The room is light.

(AN-ge-naym)
angenehm   pleasant   **Das Wetter ist angenehm.**   The weather is pleasant.

(hüpsh)
hübsch   pretty   **Das Mädchen ist hübsch.**   The girl is pretty.

(ZOW-beR)
sauber   clean   **Die Hand ist sauber.**   The hand is clean.

(HES-liç) **häßlich**	ugly	**Der Mann ist häßlich.**	The man is ugly.
(SHMU-tsiç) **schmutzig**	dirty	**Der Wagen ist schmutzig.**	The car is dirty.
(Of-en) **offen**	open	**Die Tür ist offen.**	The door is open.
(ge-SHLO-sen) **geschlossen**	closed	**Die Tür ist geschlossen.**	The door is closed.
(MÜ-deh) **müde**	tired	**Ich bin müde.**	I am tired.
(tsoo-FREE-den) **zufrieden**	satisfied	**Er ist zufrieden.**	He is satisfied.
(TSOR-niç) **zornig**	furious	**Sie ist zornig.**	She is furious.
(alt) **alt**	old	**Er ist alt.**	He is old.
(yung) **jung**	young	**Das Kind ist jung.**	The child is young.

(be-KVAYM)
groß, klein, laut, bequem
big, little, noisy, comfortable

Mein Zimmer ist groß, klein, laut, bequem

(LEK-eR)
lecker — delicious

Das Abendessen ist lecker.
The dinner is delicious.

(be-REIT)
bereit — ready

Das Abendessen ist bereit.
Dinner is ready.

(REIÇ-liç)
reichlich — ample

Das Abendessen ist reichlich.
The dinner is ample.

(TAH-del-lohs)
tadellos — perfect

Das Abendessen ist tadellos.
The dinner is perfect.

(leiçt)
leicht — light

Das Abendessen ist leicht.
The dinner is light.

You probably noticed that in every example above the adjective followed the noun and was preceded by *ist*. We could also have formed the plural by saying, for instance, Die Mädchen *sind* hübsch. The adjective stays the same in the plural in this type of sentence. Remember, however, that if the adjective precedes the noun it must agree with it. Thus, it would be Die hübschen Mädchen.

Here's a short dialogue set in a hotel room:

ANN **Wieviel Uhr ist es?**   What time is it?

SUSAN **Sieben Uhr dreißig.**   7:30.

ANN *(DON-eR-vet-eR)*
Donnerwetter!   My gosh!

(shpayt)
Schon so spät?   (*lit.* thunder-

(SHÖ-neR)
Ist es ein schöner Tag?   storm) So late already? Is it a beautiful day?

SUSAN *(ZON-en-owf-gang)*
Herrlich! Und der Sonnenaufgang!   Superb! And that sunrise! The sky is cloudless.
(VOL-ken-frei)
Der Himmel ist wolkenfrei. Was hast   What do you have there?

du dort?

ANN *(VET-eR-fohR-ows-za-geh)*
Die Wettervoraussage: Sonnig den   The weather forecast: Sunny all day.
(GAN-tsen)
ganzen Tag.

SUSAN *(RAY-gen)*
Kein Regen?   No rain?

ANN *(fee-LEIÇT)*   *(AH-bent)*
Vielleicht am Abend.   Maybe in the evening.

SUSAN *(HUN-griç)*
Ich steh auf; ich bin sehr hungrig.   I'm getting up; I am very hungry.

Die Wettervoraussage
Weather forecast

(HOHCH-druk-ge-beet)
H = **Hochdruckgebiet**
High pressure area

(ZON-eh) SONNE sun
(RAY-gen) REGEN rain
(ge-VIT-er) GEWITTER thunderstorms
(SHOW-er) SCHAUER showers
(NAY-bel) NEBEL fog
(shnay) SCHNEE snow

(TEEF-druk-ge-beet)
T = **Tiefdruckgebiet**
Low pressure area

102

WENN HEUTE DIENSTAG IST, DANN . . .

(ven) *(HOY-teh)* *(DEENS-tahk)*

If Today is Tuesday, then . . .

Let's learn the days of the week.

(MOHN-tahk)
Am *Montag* besuche ich meine Mutter.

On Monday I visit my mother.

(DEENS-tahk)
Am *Dienstag* gehe ich ins Kino.

On Tuesday I go to the movies.

(MIT-voch)
Am *Mittwoch* esse ich Wiener Schnitzel.

On Wednesday I eat Wiener schnitzel.

(DO-ners-tahk) *(SHPEE-leh)*
Am *Donnerstag* spiele ich Bridge.

On Thursday I play bridge.

(FREI-tahk)
Am *Freitag* esse ich Fisch.

On Friday I eat fish.

(BLEI-beh)
Am Freitag dem dreizehnten bleibe ich

On Friday the 13th I stay in bed

(AH-beR-gloy-bish)
im Bett (ich bin abergläubisch).

(I am superstitious).

(ZAMS-tahk) *(ZON-ah-bent)*
Am *Samstag* (oder *Sonnabend*)

On Saturday I go dancing.

(TANT-sen)
gehe ich tanzen.

(MÜ-deh)
Am *Sonntag* bin ich müde vom Samstag.

On Sunday I am tired from Saturday.

103

Now let's learn the names of the months in German. This should be easy. There are many similarities with English.

(YA-noo-aR) *(ge-VÖN-liç)*
Im *Januar* ist es gewöhnlich sehr kalt.
In January it usually is very cold.

(FAY-broo-ar) *(freert)*
Im *Februar* friert man auch, aber es
In February one freezes also, but it is a

(KUR-tser)
ist ein kurzer Monat.
short month.

(AN-ge-pliç) *(FRÜ-ling)*
Im *März* beginnt angeblich der Frühling.
In March spring allegedly begins.

(ge-BURTS-tahk)
Ich habe am ersten (1.) *März* Geburtstag.
March 1 is my birthday.

(ah-PRIL) *(BINT-fay-den)*
Im *April* regnet es Bindfäden.
In April it rains cats and dogs.

(mei) *(HEI-rah-ten)*
Im *Mai* soll man nicht heiraten.

In May one should not marry.

(YOO-nee) *(HOCH-tsei-ten)*
Im *Juni* sind die meisten Hochzeiten.
In June most weddings are held.

(YOO-lee) *(VAHN-zin-iç)*
Im *Juli* ist es wahnsinnig heiß.
In July it is insanely hot.

(ow-GUST) *(OOR-lowp)*
Im *August* fährt man auf Urlaub.
In August one goes on vacation.

(zep-TEM-beR) *(TROW-riç)*
Im *September* ist man traurig, daß der
In September one is sad that summer is over.

(vohr-Ü-beR)
Sommer vorüber ist.

(ok-TOH-beR) *(glük)*
Im *Oktober* hat man Glück, wenn die
In October one is lucky if the sun is

(sheint)
Sonne scheint.
shining.

(noh-VEM-beR)
Im *November* ist es neblig und naß.
In November it is foggy and wet.

(dayts-EM-beR)
Im *Dezember* gibt man eine Menge
In December one spends a lot

Geld aus.
of money.

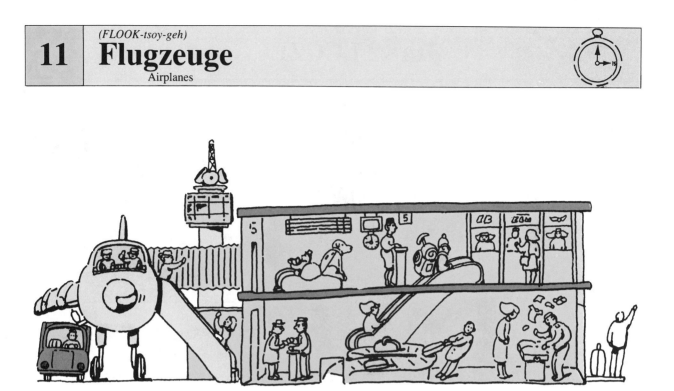

See if you can find the following in this picture.

(FLOOK-kar-ten-shal-teR) **der Flugkartenschalter**	ticket counter	**das Gepäck**	luggage
die Uhr	clock	*(pee-LOHT)* **der Pilot**	pilot
(ROL-trep-eh) **die Rolltreppe**	escalator	*(KOH-pee-loht)* **der Kopilot**	copilot
(FLEES-bant) **das Fließband**	conveyor belt	*(FLOOK-be-glei-teR-in)* **die Flugbegleiterin**	flight attendant (fem.)
(TSOL-be-am-teh) **der Zollbeamte**	customs inspector	*(kon-TROL-turm)* **der Kontrollturm**	control tower
(PAS-kon-tro-leh) **die Paßkontrolle**	passport control	*(FLOOK-shteik)* **der Flugsteig**	gate

(FLOOK-tsoyk)
DAS FLUGZEUG
The Plane

Can you find these items in the picture?

(zits)
der Sitz — the seat

(ROW-cheR-ap-teil)
das Raucherabteil — smoking section

(NIÇT-row-cher-ap-teil)
das Nichtraucherabteil — non-smoking section

(ZIÇ-eR-heits-gurt)
der Sicherheitsgurt — seat belt

(ka-BEE-neh)
die Kabine — cabin

(rumpf)
der Rumpf — fuselage

(NOHT-ows-gang)
der Notausgang — emergency exit

(pa-sa-ŽEER)
der Passagier — passenger

(START-bahn)
die Startbahn — runway

(be-ZAT-sung)
die Besatzung — crew

(ta-BLET)
das Tablett — tray

(FEN-steR)
das Fenster — window

Now watch how the vocabulary on flying is used in the following dialogue.

PILOT **Wir fliegen in ein paar Minuten** — We take off from Boston in a few minutes.

von Boston ab. Bitte machen Sie Ihren — Please fasten your seat belt. And please do not

Sicherheitsgurt fest. Und bitte nicht — smoke during takeoff.

(VAY-rent)
rauchen während des Abfliegens.

ERSTER PASSAGIER *(pa-sa-ŽEER)* **Ist es das erste Mal, daß**

Sie Deutschland besuchen?

Is this the first time you are visiting Germany?

ZWEITER PASSAGIER **Ja. Und es ist auch das**

erste Mal, daß ich über den Atlantik *(at-LAN-tik)*

fliege.

Yes. And it is also the first time I fly

across the Atlantic Ocean.

PILOT **Wir werden um vierzehn Uhr**

dreißig in Frankfurt landen. Wir

fliegen in einer Höhe von 10 000 *(HÖ-eh)*

Meter. Das Wetter in Frankfurt ist

wolkig und regnerisch und die *(VOL-kiç)* *(RAYG-neR-ish)*

Temperatur ist 25 Grad Celsius. *(tem-pe-rah-TOOR)* *(graht)* *(TSEL-see-us)*

We will land in Frankfurt at 14.30 (2:30 p.m.)

We are flying at an altitude of 10,000 meters.

The weather at Frankfurt is cloudy and rainy, and

the temperature is 25 degrees Celsius (77°

Fahrenheit).

ERSTER PASSAGIER **Fräulein, servieren Sie** *(FROY-lein)* *(seR-VEER-en)*

uns das Abendessen? *(AH-bent-es-en)*

Miss, are you going to serve us dinner?

FLUGBEGLEITERIN **Ich bringe es Ihnen in ein**

paar Minuten.

I am bringing it to you in a couple minutes.

ZWEITER PASSAGIER **Wunderbar! Im** *(VUN-der-baR)*

Flugzeug esse ich sehr gern, es vertreibt *(feR-TREIPT)*

die Zeit.

Great! I love eating on planes. It makes time go

faster.

Etwas Grammatik
Some Grammar

We have talked about pronouns before. Now let's focus on pronouns in the accusative case.

DIRECT OBJECT PRONOUNS

mich	me		**uns**	us
dich	you (familiar)		**euch**	you
ihn	him, it			
sie	her, it		**sie**	them
es	it			

Sie   you (polite)

The personal pronouns are in the accusative case when they are the direct objects of verbs.

What is a direct object?
Take a sentence like:

Paul	loves	Pauline.
Paul	liebt	Pauline.
subject	*verb*	*direct object*

Whom does Paul love: Pauline.
Pauline obviously is the object, the *direct object* of his affection.

Now let's go one step further. Instead of the name, the noun *Pauline*, you can use a form that takes it place, a pronoun. In this particular case it would be—you guessed it—*her*, in German, *sie*:

Paul	loves	her.
Paul	liebt	sie.
subject	*verb*	*direct object*

Nothing much has changed, except that we have replaced the direct object noun by a direct object pronoun.

Let's practice this:

1. Karl braucht _____.
   _{him}

2. Er ißt _____.
   _{it (das Brot)}

3. Anton sieht _____.
   _{you (familiar)}

4. Susan besucht _____.
   _{me}

5. Siehst du _____?
   _{them}

Of course, the direct object can be either a person or a thing. Let's replace some more nouns with direct-object pronouns. Number 6 is done for you.

6. Er liest ___es___.
   _{das Buch}

7. Er sieht _____.
   _{you (polite)}

8. Ich brauche _____.
   _{you (my son)}

9. Er liebt _____.
   _{you (familiar)}

10. Er hat _____.
    _{den Schlüssel}

11. Sie kauft _____.
    _{die Blumen}

ANSWERS

Practice.
1. ihn 2. es 3. dich 4. mich 5. sie 7. Sie 8. dich 9. dich 10. ihn 11. sie

ENTERTAINMENT
(UN-teR-hal-tung)
Unterhaltung

	(tay-AH-teR)	*(KEE-noh)*	*(FEI-eR-tahg-eh)*	
12	**Theater** /	**Kino** /	**Feiertage**	
	Theater	Movies	Holidays	

THEATER
Theater

John and Mary are a middle-aged couple from Omaha, Nebraska, who are making their first trip to Germany. They like the theater. The place is Munich on the second day of their stay. Being of German descent, they both speak German quite well. ''Not one word of English during our vacation,'' they decide.

(In the hotel:)

JOHN **Möchtest du heute abend ins Theater**   Would you like to go to the theatre tonight?
(GERT-neR)
gehen? Im Theater am Gärtnerplatz   In the theatre on Gärtnerplatz they are playing
(LUS-tig-eh) (VIT-veh)
spielt man *Die lustige   Witwe*   *The Merry Widow* by Franz Lehar.
(frants) (LAY-har)
von Franz Lehar.
(kays)
MARY **Diesen alten Käs?**   That old warhorse?
(me-loh-DEE-en)
JOHN **Ja, aber die Melodien sind sehr**   Yes, but the melodies are very beautiful. And the
(tekst)   (dum)
schön. Und der Text ist so dumm,   words are so dumb, it doesn't matter
(ROL-eh)
es spielt keine Rolle, wenn man ihn   if you don't understand.

nicht versteht. Ich möchte auch   I would like to hear

Siegfried hören.   *Siegfried*, also.
(VAHG-neR)
MARY **Die Wagner-Oper?**   The Wagner opera?

109

JOHN **Ja.**	Yes.
MARY **Fünf Stunden dort sitzen? Mir ist** *(LANG-vei-liç)* *(in-TSVISH-en)* **das zu langweilig. Ich gehe inzwischen** *(ZOH-fee)* *(mahkst)* **zu Tante Sophie, die du eh nicht magst.** *(BEID-eh)* **Dann sind wir beide glücklich.**	To sit there for five hours? That's too boring for me. I'll go in the meantime to Aunt Sophie, whom you don't like anyway. Then both of us are happy.
JOHN **Gute Idee!** *(KOW-feh)* *(KAR-ten)* **Wo kaufe ich die Karten?**	Good idea. Where do I buy the tickets?
MARY *(UN-ten)* **Der Kartenverkauf ist unten im** *(hoh-TEL)* **Hotel. Also bis später. Ich muß** *(fri-ZÖR)* **zum Friseur.**	The ticket office is downstairs in the hotel. See you later. I must go to the hairdresser.
JOHN **Wiedersehen.**	See you.

Notice how similar these words are in English and German:

das Hotel
hotel

(ee-DAY)
die Idee
idea

das Theater
theater

(me-lo-DEE)
die Melodie
melody

der Text
text, words

sitzen
to sit

(veR-GES-en)
Bitte nicht vergessen . . .
Please don't forget . . .

möchtest du gern, möchten Sie gern	would you like to
Diesen alten Käs?	Here **Käse** (Cheese) means this old warhorse or old chestnut; it has nothing to do with cheese.

Es (das) spielt keine Rolle.
Es (das) macht nichts.

It doesn't matter.

Ich muß zum Friseur (gehen).

I must go to the hairdresser.

Willst du *mir* das Geld geben?

Will you give the money *to me*?

In the previous unit you learned how to say "me, him, them," etc. Now you will learn how to say "to me, to him, to them," etc. These are called "indirect object pronouns."

INDIRECT OBJECT PRONOUNS

mir	to me	**uns**	to us
dir	to you (familiar)	**euch**	to you (familiar)
ihm	to him, it		
ihr	to her, it	**ihnen**	to them

Ihnen   to you (polite)

In German the indirect object stands before the direct object in a sentence.

	Indirect object	**Direct object**
Mary gives	(to) the boy	a book.
Mary gibt	**dem Jungen**	**ein Buch.**
He gives	to him	the money.
Er gibt	**ihm**	**das Geld.**
I send	(to) my mother	flowers.
Ich sende	**meiner Mutter**	**Blumen.**

111

DAS KINO
The Movies

MARY	**Ein Kino ist links um die Ecke.**	A movie theater is to the left around the corner.
	Möchtest du einen Film sehen?	Would you like to see a film?
JOHN	*(loyft)* **Was läuft?**	What is playing?
MARY	**Ein deutscher Film.**	A German film.
JOHN	**Mit Untertiteln?**	With subtitles?
MARY	**In Deutschland? Nein.**	In Germany? No.
JOHN	**Glaubst du, wir verstehen den Film?**	Do you believe we'll understand the picture?
MARY	**Ich glaube schon.**	I think so.
JOHN	*(bong-BONGS)* **Ich kaufe Bonbons.**	I'll buy candy.

(two hours later)

MARY	**Ich bin froh, es ist zu Ende.**	I am glad it is over. Do you know something?
	Weißt du was? Auch die Deutschen *(LANG-veil-i-geh)* **machen langweilige Filme.**	The Germans, too, make boring pictures.
JOHN	**Und dafür müssen wir 8000** **Kilometer herfliegen.**	And for that we have to fly 8000 kilometers.

Bitte nicht vergessen . . .
Please don't forget . . .

links um die Ecke   to the left around the corner

Ich glaube schon.   I think so.

Draw lines between the matching English and German words or expressions.

1. zu Ende   a. subtitles
2. Ecke   b. glad
3. kaufen   c. over
4. Untertitel   d. candy
5. froh   e. corner
6. Bonbons   f. to buy

True or false?

7. _____ John und Mary möchten ins Theater gehen.

8. _____ *Siegfried* dauert zwei Stunden.

9. _____ Mary muß zum Friseur.

10. _____ Sie sehen einen amerikanischen Film.

11. _____ Mary und John gehen ins Kino.

12. _____ Der Film hat Untertitel.

(FEI-eR-tah-geh)

FEIERTAGE
Holidays

JOHN   *(in-te-re-SANT)*
Es ist interessant, die deutschen   It is interesting to compare the German

Feiertage mit den   holidays with the American ones.

(feR-GLEI-çen)
amerikanischen zu vergleichen.   Well, New Year's Day, of course,

(NOY-yahRs-tahk)
Also der Neujahrstag   is international.

ist natürlich international.

(HEI-li-geh)
Dann kommt der 6. Januar, die Heiligen   Next comes January 6, Epiphany.

(KÖ-ni-geh)
Drei Könige.

MARY	*(OS-tern)* **Ostern feiern sie zwei Tage lang,**	They celebrate Easter for two days,
	Sonntag und Montag.	Sunday and Monday.
	(PFING-sten) **Auch Pfingsten.**	Pentecost, too.
JOHN	*(gahR)* **Im Juli und August ist fast gar nichts**	In July and August there is
	los.	almost nothing going on.
MARY	**Um diese Zeit gehen die Deutschen** *(vahR-SHEIN-liç)* *(OOR-lowp)* **wahrscheinlich auf Urlaub.**	At that time Germans probably go on vacation.
JOHN	**Und dann nichts bis November.**	And then nothing till November.
MARY	**Die armen Deutschen! Wie können** *(OWS-halt-en)* **sie das so lange aushalten?**	The poor Germans! How can they stand it that long?
JOHN	*(AL-eR-hei-li-gen)* **Am 1. November ist Allerheiligen,**	On November 1 is All Saints' Day,
	und dann . . .	and then . . .
MARY	*(VEI-naç-ten)* **. . . kommt Weihnachten.**	comes Christmas.
JOHN	*(vee-deR)* **Wieder zwei Tage, am 25. und 26.**	Two days again,
	Dezember.	on December 25 and 26.
MARY	*(ZIL-ves-teR)* **Und am 31. Dezember, Silvester. Die**	And on December 31, New Year's Eve. The
	Deutschen feiern wie die Amerikaner—	Germans celebrate like Americans—far into the
	bis tief in die Nacht hinein.	night.

Let's see how much you remember from the dialogues. Fill in the correct German word.

1. Inzwischen besucht Mary ihre _____ .
   Aunt Sophie

2. Das Kino ist links um die _____ .
   corner

3. Sie sehen einen _____ .
   German film

4. John kauft _____ .
   candy

5. _____ ist am 25. und 26.
   Christmas
   Dezember.

(RAYT-sel)

Ein Rätsel

A puzzle

Complete the German words.

1. again
2. indefinite article
3. interesting
4. half
5. a holiday
6. another holiday
7. temperature scale
8. hand
9. theater
10. first
11. a month

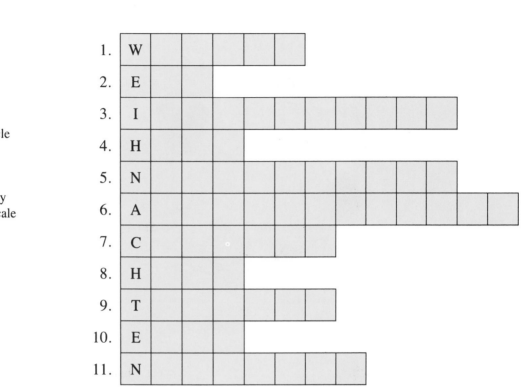

1. W
2. E
3. I
4. H
5. N
6. A
7. C
8. H
9. T
10. E
11. N

ANSWERS

Puzzle.
1. wieder 2. ein 3. interessant 4. halb 5. Neujahrstag 6. Allerheiligen 7. Celsius 8. Hand 9. Theater 10. Erst 11. November

(VAN-dern) (DJOG-ging)
WANDERN UND JOGGING
Hiking and Jogging

REPORTER	**Herr Dr. Steiner?**	Dr. Steiner?
STEINER	**Ja, das bin ich.**	Yes, that's me.
REPORTER	**Ich bin Karl Frank, Reporter vom *Morgen am Abend* aus Cincinnati, Ohio.**	I am Karl Frank, a reporter of *Morgen am Abend* from Cincinnati, Ohio.
STEINER	**Sie wollen ein Interview?**	You want an interview?
REPORTER	**Genau.**	Exactly.
STEINER	**Und worüber, wenn ich bitten darf?**	And what about, if I may ask?
REPORTER	**Als Präsident des Deutschen Amateursportverbandes sind Sie bestimmt über Jogging, Wandern, Radfahren und Schwimmen sehr gut informiert.**	As the president of the German Amateur Sports League you are surely very well informed about jogging, hiking, bicycle riding and swimming.
STEINER	*(SHMEI-çeln)* **Sie schmeicheln mir.**	You flatter me.

116

REPORTER   **Ich möchte darüber einen Artikel**
             (ZAM-leh) *(mah-tay-ree-AL)*
schreiben und sammle Material.
   (SHEE-sen)

STEINER **Schießen Sie los!**

REPORTER   **Zunächst über das Jogging.**

STEINER   **Ja, das ist hier sehr populär. Wie**

vieles andere, kommt das natürlich auch
                    (oy-ROH-pa)
aus Amerika und jetzt ist ganz Europa
(ver-RÜKT)
verrückt danach.
(zoh-GAHR)
Sogar das *Wort*
(im-por-TEE-ren)
importieren wir.
   (loyft)
Man läuft nicht mehr,
    (djogt)
man joggt.

REPORTER **Sie auch, Herr Doktor?**
   (klahr)   *(ge-ZUN-deR)*
STEINER **Klar. Jogging ist ein gesunder und**
(BI-li-geR)
billiger Sport. Alles, was Sie da kaufen

müssen, ist ein Sweatshirt und ein paar

bequeme Joggingschuhe.

REPORTER   **Wie steht's mit dem Wandern,**

Herr Doktor?

I would like to write an article about these

things and I am collecting material.

Shoot!

First about jogging.

Yes, that's very popular. Like many other

things, this too, naturally, comes from

America, and now all of Europe is crazy

about it.

We even import the word.

One doesn't run anymore,

one jogs.

You, too, sir?

You bet. Jogging is a healthy and inexpensive

sport. All you have to buy is a sweat shirt

and a pair of comfortable jogging shoes.

How about hiking, sir?

STEINER   **Ein herrlicher Sport.**

Und hier in Deutschland
(be-DOY-tung)
von großer Bedeutung.

Alle unsere Wanderwege
(mar-KEERT)
sind markiert; es ist

unmöglich sich zu verirren.

A marvelous sport, and here in Germany of

great importance. All our trails are

marked; it's impossible

to lose one's way.

REPORTER   **Was brauche ich für den Sport?**
(RUK-zak)

STEINER   **Einen Rucksack und ein Paar**
(KREF-ti-geh)
kräftige Beine mit

guten Wanderschuhen.

What do I need for the sport?

A backpack and a strong pair of legs with

good hiking shoes.

(AYR-gei-tsiç)
Wenn Sie ehrgeizig sind, vielleicht
(KOCH-ge-shir)
Schlafsack, Kochgeschirr
(FELT-fla-sheh)
und Feldflasche.

If you are ambitious,

maybe a sleeping bag, mess kit

and a canteen.

Bitte nicht vergessen . . .
Please don't forget . . .

Worüber wollen Sie sprechen?

Worum handelt es sich?

Wozu brauchen Sie das?

What do you want to talk about?

What is it about?

To what purpose (why) do you need this?

Please note:

Wir *importieren* ein Wort.   We *import* a word.

Verbs that end in **-ieren** are stressed on the next to last syllable, and are regular weak verbs. They don't change their vowels.

You have no doubt noticed that there are now a great number of American words being used as

German words. Examples of such foreign words *(Fremdwörter)* are *Jogging* and *Sweatshirt*.
(FREMT-vör-teR)

Let's learn a new verb.

SAMMELN (TO COLLECT)

ich samm*le*	I collect, am collecting
du samm*elst*	you collect, are collecting
er, sie, es samm*elt*	he, she, it collects, is collecting
wir samm*eln*	we collect, are collecting
ihr samm*elt*	you collect, are collecting
sie samm*eln*	they collect, are collecting
Sie samm*eln*	You (polite) collect, are collecting

(RAT-fah-ren)   *(SHVI-men)*
RADFAHREN UND SCHWIMMEN
Bicycling and Swimming

REPORTER **Was halten Sie vom Radfahren,**   What do you think of bicycle riding,

Herr Doktor?   sir?

STEINER   *(BLÖD-eR)* *(UN-tsoo-leng-liç-es)*
Ein blöder Sport, ein unzulängliches

(trans-PORT-mit-el) *(tsahm)*
Transportmittel. Ist doch viel zu zahm.

(ge-SHVIN-diç-keit)
Keine Geschwindigkeit, nichts.

(BAYRK-owf)
Wenn's bergauf geht,

(ding)
muß man das Ding schieben.

(SHTREN-gen) *(RAY-geln)*
Und diese strengen   Regeln!

(FOR-deR) *(RÜK-liçt)*
Müssen Sie Vorder- und Rücklicht in

Amerika haben?

REPORTER   **Nein.**

A stupid sport, an unsatisfactory means of

transportation. It's much too tame.

No speed, nothing.

Uphill you have

to push the thing.

And these strict rules!

Do you need front and back lights in

America?

No.

REPORTER   **Was halten Sie vom Schwimmen?**

(be-GEIS-tert)
STEINER   **Ich bin begeistert davon.**

(artst)
Mein Arzt sagt mir,

(BES-teh)
das ist der beste und der

(ge-ZÜND-es-teh)
gesündeste Sport, den es gibt.

(MI-ni-mum)
Auch hier investieren Sie ein Minimum:

(BAH-deh-hoh-zeh) *(BAH-deh-an-tsook)*
Eine Badehose oder einen Badeanzug—

(ay-ven-too-EL) *(bi-KEE-nee)*
REPORTER   **eventuell einen Bikini—**

What do you think of swimming?

I am enthusiastic about it.

My doctor tells me,

this is the best and the healthiest

sport there is.

Here, too, you invest a minimum:

bathing trunks or bathing suit—

perhaps a bikini—

STEINER **Das ist alles. Vielleicht eine**
(TOW-cheR-bri-leh)
Taucherbrille—

That's all. Maybe diving-goggles—

(fenkt)   *(NOY-ling)*
REPORTER **Wie fängt ein Neuling hier mit dem**

Schwimmen an?

How does a beginner start swimming here?

(BRUST-shvim-en)
STEINER **Mit dem Brustschwimmen.**

With the breast stroke.

(KROWL-en)
Dann kommt das Kraulen

Then comes the crawl

(RÜK-en-shvim-en)
und das Rückenschwimmen.

and the back stroke.

(RAY-gel-may-si-geh)
REPORTER **Haben Sie regelmäßige**
(PRÜ-fun-gen)
Prüfungen?

Do you have regular tests?

(ap-sòh-LOOT)
STEINER **Absolut. Wenn einer die Prüfung**
(be-STAYT)
fürs Freischwimmen besteht, kann er sich
(AP-tsei-çen)   *(shtolts)*
ein kleines Abzeichen stolz auf
(NAY-en)
die Badehose nähen.

Absolutely. If someone passes the free-

swimming test, he can proudly sew a little

badge on his bathing trunks.

REPORTER **Herr Doktor, ich danke Ihnen für**
(ge-SHPRAYÇ)
das Gespräch.

Sir, I thank you for the interview.

Bitte nicht vergessen . . .

Please don't forget . . .

Watch the word | **eventuell** | and how you use it. In German it means *possibly* or *perhaps*. The English word *eventual* means *ultimate, final.*

Gewiß, bestimmt, freilich, natürlich, selbstverständlich, absolut, klar—they all mean more or less the same thing, the equivalent of *sure, certainly, naturally, of course, you bet, yes indeed.*

Note that the stress in most of these words is on a syllable other than the first.

Also, notice that in Germany persons who have earned a doctorate (PhD) are addressed as "Herr Doktor" not just "Herr." Titles are very important in Germany, and a person would feel hurt, even insulted, if this "Doktor" were left out.

1. Was ist das? Das ist ein _____

2. Was ist das? Das ist eine _____

3. Was ist das? Das ist _____

4. Was ist das? Das ist _____

5. Was ist das? Das ist _____

122

Draw lines between the matching English words or expressions:

1. Wochenblatt
2. zunächst
3. verrückt
4. fliegen
5. eigentlich
6. Prüfung
7. bequem
8. Schlafsack
9. schieben
10. Brille

A. crazy
B. actually
C. comfortable
D. weekly
E. first of all
F. glasses (goggles)
G. test
H. to fly
I. sleeping bag
J. to push

ORDERING FOOD

(ES-en) *(be-SHTEL-en)*
Essen bestellen

14	*(MAHL-tsei-ten)* *(SHPEI-zen)* **Mahlzeiten / Speisen** Meals Food	

Was man sagt, wenn
(gern)   *(mahk)*
man etwas *gern mag*
What to Say When You *Like* Something

Verb + GERN	
Ich esse gern.	I like to eat.
Ich esse nicht gern.	I do not like to eat.

I like ice cream.

Ich esse gern Eis.

I don't like vegetables.

Ich esse nicht gern Gemüse.

Gern, being an adverb, always modifies a verb:
Ich esse gern. Or: **Ich esse nicht gern.**

If the object of ''to like'' is a person, we use **haben**:
                                (klows)   *(ROY-beR)*
Ich habe meine Schwester gern.   **Ich habe Klaus gern.**   **Ich habe die Räuber nicht gern.**
                                                                            robbers

As you can see, the object (Schwester, Klaus, die Räuber) always stands between the verb **habe** and the adverb **gern** (or **nicht gern**). The negative **nicht** always precedes the **gern**.
(Mö-gen)
If the object of ''to like'' is a thing, we use **mögen**:
     Ich mag gern Eis.   **Ich mag nicht gern Gemüse.**
You probably noticed that the object follows the verb **mag** and the adverb **gern**; it can also stand between them.

To convey the idea of preferring something, we frequently use the comparative form of **gern**,
(LEE-beR)
which is **lieber**:

I prefer to eat at eight.	Ich esse lieber um acht.
	(toh-MAH-ten-zaft)
I prefer tomato juice.	Ich **mag** Tomatensaft lieber.
	(tay)
I prefer to drink tea.	Ich trinke lieber Tee.
	(am LEEP-sten)
I like coffee most.	Ich **mag** Kaffee *am liebsten*.

ESSEN
Eating

ESSEN					
		to eat			
ich	esse	I eat, am eating	wir	essen	we eat, are eating
	(ist)				
du	ißt	you eat, are eating	ihr	eßt	you eat, are eating
er, sie, es	ißt	he, she, it eats, is eating	sie	essen	they eat, are eating
	Sie	essen	You (polite) eat, are eating		

FRÜHSTÜCK
Breakfast

Frühstück essen
Eating breakfast

(KA-fay-tas-eh)
die Kaffeetasse
coffee cup

der Kaffee
coffee
(ZAH-neh)
mit Sahne
with cream

(TAY-ta-seh)
die Teetasse
tea cup
(TAY-boy-tel)
der Teebeutel
tea bag

PAUL	**Um wieviel Uhr ißt du gern Frühstück?**	At what time do you like to eat breakfast?
ANNA	**Ich esse Frühstück gern um acht.**	I like to eat breakfast at eight.
PAUL	**Ich esse Frühstück lieber um 7.45.**	I prefer to eat breakfast at 7:45.
ANNA	**Magst du lieber Kaffee mit** *(ZAH-neh)* *(SHVAR-tsen)* **Sahne oder schwarzen Kaffee?**	Do you prefer coffee with cream or black coffee?

(tohst)
der Toast

(mar-me-LAH-deh)
die Marmelade
marmalade

(BUT-eR)
die Butter

(ZE-mel)
die Semmel
or
(BRÖT-çen)
das Brötchen
roll

ein Glas
a glass of
(oh-RANŽ-en-zaft)
Orangensaft
orange juice

ein Glas
a glass of
(toh-MAH-ten-zaft)
Tomatensaft
tomato juice

PAUL   **Ich mag Kaffee nicht gern, auch Milch nicht. Ich trinke lieber Tee.**

I don't like to drink coffee, also not milk. I prefer to drink tea.

ANNA   *(tohst)* **Ißt du Toast mit Butter** *(mar-me-LAH-deh)* **und Marmelade?**

Do you eat toast with butter and marmalade?

PAUL   **Nein! Ich mag Toast nicht gern; ich esse lieber** *(KOO-chen)* *(ZEM-eln)* **Kuchen oder Semmeln.**

No! I don't like toast; I prefer to eat cake or rolls.

ANNA   **Und Orangensaft? Magst du ihn gern?**

And orange juice? Do you like it?

PAUL   **Ich mag Tomatensaft lieber.**

I prefer tomato juice.

ANNA   *(GOT-tes)(VIL-en)* **Um Gottes willen! Wie** *(YAY-mals)* **können wir da jemals** *(MIT-ein-an-deR)* **miteinander reisen?**

Good heavens! How can we ever travel together?

Try to complete the following sentences:

1. I like to swim.

2. I don't like to dance.

3. I like Michael.

4. I don't like my auto.

Ich schwimme _____.

Ich tanze _____ _____.

(MIÇ-ah-ayl)
Ich _____ Michael _____.

Ich _____ _____ _____ mein Auto.

126

Let's practice *gern* and *lieber*. See how much of the conversation you remember by filling in the blanks with the missing word. Then read the sentence aloud.

1. Anna sagt: Ich esse Frühstück _____ um acht.

2. Paul sagt: Ich esse Frühstück _____ um 7.45.
   preferably

3. Paul sagt: Ich mag Kaffee _____ _____.

4. Paul trinkt _____ Tee.
   preferably

5. Paul mag Toast _____ _____.

6. Er ißt _____ Kuchen oder Semmeln.

Fill in the blanks as indicated. Be sure to say the words aloud.

(HEIS-eh) (ge-TREN-keh)
7. 2 heiße Getränke _____ , _____

(FRUCHT-sef-teh)
8. 2 Fruchtsäfte (juices) _____ , _____

(ZACH-en)
9. 2 Sachen von der Bäckerei _____ , _____
   items

10. Was ist auf dem Toast oder der Semmel? _____ und _____

Using the pictures and the words and phrases from Anna and Paul's conversation, try answering these questions:

1. Wann essen Sie Frühstück? _____

(Mȫ-gen)
2. Was mögen Sie lieber, Kaffee mit Sahne, schwarzen Kaffee oder Tee?

_____

3. Mögen Sie Orangensaft oder Tomatensaft?

_____

4. Was ist auf Ihrem Toast? _____

DER TISCH
(tish)

The Table

(VEIN-glas)
das Weinglas
wine glass

(zalts)
das Salz
salt

(PFEF-eR)
der Pfeffer
pepper

(TAS-eh)
die Tasse
cup

(UN-teR-tas-eh)
die Untertasse
saucer

das Glas
glass

(sayr-vy-ET-eh)
die Serviette
napkin

(TSU-keR)
der Zucker
sugar

(GAH-bel)
die Gabel
fork

(LÖF-el)
der Löffel
spoon

(TEL-eR)
der Teller
plate

(MES-eR)
das Messer
knife

Here's a little fun. And a little learning. Draw a line from each item in Column 1 to the item in Column 2 you associate it with.

1. Gabel

2. Frühstück

3. Tasse

4. Orangensaft

(AP-vi-shen)
5. den Mund abwischen
   to wipe

6. Glas

7. Salz

A. Fruchtsaft

B. Serviette

C. Tee

D. Toast und Kaffee

E. Pfeffer

F. Messer

G. Tomatensaft

ANSWERS

Matching 1. F 2. D 3. C 4. A 5. B 6. G 7. E

128

DIE HAUPTMAHLZEIT
(HOWPT-mahl-tseit)
The Main Meal

DAS MITTAGESSEN
(MI-tag-es-en)
The Noon Meal

An ample Sunday meal:

das Kraut *(krowt)*
cabbage

der Knödel *(KNÖ-del)*
dumpling

der Fisch *(fish)*

der Nachtisch *(NACH-tish)*
dessert

der Kuchen *(KU-chen)*
cake

die Torte *(TOR-teh)*
pie

die Suppe *(ZU-peh)*
soup

das Gemüse *(ge-mü-zeh)*
vegetable

die Kartoffeln *(kaR-TOF-eln)*
potatoes

das Fleisch *(fleish)*
meat

der Schweinebraten *(SHVEI-neh-brah-ten)*
roast pork

Depending on the region, you drink beer or wine with your meat. Coffee is hardly ever served with it. *Vorspeisen* *(FOHR-shpei-zen)* (appetizers) are relatively unpopular in Germany and Austria, and the main meal of the day usually begins with soup instead. Salads are not too much in demand.

1. Was trinken Sie gewöhnlich *(ge-VÖN-liç)* aus einem Glas?
   usually

   _____

2. Was schneiden Sie gewöhnlich mit einem Messer?

   _____

3. Was trinken Sie gewöhnlich aus einer Tasse?

   _____

4. Was für Gänge *(GEN-geh)* kommen vor dem Hauptgang? *(HOWPT-gang)*
   courses   main course

   _____

5. Was ist der letzte Gang? _____

129

Try answering these questions about the meal:

1. Was ist der erste Gang der Mahlzeit? _____
   (VEL-çen)
2. Welchen Gang haben Sie am liebsten? _____
   which   *(FOR-tsee-hen)*
3. Ziehen Sie Fisch oder Fleisch vor (vorziehen)?
                                    to prefer

_____

(FROYN-deh)
4. Was haben Ihre Freunde gern?
   friends

_____

MAHLZEITEN IN DEUTSCHLAND UND ÖSTERREICH
Meals in Germany and Austria

Meals in Germany and Austria are taken at about the same time as in America. But while lunch in the United States usually is of no great
(MI-tag-es-en)
consequence, lunch *(das Mittagessen)* in Germany   *(AH-bent-es-en)*
and Austria is the major meal of the day. The evening meal *(das Abendessen)* is of lesser importance. It is more like a light supper or like the American lunch, often consisting mainly of bread, cold cuts, and cheeses with perhaps a salad or dessert as well. It is sometimes called
(AH-bent-broht)
Abendbrot ("evening bread"), and this name accurately reflects the nature of this meal.
   There also are in-between meals, especially in southern German-speaking areas. For
       (GAH-bel-frü-shtük)
instance, *Gabelfrühstück*, served at about ten in the morning, is a warm meal, maybe goulash
           (YOW-zeh)
and beer. In Austria, *Jause*, served at about four in the afternoon, is a snack consisting of coffee and cake. In Germany this is called *Kaffeetrinken*.

ANSWERS

1. Vorspeise *or* Suppe 2. Vorspeise, Suppe, Hauptgang, *or* Nachtisch 3. Ich ziehe —— vor. 4. Meine Freunde haben —— gern.

130

Let's try some exercises about meals.

What are the names of the morning, noon, and evening meals?

das _____ , das _____ , das _____ .

Can you show the correctness of these statements by writing TRUE or FALSE after them?

1. In Deutschland servieren sie die Hauptmahlzeit um 9 Uhr abends. _____

2. Wenn ich hungrig bin, trinke ich Wasser. _____

(SHIN-ken-broht)
3. Wenn ich durstig bin, esse ich ein Schinkenbrot. _____
ham sandwich

(IM-bis)
4. Es ist möglich, einen Imbiß zwischen der Hauptmahlzeit und dem Abendessen zu essen.
snack

_____

5. Es gibt eine leichte Mahlzeit zwischen dem Frühstück und der Hauptmahlzeit. _____

See if you can supply the missing letter(s) in the following sentences.

1. Ich esse ge____n Toa____t mit Marm____lad____ und Bu____ ____er.

2. Paul i____t li____ber Kuchen.

3. Sie____ ____ink____ gern Kaf____e ____ .

4. Sie ser____ie____t das Fr____ ____st____ck um si____ben.

5. Wir es____en am A____end um s____chs.

Try answering these questions:
1. Was tun Sie, wenn Sie hungrig sind?

_____

2. Was tun Sie, wenn Sie durstig sind?

_____

131

Can you find the hidden words? There are 5 of them, not counting the example. The words are very similar to the English ones.

S	A	L	A	T	G	G	O	G	E	L
N	W	O	C	E	N	L	M	N	P	U
M	A	R	M	E	L	A	D	E	N	F
P	S	O	I	S	F	S	U	P	P	E
L	S	E	L	T	O	M	G	X	N	A
A	E	N	C	B	R	O	M	L	S	E
O	R	E	H	N	S	O	P	Z	L	A

(GAY-ben) (NAY-men)
Geben und Nehmen
to give to take

These are two important and quite common verbs worth repeating and remembering.

Let's practice them:

Ich gebe **dir ein Buch.**
Du gibst **mir die Zeitung.**
Er (sie, es) gibt **mir ein Glas.**
Wir geben **ihr Blumen.**
Ihr gebt **uns den Schlüssel.**
Sie geben **uns das Messer.**
Geben Sie **uns die Speisekarte!**
Was für einen Salat *gibt es?*

I give you a book.
You give me the newspaper.
He (she, it) gives me a glass.
We give her flowers.
You give us the key.
They give us the knife.
Give us the menu.
What kind of salad is there?

Ich nehme **gefüllte Eier.**
Du nimmst **lieber Fisch.**
Er (sie, es) nimmt **Fleisch.**
Wir nehmen **Suppe.**
Ihr nehmt **Kartoffeln.**
Sie nehmen **Salat.**
Nehmen Sie **Backhuhn!**

I'll take deviled eggs.
You prefer fish.
He (she, it) takes meat.
We take soup.
You take potatoes.
They take salad.
Take fried chicken.

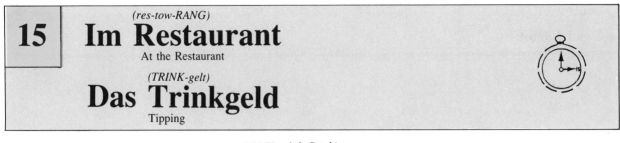
Die Speisekarte bitte!
(SHPEI-zeh-kaR-teh)

The menu, please

After carefully perusing the voluminous menu laid before them by the waiter, Karl and Josef decide to make their choice from the following items:

Vorspeisen:	Appetizers:
Norwegischer Lachs mit Toast *(laks)*	Norwegian salmon with toast
Gefüllte Eier *(ge-FÜL-teh) (EI-eR)*	deviled eggs
Suppen:	Soups:
Ochsenschwanzsuppe *(OK-sen-shvants)*	oxtail soup
Zwiebelsuppe *(TSVEE-bel-su-peh)*	onion soup
Fleischspeisen:	Meat Dishes:
Backhuhn *(BAK-hoon)*	baked chicken
Kalbsbraten *(KALPS-brah-ten)*	roast veal
Zwiebelrostbraten *(TSVEE-bel-rost-brah-ten)*	roast beef with onions

Gemüse:	Vegetables:
Salzkartoffeln	boiled potatoes
(reis)	
Reis	rice
(SHPAR-gel)	
Spargel	asparagus

Salate:	Salads:
(GUR-ken)	
Gurken mit Tomaten	cucumbers with tomatoes
Kohlsalat	cole slaw

Nachtisch:	Dessert:
Käsekuchen	cheese cake
(ZA-cheR-tor-teh)	
Sachertorte	Sacher torte

Getränke:	Beverages:
(PILS-neR)	
Pilsner Bier	Pilsen beer
(REIN-vein)	
Rheinwein	Rhine wine

On a separate page they find also "Specialties of the House," among which they have a hard time choosing.

(FISH-ge-riç-teh)
Fischgerichte:
fish dishes

(pa-NEER-teR) (KAR-pfen)	
panierter Karpfen	breaded carp
(fo-REL-eh)	
Forelle	trout
(SHOL-eh)	
Scholle	flounder

Finally they are ready to order. The waiter approaches the table.

(be-SHTEL-en)
KELLNER   **Möchten Sie bestellen,**   Would you like to order, gentlemen?

meine Herren? Das Backhuhn   *(BAK-hoon)*   I highly recommend the baked chicken.
(emp-FAY-len)   **das Backhuhn**
kann ich bestens empfehlen.   baked chicken

JOSEF	**Wie sind Ihre gefüllten**	How are your deviled eggs?
	Eier?	

(ge-FÜL-teh EI-eR)
gefüllte Eier
deviled eggs

	(OWS-ge-tseiç-net)	
KELLNER	**Ausgezeichnet, mein**	Excellent, sir.
	Herr.	
JOSEF	**Also gefüllte Eier und**	So, deviled eggs and then oxtail soup.
	dann Ochsenschwanzsuppe.	And, for me, half a baked chicken. Do
	Und für mich ein halbes	you prefer to order fish, Karl?
	Backhuhn. Bestellst du lieber	
	Fisch, Karl?	

(ZU-peh)
die Suppe
soup

die Forelle
trout

KARL	**Ja. Wie ist die Forelle?**	Yes. How is the trout?
	(shpe-tsee-a-lee-TAYT)	
KELLNER	Unsere Spezialität.	Our specialty.
KARL	**Also gut. Forelle für mich.**	Good! Trout for me. With boiled
	Mit Salzkartoffeln.	potatoes.

(salts)   (PFEF-eR)
Salz und Pfeffer
salt and pepper

JOSEF	**Was für einen Salat gibt es?**	What kind of salad do you have?
KELLNER	**Gurken mit Tomaten.**	Cucumbers and tomatoes.
JOSEF	**Gut.**	Good.

(zah-LAT)
der Salat
salad

KELLNER	**Der andere Herr nimmt**	Does the other gentleman also want
	auch einen?	one?

(SHVARTS-broht)
das Schwarzbrot
dark bread

KARL	**Ja. Zwei Salate.**	Yes. Two salads.
KELLNER	**Und zum Nachtisch?**	And for dessert?
JOSEF	Geben Sie uns noch	Give us the menu again.
	einmal die Speisekarte.	

(KAY-zeh)
der Käse
cheese

(Er nimmt sie und liest.)
(SACH-eR-tor-teh)
Möchtest du Sachertorte,
Karl?

(VEIN-trow-ben)
die Weintrauben
grapes

(He takes it and reads.)

Would you like Sachertorte,

Karl?

KARL **Gute Idee. Sachertorte mit**
(SHLAK-zah-neh)
Schlagsahne.

Good idea. Sachertorte with whipped
cream.

JOSEF **Also Sachertorte mit**

Schlagsahne.

(vein)
der Wein
wine

So, Sachertorte with whipped cream.

KARL **Zum Fisch einen guten**

Rheinwein.

With fish a good Rhine wine.

(beeR)
das Bier
beer

JOSEF **Und für mich ein großes**

Glas Bier.

And for me a large glass of beer.

Let's look at an important reflexive verb.

(FÜ-len)
WIE FÜHLEN SIE SICH?
How do you feel?

SICH FÜHLEN

Ich fühle mich (nicht) wohl	I (don't) feel well
Du fühlst dich (nicht) wohl	You (don't) feel well
Er, sie, es fühlt sich (nicht) wohl	He, she (doesn't) feel well
Wir fühlen uns (nicht) wohl	We (don't) feel well
Ihr fühlt euch (nicht) wohl	You (don't) feel well
Sie fühlen sich (nicht) wohl	They (don't) feel well
Sie fühlen sich (nicht) wohl	You (don't) feel well (polite)

Damen
Women

Herren
Men

Here are a few exercises based on what we've learned about eating in a restaurant. You're well into your new language, so the exercises should be easy. Like a piece of cake.

Place the numbers of the courses in front of the dishes and drinks to show in which course(s) each is typically served.

1. Vorspeisen   2. Suppe   3. Salat
4. Fisch   5. Fleisch   6. Nachtisch

a. _____ Gurken mit Tomaten   b. _____ Backhuhn   c. _____ Bier

d. _____ Sachertorte   e. _____ Rheinwein   f. _____ Reis

g. _____ Salzkartoffeln   h. _____ gefüllte Eier   i. _____ Brötchen

j. _____ Zwiebelsuppe   k. _____ Gemüse.

Now try to fill in the blanks with the German version of the English words in parentheses.

1. _____ (The waiter) gibt Josef die Speisekarte.

2. _____ (He gives him) die Speisekarte.

3. _____ (He takes) die Speisekarte.

4. Der Kellner empfiehlt _____ (baked chicken).

5. Karl (prefers) _____ Forelle _____.

6. Er trinkt eine _____ (bottle) Rheinwein.

(FOL-gen-deh)
Wie sagt man das Folgende auf Deutsch?
following

1. Where are the restrooms? _____

2. Please bring . . . to me. _____

The answers section is printed upside down at the bottom.

ANSWERS

Courses.
a. 3 b. 5 c. 5 d. 6 e. 4 f. 4,5 g. 4,5 h. 1 i. 1,4,5 j. 2 k. 4,5

Fill-ins.
1. Der Kellner 2. Er gibt ihm 3. Er nimmt 4. Backhuhn 5. zieht, vor 6. Flasche

Auf Deutsch. 1. Wo sind die Toiletten? 2. Bitte bringen Sie mir . . . .

137

VORSPEISEN	SUPPEN	SALATE

(ge-ROYCH-eR-teR) (HAY-ring)
Geräucherter Hering
smoked herring

(FLEISH-brü-eh)
die Fleischbrühe mit Nudeln
beef broth with noodles

(KOPF-za-lat)
der Kopfsalat
lettuce

(ge-BA-ke-neh)(PIL-tseh)
Gebackene Pilze
baked mushrooms

(ERP-sen-zu-peh)
Erbsensuppe
pea soup

(BOH-nen-za-lat)
der Bohnensalat
bean salad

Now here's a chance for creativity. Name some foods you would eat in the following cases.

1. Sie wollen abnehmen. _____ , _____ ,
     lose weight
_____

2. Sie wollen zunehmen. _____ , _____ ,
     gain weight
_____

(vits)
EIN WITZ
A joke

KELLNER   Tee oder Kaffee?

GAST   Kaffee ohne Sahne.

KELLNER   Sie müssen ihn ohne Milch nehmen. Wir haben keine Sahne.

Many restaurants and lunch counters serve a plate of the day which is quite inexpensive. It is especially good for tourists who wish to economize. Nowadays the North American influence is seen in fast-food restaurants and in the food they serve. If you have a yen for a hamburger, you can find it in Germany and Austria. It isn't expensive. But you may prefer to try out the food of the country. If you feel like having a soft drink of a North American brand, it is possible to find it at any café or restaurant. You can stay there a long time, and you don't have to drink up in a hurry. When you pay the bill, you should check if the service (**Bedienung**) is included. If not, you should leave a tip of 10%–15% for the waiter or waitress. In restaurants, service is usually included, but you should still leave a small tip.

ANSWERS
Things to eat. 1. Fisch, Gemüse, Salat   2. Backhuhn, Kartoffeln, Torte

138

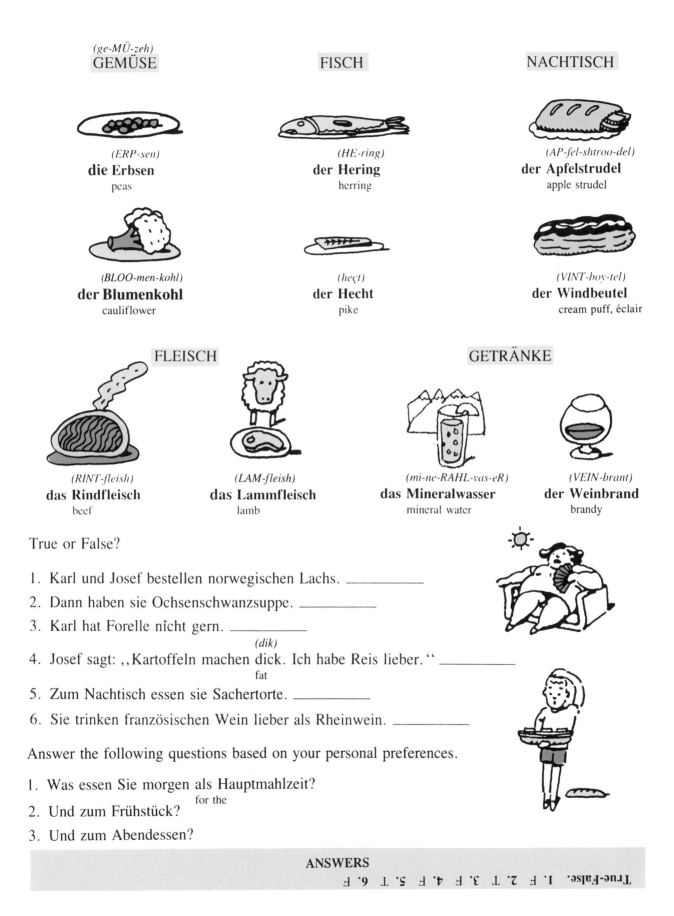

(ge-MÜ-zeh)
GEMÜSE

FISCH

NACHTISCH

(ERP-sen)
die Erbsen
peas

(HE-ring)
der Hering
herring

(AP-fel-shtroo-del)
der Apfelstrudel
apple strudel

(BLOO-men-kohl)
der Blumenkohl
cauliflower

(heçt)
der Hecht
pike

(VINT-boy-tel)
der Windbeutel
cream puff, éclair

FLEISCH

GETRÄNKE

(RINT-fleish)
das Rindfleisch
beef

(LAM-fleish)
das Lammfleisch
lamb

(mi-ne-RAHL-vas-eR)
das Mineralwasser
mineral water

(VEIN-brant)
der Weinbrand
brandy

True or False?

1. Karl und Josef bestellen norwegischen Lachs. _____

2. Dann haben sie Ochsenschwanzsuppe. _____

3. Karl hat Forelle nicht gern. _____

4. Josef sagt: ,,Kartoffeln machen dick. Ich habe Reis lieber.'' _____
   _(dik)
   fat

5. Zum Nachtisch essen sie Sachertorte. _____

6. Sie trinken französischen Wein lieber als Rheinwein. _____

Answer the following questions based on your personal preferences.

1. Was essen Sie morgen als Hauptmahlzeit?

2. Und zum Frühstück?
   for the

3. Und zum Abendessen?

139

Try putting the words together in the right order so they make sense:

1. empfehlen, kann, das, bestens, ich, Backhuhn

_____

2. bestellen, meine, Sie, möchten, Herren?

_____

3. Salat, was, es, gibt, einen, für?

_____

4. für, Glas, und, ein, Bier, mich, großes

_____

(GOO-ten)   *(a-pe-TEET)*   *(MAHL-tseit)*

Guten Appetit! Mahlzeit!

Enjoy your meal!

Congratulations. We hear you have just been named Chef of the Year. All of your friends are coming over tonight for a very special dinner which you are preparing to celebrate the occasion. Draw up a menu, course by course, of what you plan to serve.

die Vorspeise _____   der Fisch _____

die Suppe _____   das Fleisch _____

der Salat _____   der Nachtisch _____

das Gemüse _____   die Getränke (pl) _____

ANSWERS

1. Ich kann das Backhuhn bestens empfehlen.   2. Möchten Sie bestellen, meine Herren?   3. Was für einen Salat gibt es?   4. Und ein großes Glas Bier für mich.

140

HOW'RE WE DOING?
Na, wie geht's?

You're now more than halfway through.
You've come a long way — you've learned a lot.

It's a good idea to go through the first part of the book, reviewing the vocabulary and rereading the dialogues. If you're confused about a point, study it closely—you'll catch on soon enough!

After you've reviewed the material, try to complete the following quiz. It'll probably be easy. If you have any difficulty, reread the appropriate section of the book.

(feel) (glük)   *(spahs)*
Viel Glück—und viel Spaß!
Good luck   lots of fun

Exercise 1
Fill in the proper article:

1. _____ Katze
   a

2. _____ Spiegel
   the

3. _____ Mädchen
   the (plural)

4. _____ Haus
   a

5. _____ Onkel
   the

6. _____ Blume
   a

Fill in the correct endings:

7. Der Vater sing_____.

8. Das Mädchen komm_____.

9. Wir sing_____ schön.

10. Du wohn_____ in Berlin.

11. Sie sprech_____ viel.

12. Ihr komm_____ heute.

Exercise 2
Fill in the correct prepositions:

1. Er kommt _____ New York.
   from

2. Die Katze ist _____ dem Stuhl.
   behind

3. Sie geht _____ John.
   with

4. Der Baum ist _____ dem Haus.
   in front of

5. John kommt _____ Mary.
   without

6. Das Buch ist _____ dem Tisch.
   under

ANSWERS

Exercise 1.
1. eine 2. der 3. die 4. ein 5. der 6. eine 7. t (singt) 8. t (kommt) 9. en (singen) 10. st (wohnst) 11. en (sprechen) 12. t (kommt)

Exercise 2.
1. aus 2. hinter 3. mit 4. vor 5. ohne 6. unter

141

Exercise 2
Fill in the verbs with the correct endings:

7. Ich _____ nicht.
   speak

8. Du _____ gut.
   see

9. Sie _____ nicht.
   speak (polite form)

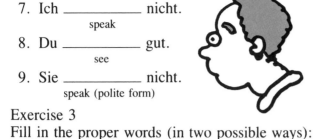

10. Er _____ das Mädchen.
    see

11. Du _____ schnell.
    speak

12. Sie _____ den Mann.
    sees

Exercise 3
Fill in the proper words (in two possible ways):

1. _____ or _____ Katze
   this

2. _____ or _____ Vater
   this

3. _____ or _____ Mädchen
   this

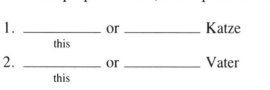

4. _____ or _____ Häuser
   these

5. _____ or _____ Füße
   these

6. _____ or _____ Blumen
   these

Fill in the verbs with the correct endings:

7. Er _____ zwanzig Mark.
   takes

8. Du _____ acht Stunden.
   sleep

9. Sie _____ nach Wien.
   travels

10. Das _____ zu viel.
    costs

11. Er _____ das Auto.
    washes

12. Wir _____ das Buch.
    take

Exercise 4
Fill in the proper words:

1. Sie müssen hier _____. (to get off)

2. Er _____ hier _____. (to get on)

3. Der Bus _____ hier _____. (to stop)

4. Wir _____ hier _____. (to transfer)

5. Eine _____, bitte.
   ticket

6. Das ist die _____.
   stop

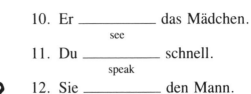

ANSWERS

Exercise 2.
7. spreche 8. siehst 9. sprechen 10. sieht 11. sprichst 12. sieht

Exercise 3.
1. diese, die 2. dieser, der 3. dieses, das 4. diese, die 5. diese, die 6. diese, die 7. nimmt
8. schläfst 9. fährt 10. kostet 11. wäscht 12. nehmen

Exercise 4.
1. aussteigen 2. steigt, ein 3. bleibt, stehen 4. steigen, um 5. Fahrkarte 6. Haltestelle

142

Exercise 4

Fill in the correct verb form of *sein* and of *haben*:

7. Er _____ ein Junge. (sein)

8. Du _____ ein Mädchen. (sein)

9. Wir _____ Frauen. (sein)

10. Sie _____ ein Mann. (polite, sein)

11. Du _____ ein Buch. (haben)

12. Er _____ eine Katze. (haben)

Exercise 5

Try these contractions:

1. Er kommt ____beim____ Haus an.
   bei dem

2. Die Katze springt _____ Sofa.
   über das

3. Er geht _____ Kino.
   in das

4. Wir fahren _____ Markt.
   zu dem

5. Der Hund ist _____ Haus.
   in dem

6. Das Kind kommt _____ Mutter.
   zu der

Exercise 6

Wieviel Uhr ist es?

1. Es ist _____ or
   _____ .

2. Es ist _____ or
   _____ .

3. Es ist _____ or
   _____ .

4. Es ist _____ or
   _____ .

5. Es ist _____ or
   _____ .

6. Es ist _____ .

143

Exercise 7
Fill in the correct pronouns:

1. Er ist _____ Sohn.
   my
2. Sie ist _____ Tochter.
   our
3. Das ist _____ Freund.
   her

4. Er ist _____ Vater.
   his
5. Das ist _____ Haus.
   your (polite)
6. Ist das _____ Uhr?
   your (familiar)

Insert the correct form:

7. _____ Blumen?
   do you want (polite)
8. Er _____ ein Glas Bier.
   would like
9. Wir _____ aussteigen.
   would like

10. Sie _____ ins Kino gehen.
    wants
11. Du _____ eine Fahrkarte.
    want
12. _____ jetzt essen?
    do you want (familiar)

Exercise 8
Fill in the correct reflexive pronouns:

1. Wir waschen _____.
   ourselves
2. Sie rasieren _____.
   themselves
3. Er entschuldigt _____.
   himself
4. Du erinnerst _____.
   yourself
5. Ihr amüsiert _____.
   yourselves
6. Ich erinnere _____.
   myself

Complete the following sentences:

7. Ich möchte _____.
   rent a car
8. _____ den Polizisten
   ask (you, polite)
   _____.
   over there
9. Wie funktioniert _____?
   the brake
10. Er braucht _____.
    a book
11. Gibt es _____ in der Nähe?
    a service station
12. Gibt es _____ hier?
    toilets

Exercise 9
Personal Pronouns again:

1. Karl sieht _____.
   you (polite)

2. Wir lesen _____.
   it (the book)

3. Er hört _____.
   us

4. Sie kauft _____.
   them

5. Mary besucht _____.
   me

6. Ich liebe _____.
   you (my daughter)

"Will you give it to me. . . ." (the indirect object):

7. Er gibt _____ das Geld.
   to us

8. Sie sendet _____ Bonbons.
   to me

9. Ich gebe _____ Blumen.
   to her

10. Ich kaufe _____ ein Buch.
    for you (polite)

11. Er dankt _____ für die Karte.
    to you (familiar)

12. Du gibst _____ eine Krawatte.
    to him

Exercise 10
Fill in the blanks:

1. _____ wollen Sie sprechen?
   about what

2. _____ sammeln Sie das?
   to what purpose

Try to translate these idiomatic expressions so that they sound as natural in German as they do in English:

3. That doesn't matter. _____

4. What is it about? _____?

5. Turn left (right). _____

6. Drive straight ahead! _____!

7. I am lost. _____

8. I passed the test. _____

9. He has the right-of-way. _____

10. Fill it up, please! _____

11. You are right. _____

12. Over there. _____

Exercise 11
True or False?

1. _____ Ein Reporter schreibt für eine Zeitung.

2. _____ Zum Wandern braucht man einen Koffer.

3. _____ Die meisten Deutschen gehen im März auf Urlaub.

4. _____ Deutsche feiern Weihnachten zwei Tage lang.

5. _____ Jogging ist ein sehr teurer Sport.

6. _____ Die Deutschen wandern sehr gern.

7. _____ Eine Trainingsbluse ist dasselbe wie ein Sweatshirt.

8. _____ In Deutschland braucht man kein Rücklicht für Fahrräder.

9. _____ Brustschwimmen lernt man im allgemeinen zuerst.

10. _____ *Eventuell* heißt auf Englisch *eventual*.

11. _____ Fisch schneidet man immer mit dem Messer.

12. _____ Das Mittagessen ist die wichtigste Mahlzeit in Deutschland.

Exercise 12
Circle the correct answer.

1. Wohin gehen Sie, wenn Sie essen wollen?
   a. in die Garage   b. ins Theater   c. ins Restaurant

2. Die Tasse steht gewöhnlich auf
   a. dem Auto   b. der Untertasse   c. der Serviette

3. Knödel ißt man oft mit
   a. Kraut   b. Sachertorte   c. Tomatensaft

4. In Deutschland ist der erste Gang gewöhnlich
   a. Kuchen   b. Fisch   c. Suppe

5. Jause hat man gewöhnlich um
   a. zehn Uhr   b. sechzehn Uhr   c. zwölf Uhr mittag

6. Wasser trinkt man gewöhnlich
   a. aus einer Tasse   b. aus einem Glas   c. aus einem Teller

Pick the right word and insert it where it belongs. Choose among:
Bäckerei, Abzeichen, Glas, abwischen, Wanderpfade, Sport.

7. Schwimmen ist ein sehr gesunder _____ .

8. Die deutschen _____ sind sehr gut markiert.

9. Man näht sich ein _____ auf die Badehose.

10. Brötchen kauft man in der _____ .

11. Mit der Serviette kann man sich den Mund _____ .

12. Er bestellt ein großes _____ Bier.

AT THE STORE

(im) *(ge-SHEFT)*
Im Geschäft

<table>
<tr><td>

16

</td><td>

(be-KLEI-dungs-ge-shef-teh)
Bekleidungsgeschäfte
Clothing Stores

(GRÖ-sen)   *(MAH-seh)*   *(GRUNT-far-ben)*
Größen, Maße, Grundfarben
Sizes, Measurements, Basic Colors

</td></tr>
</table>

(TSEE-eh)
Ich ziehe mir einen
(UN-teR-rok)
Unterrock an.

I am putting on my slip.

Ich ziehe mir das
(hemt)
Hemd aus.

I am taking off my shirt.

(AN-klei-den)   *(OWS-klei-den)*
SICH ANKLEIDEN—SICH AUSKLEIDEN
to get dressed / undressed

(KLEI-deR)   *(AN-proh-bee-ren)*
Kleider anprobieren
Trying on clothes

*Ich kleide **mich** an, du kleidest **dich** aus, er kleidet **sich** aus:* These are reflexive verbs taking the reflexive pronoun in the accusative (plural: *uns, euch, sich*).

In the case of articles of clothing:

*Ich ziehe **mir** etwas an, du ziehst **dir** etwas an, er probiert **sich** etwas an:* Here we have reflexive verbs taking the reflexive pronoun in the dative (plural: *uns, euch, sich*).

These verbs also have separable prefixes, which are separated from the verb under certain conditions. The position of the separable prefix is always at the end of the clause.

Ich kleide mich an. Ich kleide mich aus.

(MIT-gay-en) (tsoo-RÜK-kom-en)   *(TSOO-hö-ren)*
A few other verbs with separable prefixes are *mitgehen, zurückkommen,* and *zuhören.* Note how they are used in sentences.

Sie geht mit.   Er kommt zurück.   Er hört zu.
along   back   listens

HERRENBEKLEIDUNG

Men's Clothes

Here are the German words for some basic items of men's clothing.

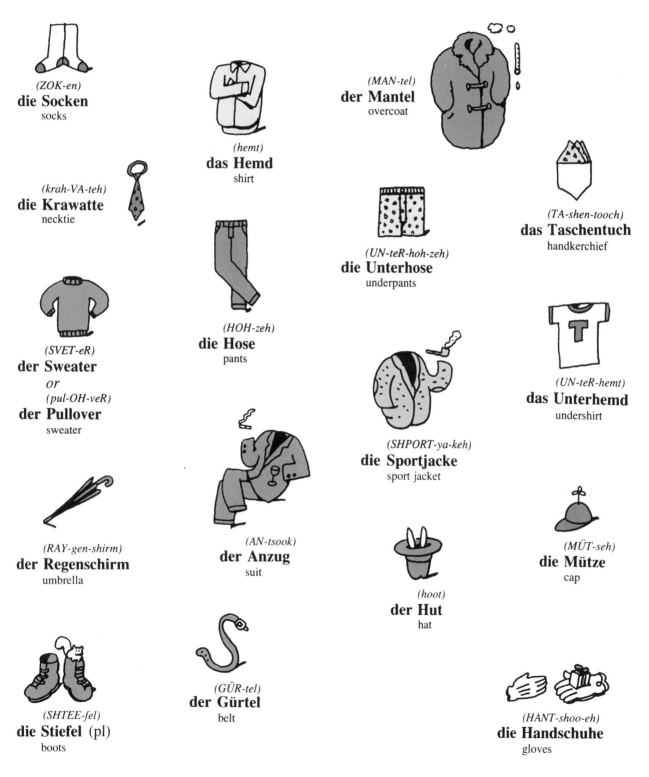

(ZOK-en)
die Socken
socks

(krah-VA-teh)
die Krawatte
necktie

(SVET-eR)
der Sweater
or
(pul-OH-veR)
der Pullover
sweater

(RAY-gen-shirm)
der Regenschirm
umbrella

(SHTEE-fel)
die Stiefel (pl)
boots

(hemt)
das Hemd
shirt

(HOH-zeh)
die Hose
pants

(AN-tsook)
der Anzug
suit

(GÜR-tel)
der Gürtel
belt

(MAN-tel)
der Mantel
overcoat

(UN-teR-hoh-zeh)
die Unterhose
underpants

(SHPORT-ya-keh)
die Sportjacke
sport jacket

(hoot)
der Hut
hat

(TA-shen-tooch)
das Taschentuch
handkerchief

(UN-teR-hemt)
das Unterhemd
undershirt

(MÜT-seh)
die Mütze
cap

(HANT-shoo-eh)
die Handschuhe
gloves

149

A villager goes to a men's clothing store in the big city:

(feR-KOY-feR)   *(voh-MIT)*

VERKÄUFER   **Womit kann ich Ihnen dienen,**   What would you like, sir?
clerk

    mein Herr?

(KUN-deh)   *(HEI-ra-teh)*   *(VO-chen-en-deh)*

KUNDE   **Ich heirate dieses Wochenende**   I'm getting married this weekend and need new
customer

    und brauche etwas Neues zum   clothes. I need undershorts and undershirts, also a

    Anziehen. Ich brauche Unterhosen   white shirt and a black tie.

    und Unterhemden, auch ein weißes

    Hemd und eine schwarze Krawatte.

VERKÄUFER   **Brauchen Sie auch einen neuen**   Do you need a new suit, too?

    Anzug?

KUNDE   **Ja. Zeigen Sie mir bitte einen**   Yes. Show me a black suit, please. I wear

                 (TRAH-geh)

    schwarzen Anzug. Ich trage Größe 44.   size 44.

VERKÄUFER   **Wir haben keinen Anzug in**   We don't have a suit in that size. Can I show you

    dieser Größe. Kann ich Ihnen eine   a sport jacket and slacks?

    Sportjacke und eine Sporthose zeigen?

KUNDE   **Gut. Kann ich sie anprobieren?**   Good. Can I try them on?

    (He tries them on, and they are too big
    for him.)

VERKÄUFER   **Sie passen Ihnen ausgezeichnet.**   They fit you beautifully.

    Jetzt, glaube ich, brauchen Sie einen   Now, I think, you need

    neuen Gürtel!   a new belt!

Can you tell me if these statements are correct? Write SIE HABEN RECHT *(reçt)* or SIE HABEN
UNRECHT.

are correct (over RECHT)
not correct (under UNRECHT)
are (over SIE HABEN, right)

1. Der Mann vom Land (villager) braucht neue Kleidung. _____

2. Er trägt Größe 54. _____

3. Er probiert die Hose an. _____

4. Die Hose ist ihm zu klein. _____

5. Er braucht keine Unterhosen. _____

When a man gets dressed in the morning, in what order does he put his clothes on? Write
numbers over the items to show the sequence:

der Gürtel,   die Socken,   der Hut,   die Unterhose,   die Krawatte,   das Hemd,   die Hose

Fill in the blanks with the right form of the verb in parenthesis.

1. _____ ein Sportjacke.
   (I need)
2. Die Hosen _____ mir nicht.
   (fit)
3. _____ mir morgens
   (I put)
   die Kleider _____ .
   (on)

4. _____ mir abends die
   (I take)
   Kleider _____ .
   (off)
5. Darf ich den Anzug _____ ?
   (try on)

Can you answer these questions?

1. Warum braucht der Mann neue Kleider?

_____

2. Was für einen Anzug will er?

_____

3. Was zeigt man ihm?

_____

4. Was probiert er an?

_____

Herrengrößen
Men's clothing sizes

Hemden (Shirts)

AMERICAN SIZE	14	14½	15	15½	16	16½	17	17½
EUROPEAN SIZE	36	37	38	39	40	41	42	43

(AN-de-reh)
Andere Kleidung (Other clothing)

AMERICAN SIZE	34	36	38	40	42	44	46	48
EUROPEAN SIZE	44	46	48	50	52	54	56	58

If you are a man, what size shirt do you wear? Ich trage Größe _____.

What size pants, suit and jacket do you wear? Ich trage Größe _____.

If you are a woman, look for the sizes of a male friend or relative:

Er trägt Größe _____ für seine Hemden und Größe _____
für seine Hosen, Jacken und Anzüge.

Try saying these set phrases which will help you in purchasing clothes. Place the article of clothing of your choice in the blanks:

Wollen Sie mir bitte _____ zeigen?

Kann ich _____ anprobieren?

(UM-en-dern)
Können Sie den _____ umändern?
alter

Dieser _____ paßt mir nicht gut.

Fill in the blanks with the words depicted:

1. Wenn es kalt ist, trage ich einen

   _____ .

2. Wenn es kühl ist, ziehe ich mir meinen Mantel aus und ziehe mir

   einen _____ an.

3. Wenn es schneit, ziehe ich mir

   meine _____ an.

4. Wenn es regnet, ziehe ich mir meinen Mantel aus und ziehe mir

   meinen _____ an.

5. Wenn es regnet, nehme ich auch

   meinen _____ mit.

6. Wenn es heiß ist, trage ich

   _____

ANSWERS
1. Mantel   2. Sweater   3. Stiefel   4. Regenmantel   5. Regenschirm   6. kurze Hosen

DAMENBEKLEIDUNG
Women's clothes

Grundfarben
Basic Colors

(GEL-beh) (BÜS-ten-hal-terR)
der gelbe Büstenhalter

or

(bay-hah)
der gelbe BH
yellow bra

(ROH-teh) (HANT-ta-sheh)
die rote Handtasche
red   handbag

(BLOW-eh) (kleit)
das blaue Kleid
blue   dress

(GRÜ-neh) (TA-shen-tooch)
das grüne Taschentuch
green   handkerchief

(GEL-beh) (HŌS-çen)
das gelbe Höschen
yellow   panties

(VEI-seh) (UN-teR-rok)
der weiße Unterrock
white   slip

(GRÜ-neh) (BLOO-zeh)
die grüne Bluse
green   blouse

(ROH-teh) (rok)
der rote Rock
red   skirt

Can you answer these questions? Example: What color is the skirt? The skirt is red. (Was für eine Farbe hat der Rock? Der Rock ist rot.)

1. Was für eine Farbe hat das Taschentuch?

_____

2. Was für eine Farbe hat die Bluse?

_____

Can you continue by asking and answering similar questions about the remaining items of clothing above?

Damengrößen
Women's clothing sizes

Blusen (Blouses)

AMERICAN SIZE	32	34	36	38	40	42	44
EUROPEAN SIZE	40	42	44	46	48	50	52

Andere Kleidung (Other clothing)

AMERICAN SIZE	8	10	12	14	16	18
EUROPEAN SIZE	36	38	40	42	44	46

DAMEN- UND HERRENSCHUHE
Shoes for Men and Women

(eng)
Sie sind mir zu eng.
They are too narrow for me.

(DRÜ-ken)
Sie drücken mich.
They pinch me.

Sie sind mir zu groß.
They are too big for me.

Schuhgrößen
Shoe Sizes

Footwear for Men (shoes, boots, sandals)

AMERICAN SIZE	7	7½	8	8½	9	9½	10	10½	11	11½
GERMAN SIZE	40	41	41	42	43	43	44	44	45	46

Footwear for women

AMERICAN SIZE	5	5½	6	6½	7	7½	8	8½	9
GERMAN SIZE	36	36½	37	37½	38	38½	39	39½	40

Welche Größe tragen Sie?
What size do you wear?

KLEIDUNG FÜR DIE PARTY

(KLEI-dung) *(PAR-tee)*

Clothes for the Party

Mimi zieht sich für die Party bei Therese schön an. Im Schuhgeschäft *(EIN-ig-eh)* **probiert sie viele Schuhe an. Einige sind zu eng und drücken sie. Andere sind ihr zu groß. Endlich kauft sie ein Paar, das ihr gut paßt.**

Der Verkäufer im Warenhaus bedient *(feR-KOY-feR)* *(VAH-ren-hows)* **sie. Sie kauft einen blauen Rock und eine** *(kowft)* **rosa Polyester-Bluse. Sie trägt immer rosa** *(po-lee-ES-teR)* *(traykt)* **Blusen.**

Als sie zur Party geht, findet sie, daß Therese fast dieselben Kleider anhat wie sie. Soll sie nach Hause gehen und sich andere Kleider anziehen? Oder soll sie Therese zu ihrem guten Geschmack *(ge-SHMAK)* **gratulieren?** *(grah-too-LEER-en)*

Mimi is getting all dressed up for the party at Therese's. In the shoe store she tries on many shoes. Some are too narrow and pinch her. Others are too big for her. Finally she buys a pair that fits her well.

The salesman in the department store waits on her. She buys a blue skirt and a pink polyester blouse. She always wears pink blouses.

When she goes to the party, she finds that Therese has on almost the same clothes as she does. Should she go home and put on other clothes? Or should she congratulate Therese on her good taste?

We don't suppose you're overly fussy. But if you have something particular in mind, here are some words and expressions that may be helpful:

I want something in:

(BOWM-vol-eh)	*(BOWM-vol-dril)*	*(VILT-lay-deR)*
cotton: **Baumwolle**	denim: **Baumwolldrill**	suede: **Wildleder**
(ZEI-deh)	*(NEI-lon)*	*(LAY-deR)*
silk: **Seide**	nylon: **Nylon**	leather: **Leder**

Please take my measurement.

Bitte nehmen Sie Maß.

I would like something of better quality.

Bessere Qualität, bitte.

Do you have something handmade?

(HANT-ge-mach-tes)
Haben Sie etwas Handgemachtes?

It is long (big, short, small) on me.

Es ist zu lang (groß, kurz, klein) für mich.

I don't like the color. I prefer green.

Ich habe die Farbe nicht gern. Ich habe lieber grün.

Try practicing some imaginary situations in which you might use these expressions with various articles of clothing:

You have been named the best-dressed man or woman of the year. Can you describe what you usually wear to have gained such an honor? Use expressions like *tragen, Schuhe anziehen, es paßt mir gut, die Farben, jeden Tag, ich ziehe an, ich habe lieber, ich habe gern.*

What does the worst-dressed man or woman wear? Be outrageous!

What articles of feminine clothing correspond, more or less, to the masculine items listed:

1. Hemd _____.

2. Hose _____.

3. Unterhose _____.

4. Unterhemd _____.

Food stores in West Germany carry a wide variety of items. Shopping for food can be a lot of fun, especially if you look for local specialties.

(mol-ke-REI)
die Molkerei
dairy

(mets-ge-REI)
die Metzgerei
butcher shop

(ge-MÜZ-eh-hand-lung)
die Gemüsehandlung
vegetable store

(OHPST-hand-lung)
die Obsthandlung
fruit store

(be-keh-REI)
die Bäckerei
bakery

(FISH-hand-lung)
die Fischhandlung
fish market

(SÜS-vah-ren-ge-sheft)
das Süßwarengeschäft
candy store

(kon-dee-toh-REI)
die Konditorei
pastry shop

(EIS-dee-leh)
Eisdiele
ice cream shop

(VEIN-hand-lung)
die Weinhandlung
wine store

Draw a line through the item(s) which you could *not* find in each type of store:

1. Molkerei—Butter, Käse, Wein
2. Metzgerei—Lamm, Orangen, Kalbfleisch
   (KALP-fleish)
   veal
3. Gemüsehandlung—Semmeln, Gurken, Kopfsalat
4. Obsthandlung—Weintrauben, Orangen, Brot
5. Bäckerei—Schinken, Sardellen, Brot
   (zar-DEL-en)
   anchovies
6. Fischhandlung—Marmelade, Spargel, Forelle
   (SHPAR-gel)
   asparagus

157

7. Süßwarengeschäft—Süßigkeiten, Tomaten, Mineralwasser
8. Konditorei—Reis, Milch, Torten
9. Eisdiele—Sardellen, Salate, Eis *(shpi-NAHT)*
10. Weinhandlung—Backhuhn, Flaschen, Spinat
   spinach

In West Germany there are supermarkets, but not as many as in the United States. Many Germans still do their shopping at a number of specialized stores rather than at one supermarket.

Here are some adjectives about food:

(frish)
frisch
fresh

(fer-DOR-ben)
verdorben
spoiled

(ALT-bak-en)
altbacken
stale

How could you complain about the following situations?

1. You have bought a rotten tomato. Diese Tomate ist _____.

2. The bread you bought is not fresh. Dieses Brot ist nicht _____.

3. The cake you bought is stale. Dieser Kuchen ist _____.

(ge-VIÇ-teh)   *(MAH-seh)*
GEWICHTE UND MASSE
Weights and Measures

(VEE-gen)
wiegen
to weigh

(ge-VIÇT)
das Gewicht
weight

Although it has not yet caught on fully in the U.S., the metric system is the standard means for measuring in many foreign countries, including Germany. Here are two of the most common weights and measures:

a kilogram = 2.2 U.S. pounds
(KEE-loh-gram)
das Kilogramm *or* **das Kilo**

a liter = 1.1 U.S. quarts
(LEE-teR)
das Liter

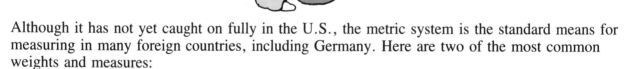

ANSWERS

Situations.
1. verdorben 2. frisch 3. altbacken

Items.
7. Tomaten, Mineralwasser 8. Reis, Milch 9. Sardellen, Salate 10. Backhuhn, Spinat

A kilogram is made up of 1000 grams; it is sometimes divided into two pounds *(das Pfund)* *(pfunt)* of 500 grams each. The German pound is slightly heavier than the U.S. pound.

How many kilos do you weigh? _____   How much water do you drink a day? _____

Here are some useful expressions to use when buying food. Try writing them out:

(DUT-sent)
ein Dutzend _____
dozen

(HAL-bes)
ein halbes Dutzend _____.
half   dozen

ein Kilo _____

ein halbes Kilo _____

ein halbes Pfund _____
half a pound

ein Liter _____

(veekt)
Wieviel wiegt es? _____
How much does it weigh?

Wieviel kostet es? _____
How much does it cost?

Es ist zu viel. _____
It's too much.

Ich möchte (gern) _____
I would like

Wieviel kosten sie per Dutzend? _____
How much are they per dozen?

IM LEBENSMITTELGESCHÄFT
At the Grocery Store

PLEASE NOTE: In German the **of** in the following expressions is not translated: A cake
(ZEI-feh)
of soap becomes **ein Stück Seife** (*not* ein Stück von Seife), a liter of milk **ein Liter Milch**.

Ask the clerk for the items in the pictures. Use the names of the containers they come in or the unit of measurement. Try asking some questions like:

Wieviel kostet das (kosten sie)?
How much does it (do they) cost?

Wieviel wiegt das (wiegen sie)?
How much does it (do they) weigh?

Wieviel kosten sie pro Dutzend, pro Kiste, etc.
How much are they per dozen, per box, etc.?

(shtük) (ZEI-feh)
ein Stück Seife
a cake of soap

(KIR-shen)   (owf) (dayR) (VAH-geh)
die Kirschen auf der   Waage
cherries on the scales

(DOH-zeh)
eine Dose Gemüse
a can of vegetables

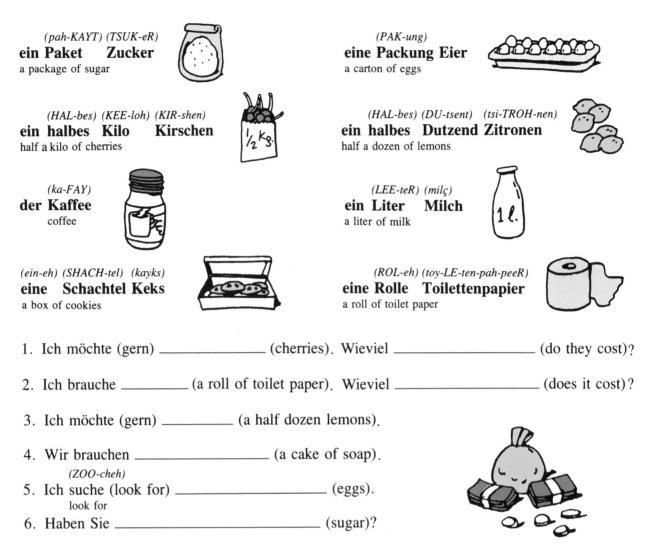

(pah-KAYT) *(TSUK-eR)*
ein Paket Zucker
a package of sugar

(PAK-ung)
eine Packung Eier
a carton of eggs

(HAL-bes) *(KEE-loh)* *(KIR-shen)*
ein halbes Kilo Kirschen
half a kilo of cherries

(HAL-bes) *(DU-tsent)* *(tsi-TROH-nen)*
ein halbes Dutzend Zitronen
half a dozen of lemons

(ka-FAY)
der Kaffee
coffee

(LEE-teR) *(milç)*
ein Liter Milch
a liter of milk

(ein-eh) *(SHACH-tel)* *(kayks)*
eine Schachtel Keks
a box of cookies

(ROL-eh) *(toy-LE-ten-pah-peeR)*
eine Rolle Toilettenpapier
a roll of toilet paper

1. Ich möchte (gern) ———————— (cherries). Wieviel ———————— (do they cost)?

2. Ich brauche ———— (a roll of toilet paper). Wieviel ———————— (does it cost)?

3. Ich möchte (gern) ———— (a half dozen lemons).

4. Wir brauchen ———————— (a cake of soap).
   (ZOO-cheh)
5. Ich suche (look for) ———————— (eggs).
   look for
6. Haben Sie ———————————— (sugar)?

Try practicing these requests further on a sheet of paper until you feel you know them.

Nowadays, it is not always necessary to go to different stores to buy groceries. Germany now has North American style supermarkets where we can buy them in one place: bakery items, meat, eggs, a box of cookies, a roll of toilet paper, a liter of milk, a half-dozen oranges, a kilo of sugar, a package of candy. But it is still interesting to go to the open-air markets to see the great variety of poultry, fruit, vegetables, and other products the farmers sell each day. It is a good way to observe the foods typical of the country or the region.

Indicate the correctness of the following statements by writing SIE HABEN RECHT or SIE HABEN UNRECHT.
(SU-peR-merk-teh)
1. Es gibt keine Supermärkte in Deutschland. ————————————————————
   supermarkets

160

2. Viele Deutsche kaufen Lebensmittel in kleinen Geschäften. _____

3. Keks kauft man in einer Schachtel. _____
      (um-GAY-bung)
4. Produkte der Umgebung kauft man nur im Supermarkt. _____
      region
5. Die Deutschen wiegen Milch auf einer Waage. _____

Suppose you're making out a grocery list. Fill in the blanks below with the things you want and the quantity. Example: Zwei Kilo Kirschen.

_____   _____   _____

_____   _____

In many German cities you can find open-air markets where local farmers sell their produce. In some cities local specialties are sold by street vendors. For instance, in Hamburg you can buy smoked eel, a local specialty, from street vendors.

As we've noted, there are numerous specialty stores in Germany. What stores would you visit to buy the following items?

1. Wir finden *Semmeln* in der _____.
     (FER-kow-fen)
2. Sie verkaufen *Schinken* in der _____.
     sell
3. Wenn wir frische *Erdbeeren* brauchen, gehen wir zur _____.
4. Sie verkaufen *Sahne* in der _____.
5. Wenn wir *Tomaten* wollen, gehen wir zur _____.
6. Wenn wir *Kuchen* brauchen, kaufen wir ihn in der _____.

ANSWERS

Recht/unrecht.
2. recht 3. recht 4. unrecht 5. unrecht

Stores.
1. Bäckerei 2. Metzgerei 3. Obsthandlung 4. Molkerei 5. Gemüsehandlung 6. Konditorei

Can you make up questions which would bring about these responses?

1. Sie kosten 2 Mark per Kilo. 2. Sie wiegen ein halbes Pfund.

_____ _____

Can you guess what we call the person who works in the following stores?

1. in der Konditorei _____ 2. in der Metzgerei _____

3. in der Bäckerei_____

Let's have a little fun.

You are on a food-shopping trip. Fill in the blanks
in the following sentences to indicate how
you'd get to various stores. You are standing near
the ice-cream shop as you start your trip.

> Do you remember?
> **links** = left
> **rechts** = right
> **geradeaus** = straight ahead

Ich möchte zuerst zur Fischhandlung. Ich gehe an der Eisdiele vorbei: und dann _____

um die Ecke. Ich kaufe zwei Forellen in der Fischhandlung. Dann möchte ich das

Süßwarengeschäft besuchen. Ich gehe links und dann _____. Dann gehe ich

_____ zur Obsthandlung, wo ich viele Äpfel kaufe. Dann muß ich _____

und dann _____, um Milch zu kaufen. Ich möchte auch Brot kaufen. Ich gehe

erst _____, dann _____ bis zur Bäckerei. Die Weinhandlung ist

in der Nähe; ich kaufe eine Flasche Wein und dann gehe ich _____ nach Hause.

IN DER DROGERIE
At the Drugstore

(HEI-dee) *(KAHR-in)*
Heidi and Karin go into a drugstore
and head for the beauty aids.
Heidi looks at herself in the mirror.

HEIDI	*(REI-ni-gungs-kraym)*	
	Ich muß eine Dose Reinigungskrem	I must buy a jar of cold
	(pah-PEER-ta-shen-tüç-eR)	
	und Papiertaschentücher kaufen.	cream and paper tissues.
KARIN	*(fer-VEN-deh)*	
	Ich verwende nie Reinigungskrem.	I never use cold cream. It's too expensive. Do
	Sie ist zu teuer. Kaufst du immer dein	you always buy your makeup here? This is a shop
	Make-up hier? Das ist ein Geschäft	for the rich;
	für die Reichen; die Artikel kosten	the articles cost a lot.
	sehr viel.	
HEIDI	*(pro-DUK-teh)*	
	Du hast recht, aber gute Produkte	You're right, but good products
	sind teuer.	are costly.
KARIN	**Ich sag dir was. Ich kaufe nichts in**	I'll tell you something. I'm not buying anything
	dieser Drogerie. Die Preise sind zu	in this drugstore. The prices are too high here.
	hoch hier.	
DER VERKÄUFER	**Guten Tag, meine**	Hello, ladies.
	Damen. Womit kann ich Ihnen	What would you like?
	dienen?	

163

HEIDI *(kam)* **Ich brauche einen Kamm, eine** *(HAHR-bürs-teh)* *(HAHR-shpray)* **Haarbürste und eine Dose Haarspray.** *(TSAHN-bürs-teh)* **Ich möchte auch gern eine Zahnbürste** *(TSAHN-pas-teh)* **und Zahnpaste kaufen. Wieviel macht das?**

I need a comb, a hair brush, and a can of hair spray. I'd also like to buy a toothbrush and toothpaste. How much does that come to?

VERKÄUFER Die Zahnbürste kostet 4 Mark und die Zahnpaste 3 Mark fünfzig.

The toothbrush costs 4 marks and the toothpaste 3 marks fifty.

KARIN Siehst du? Das kostet dich eine Menge Geld.

You see? That'll cost you a lot of money.

HEIDI Jetzt möchte ich gern das Make-up *(roož)* *(LIP-en-shtift)* **sehen. Rouge, Lippenstift,** *(ma-SKAH-ra)* *(NAH-gel-lak)* **Maskara, bitte. O ja, auch Nagellack** *(NAH-gel-lak-ent-fern-eR)* **und Nagellackentferner.**

Now I'd like to see the makeup. Rouge, lipstick, mascara, please. Oh, yes, nail polish and nail polish remover, too.

KARIN Aber du gibst zu viel aus.

But you're spending too much.

HEIDI Ja, ich weiß. Aber ich brauche *(ZA-chen)* **diese Sachen.**

Yes, I know. But I need these things.

Show whether the statements are TRUE or FALSE:

1. Ich kann Papiertaschentücher in einer Drogerie kaufen. _____
(kos-MAY-tik-ap-tei-lung)
2. Wir finden Make-up in der Kosmetikabteilung. _____
   beauty-aid section
3. Die Preise in der Drogerie sind hoch. _____

4. Karin will in der Drogerie nichts ausgeben. _____

5. Heidi kauft nie etwas in einer Drogerie. _____

ANSWERS

True/false.
1. T 2. T 3. T 4. T 5. F

164

Let's try to answer the following questions.

1. Was kann man für die Zähne in einer Drogerie kaufen? (2)

_____ , _____

(be-NUTS-en)
2. Was benutzen Frauen auf ihren Fingernägeln? (2)
use

_____ , _____

(ge-SIÇT)
3. Was sind die drei Schönheitsmittel, die Frauen auf Gesicht, Lippen und Augen benutzen? (3)
face

_____ , _____ , _____

4. Was benutzen Frauen für ihr Haar? (3)

_____ , _____ , _____

(Mü-sen)
Müssen
must, have to

The following modal verb is very useful:

ich muß	wir müssen
du mußt	ihr müßt
er sie } muß es	sie müssen
Sie müssen	

Here are a couple examples:

Ich muß etwas kaufen.
I must buy something.

(TSAHN-artst)
Sie müssen zum Zahnarzt.
You (polite) have to go to the dentist.

Can you answer the questions?

1. Wo müssen Sie Brot kaufen? _____

2. Wo muß man Fleisch kaufen? _____

(ent-FERN-en)

3. Was muß man benutzen, um Nagellack zu entfernen?
   remove

_____

4. Wohin muß man gehen, um Make-up zu kaufen?

_____

Study the following dialogue, set in a German drug store. Write the name of the toilet articles on the line indicated.

HEINRICH **Haben Sie Süßigkeiten?**

VERKÄUFER **Nein, wir haben keine**

Süßigkeiten. Um Süßigkeiten zu

kaufen, müssen Sie ins

Süßwarengeschäft gehen.

(rah-ZEER-ap-pa-raht)
der Rasierapparat
razor

_____

HEINRICH **Und wie steht es mit Zigaretten**

(SHTREIÇ-hölts-eRn)
und Streichhölzern?
matches

VERKÄUFER **Um Zigaretten zu kaufen,**

müssen Sie in die Tabakhandlung

gehen.

(rah-ZEER-kling-en)
die Rasierklingen
razor blades

_____

HEINRICH **Dann möchte ich gern ein**

Deodorantspray kaufen, einen

Rasierapparat, Rasierkrem, und einige

Rasierklingen.

(day-OH-der-ant-shpray)
das Deodorantspray

_____

VERKÄUFER Wie wäre es mit einem

elektrischen Rasierapparat?

(ALT-moh-dish)

HEINRICH Nein, dafür bin ich zu altmodisch.
old-fashioned

(eh-LEK-tri-sheh)
der elektrische
(rah-ZEER-ap-pa-raht)
Rasierapparat
electric razor

_____

Let's try a few more questions.

1. Was finden Sie in der Tabakhandlung? (2)

_____ , _____

2. Was benutzt ein Mann zum Rasieren? (3)

_____ , _____ , _____

3. Wo kauft man Süßigkeiten?

_____

IN DER APOTHEKE
At the Pharmacy

(re-TSEPT)

At the pharmacy your prescription (**das Rezept**) will be filled. Write the name of each of the drugstore items on the line indicated.

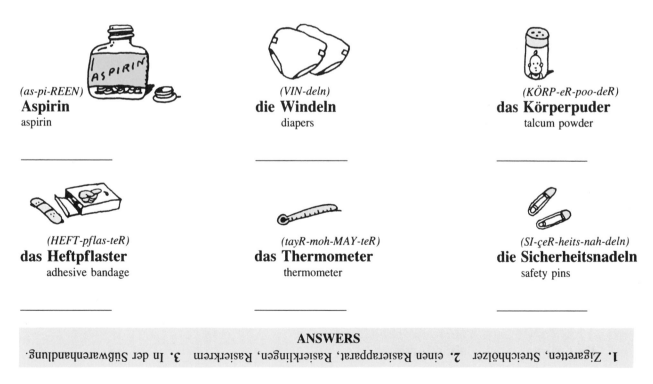

(as-pi-REEN)
Aspirin
aspirin

_____

(VIN-deln)
die Windeln
diapers

_____

(KÖRP-eR-poo-deR)
das Körperpuder
talcum powder

_____

(HEFT-pflas-teR)
das Heftpflaster
adhesive bandage

_____

(tayR-moh-MAY-teR)
das Thermometer
thermometer

_____

(SI-çeR-heits-nah-deln)
die Sicherheitsnadeln
safety pins

_____

167

Here are some useful phrases for making purchases at the pharmacy.

Ich brauche etwas *gegen* . . .

(er-KEL-tung)
eine Erkältung
cold

(fer-SHTOP-fung)
die Verstopfung
constipation

(HALS-shmer-tsen)
die Halsschmerzen
sore throat

Here's a short paragraph about Marie's trip to a pharmacy.

Marie geht in die Apotheke, um einiges
(feR-LANKT)
zu kaufen. Sie verlangt Heftpflaster,

Alkohol und ein Thermometer. Sie sagt
(KOPF-shmerts-en)
dem Verkäufer, sie hat Kopfschmerzen,

und sie verlangt auch Aspirin.
(da-TSU)
Marie sagt dazu, daß sie sich
(ÖF-teRs) *(vohl)*
morgens öfters nicht wohl fühlt
(ge-VIÇT) *(TSU-nimt)*
und daß sie Gewicht zunimmt.

Und der Verkäufer denkt, sie ist
(SHVANG-eR)
schwanger, und sagt zu Marie „Vielleicht

sollen Sie lieber Körperpuder,

Sicherheitsnadeln und Windeln für das

Baby kaufen.“

Marie goes into the pharmacy to buy a few things. She asks for bandages, rubbing alcohol, and a thermometer. She tells the clerk she has a headache, and also asks for aspirin.

Marie adds that she often doesn't feel well in the morning and that she is putting on weight.

And the clerk thinks she is pregnant, and says to Marie, "Perhaps you should rather buy talcum powder, safety pins and diapers for the baby."

Here are some useful expressions to use when going to a drugstore or pharmacy.

Ich habe . . .

(DURÇ-fal)
Durchfall
diarrhea

(TSU-keR-krank-heit)
Zuckerkrankheit
diabetes

(HOOS-ten)
Husten
cough

(FEE-beR)
Fieber
fever

(KREMP-feh)
Krämpfe
cramps

(KOPF-shmerts-en)
Kopfschmerzen
headache

(SHNIT-vun-deh)
eine Schnittwunde
cut

(ZON-en-brant)
einen Sonnenbrand
sunburn

(GRI-peh)
die Grippe
flu

(TSAHN-shmer-tsen)
Zahnschmerzen
toothache

Ich möchte... kaufen.

(MAH-gen-zoy-reh)
etwas gegen Magensäure
antacid

(an-tee-SEP-ti-kum)
ein Antiseptikum
antiseptic

(YOHT-tink-tooR)
Jodtinktur
iodine

(HEFT-pflas-teR)
Heftpflaster
bandages

(VAT-eh)
Watte
cotton

(SHAY-reh)
eine Schere
scissors

Ich muß... kaufen.

(AP-für-mi-tel)
ein Abführmittel
laxative

(MOH-nats-bin-den)
Monatsbinden
sanitary napkins

(TAM-pongs)
Tampons
tampons

(in-zu-LEEN)
Insulin
insulin

(HOO-sten-see-rup)
Hustensirup
cough syrup

Match the ailment (column 1) with the item or items (column 2) you would most likely ask for at the pharmacy.

_____ 1. Verstopfung

_____ 2. eine Schnittwunde

_____ 3. Fieber

_____ 4. Kopfschmerzen

_____ 5. Magenschmerzen

_____ 6. Zuckerkrankheit

_____ 7. Husten

(feR-DOR-be-neR)
_____ 8. ein verdorbener Magen
indigestion

A. Verbände

B. Insulin

C. ein Abführmittel

D. etwas gegen Magensäure

E. Aspirin

F. ein Antiseptikum

G. ein Thermometer

H. Hustensirup

Can you recall these items you might want to buy at the pharmacy?

1. _ _ _ _ _ _ _   2. _ _ _ _ _ _   3. _ _ _ _ _ _ _ _ _   4. _ _ _ _ _ _ _ _ _ _
   aspirin   insulin   iodine   cough syrup

Now try the same with these ailments:

1. _ _ _ _ _ _ _ _ _   2. _ _ _ _ _ _   3. _ _ _ _ _ _ _   4. _ _ _ _ _ _
    diarrhea   flu   headache   cough

Answer the following questions in German:

1. What are two items for feminine hygiene?

   _____ , _____

2. What things might you need for a minor cut or abrasion?

   _____ , _____

3. Can you name three ailments that could cause a fever?

   _____ , _____ , _____

Wäschereien und
Laundries and
(ÇAY-mish-eh) *(REI-ni-gung)*
Chemische Reinigung
Dry Cleaning

(VASH-mah-shee-neh)
die Waschmaschine
washing machine

(VASH-en)
waschen
to wash

(TROK-nen)
trocknen
to dry

(TRO-ken-ma-shee-neh)
die Trockenmaschine
drier

Hotel laundering and cleaning services in Germany, Austria, and Switzerland are more than adequate all through the year. It usually takes three days for clothing to be returned.

The better hotels offer a one-day service if the customer is willing to pay about 50% more for it. Outside the hotel, laundry and cleaning establishments are plentiful, as are self-service laundromats.

(pa-KAYT) *(VASH-pul-veR)*
das Paket   Waschpulver
box of soap powder

(BÜ-gel-bret)
das Bügelbrett
ironing board

(VASH-korp)
der Waschkorb
wash basket

(VASH-mah-shee-neh)
die Waschmaschine
washing machine

(BÜ-gel-ei-zen)
das Bügeleisen
iron

(VESH-eh-klam-ern)
die Wäscheklammern
clothes pins

WÄSCHEREI UND CHEMISCHE REINIGUNG IM HOTEL

Since you may not want to spend time in laundromats, you will probably prefer to use the laundry services of the hotels where you stay. In that case, these expressions may be useful:

Haben Sie hier eine Wäscherei?	Do you have a laundry here?
Ich habe etwas zum Waschen.	I have some laundry to wash.
Können Sie einen Knopf an meinem Hemd *(AN-nay-en)* **annähen?** sew on	Can you sew a button on my shirt?
(ER-mel) *(FLIK-en)* **Können Sie den Ärmel dieser Bluse flicken?** sleeve mend	Can you mend the sleeve of this blouse?
(SHTERK-eh) *(HEM-den)* **Ich will keine Stärke in meinen Hemden.** starch	I don't want any starch in my shirts.
(hemt) **Bitte bügeln Sie dieses Hemd noch einmal.** shirt	Please iron this shirt again.
(REI-ni-gung) **Bitte bringen Sie diesen Anzug zur Reinigung.**	Please take this suit to the cleaners.
(flek) *(her-OWS-nay-men)* **Können Sie diesen Fleck herausnehmen?** spot take out	Can you take this spot out?

Try filling in the blanks with the key words from the sentences above. Then read the sentences aloud:

1. Können Sie diesen _____ herausnehmen?

                                spot

2. Können Sie meine Hemden _____ ?

                                        wash

3. Können Sie einen Knopf an meinem Hemd _____ ?

                    sew

4. Können Sie diesen Anzug zur _____ bringen?

                    cleaners

5. Wollen Sie dieses Hemd noch einmal _____ ?

                    iron

6. Können Sie den _____ aus dieser Bluse _____ ?

                spot   take out

7. Ich habe etwas Unterwäsche zum _____ .

                    wash

8. Ich will keine _____ in meinen Hemden.

                starch

ANSWERS

Fill-ins. 1. Fleck 2. waschen 3. annähen 4. Reinigung 5. bügeln 6. Fleck, herausnehmen 7. waschen 8. Stärke

(be-SHVAYR-den)
BESCHWERDEN
complaints

Hans schickt seine Kleidung

immer zur Hotelwäscherei. Dieses

Mal gibt es Probleme. Da gibt es eine
(feR-VEKS-lung)
Verwechslung und viele

Kleidungsstücke, die man ihm
(ge-Hö-r-en)
zurückschickt, gehören einer
(payR-ZOHN) *(be-SHVAYRT)*
anderen Person. Er beschwert

sich beim Manager. Erstens
(traykt)
trägt er niemals Büstenhalter oder

Höschen. Außerdem haben

seine Hemden zu viel Stärke und
(roo-ee-NEERT) *(feR-ZENGT)*
eines ist ruiniert; es ist versengt.
(FAY-len)
Auch fehlen ihm zwei Socken,

eine rote und eine grüne. Der

Anzug, den er von der

Reinigung bekommt, hat

noch immer einen Fleck am
(grunt)
Ärmel. Er hat Grund, sich zu

beschweren, glauben Sie nicht?

Hans always sends his clothes to

the hotel laundry service. This time

there are problems. There is a

mix-up, and many of the clothes

they return to him belong to another

person. He complains to the

the manager. In the first place, he

never wears bras or panties.

Besides, his shirts have too much

starch in them and one is ruined;

it's scorched. Also, he is missing

two socks, one red and one green.

The suit he receives from the

cleaner's still has a spot on the

sleeve. He has reason to complain,

don't you think?

Here are some phrases to use if you have a complaint.

I have a complaint.
Ich habe eine Beschwerde.

There is a mix-up.
Da gibt es eine Verwechslung.

These clothes are someone else's.
Diese Kleidung gehört jemand anders.

This shirt has too much starch.
Dieses Hemd hat zuviel Stärke.

My clothes are ruined.
Meine Kleidung ist ruiniert.

This shirt is scorched.
Dieses Hemd ist versengt.

There's a button missing.
Da fehlt ein Knopf.

I'm missing a pair of socks.
Mir fehlt ein Paar Socken.

Circle the most appropriate complaint dealing with the laundry and dry cleaner.

Wäscheleine
1. Diesem Hemd fehlt ein Fleck
Knopf

rot
2. Das Hemd ist versengt
zugemacht

ein Knopf
3. Da ist eine Waschmaschine auf meinem Anzug.
ein Fleck

4. Ich habe gern
Mir fehlen meine Unterhosen.
Ich trage

Baumwolle
5. Das Hemd hat zuviel Stärke
Rouge

jemand anders
6. Diese Anzüge gehören uns
meinen Freunden

Can you put the following words in the right order to form sensible sentences?

1. Verwechslung, es, eine, da, gibt

_____

2. fehlen, drei Hemden, mir

_____

3. dieses Hemdes, flicken, können Sie, den Ärmel

_____

4. Knopf, annähen, diesen, man muß

_____

5. bügeln, Kleidung, meine, waschen, ich muß, und

_____

This should be a snap! Can you draw lines from the words in Column 1 to those in Column 2 which are related to them? Some words in Column 1 may be related to more than one entry in Column 2.

1. Waschmaschine	A. Hemd
2. Fleck	B. hängen
3. Waschkorb	C. die Wäsche trocknen
4. Beschwerde	D. Reinigungsanstalt
5. Bügeleisen	E. die Kleidung waschen
6. nähen	F. die Kleidung zur Wäscheleine tragen
7. Stärke	G. Kleider fehlen mir
8. Trockenmaschine	H. die Kleider bügeln
9. Wäscheleine	I. Knopf
10. Ärmel	J. Waschpulver

20	**Der Damensalon** (DAH-men-zah-long) The Beauty Shop	**Der Friseur** (fri-ZÖR) Hairdresser
	Der Herrensalon (HER-en-zah-long) Hair Stylist	**Der Friseur** Barber

Der Damensalon

(hahR) **das Haar** hair	*(lang)* **lang** long	*(brown)* **braun** brown	*(kurts)* **kurz** short	*(blont)* **blond** blond

Josephine goes to the hairdresser.

FRISEUR **Was wünschen Sie,** *(VÜN-shen)* **gnädige Frau?** *(GNAY-di-geh)*
wish madam

JOSEPHINE **Waschen und Legen, bitte, und** *(LAY-gen)*
set

Auffrischen. Können Sie mir auch eine *(OWF-fri-shen)*
touch up

Maniküre geben?

FRISEUR **Sie sind jetzt eine Brünette; was** *(brü-NE-teh)*

für eine Farbe wünschen Sie für die

Haarspülung? Dieselbe Farbe oder ein *(HAHR-shpü-lung)*
rinse

wenig dunkler? *(DUNK-leR)*
darker

(ge-ZIÇTS-ma-sa-žeh)
die Gesichtsmassage
facial massage

(ma-ni-KÜ-reh)
die Maniküre
manicure

(LOK-en-vik-el)
die Lockenwickel
curlers

176

JOSEPHINE   *(HEL-eR)*
Ein wenig heller, bitte. Und ich
     lighter

(LOK-en)
möchte Locken auf der Seite und
     curls

(VEL-en) *(OH-ben)*
Wellen oben. Können Sie hinten ein
waves   on top

(AP-shnei-den)
wenig abschneiden? Ich habe langes
     cut off

Haar nicht gern. Ich habe es lieber kurz.

(selbst)   *(AN-show-en)*
sich selbst im Spiegel anschauen
to look at oneself in the mirror

Eine Stunde später bürstet der

Friseur Josephines Haar aus, und

Josephine schaut sich im Spiegel an.

(HAHR-trok-neR)
der Haartrockner
hair dryer

(GO-tes) *(VI-len)*
JOSEPHINE   **Um Gottes willen! Ich bin blond!**
     good grief

(DOW-eR-vel-eh)
die Dauerwelle
permanent

NOTE: If the hairdresser is a woman, she is
(fri-ZÖ-zeh)
called *die Friseuse*.

(sham-POO)
das Shampoo
shampoo

(HAHR-bürs-teh)
die Haarbürste
brush

(BÜRS-ten)
bürsten
to brush

Here are some useful expressions a woman might want to know before she goes to the beauty
shop. Try writing them out:

I'd like to make an appointment for tomorrow.
(ter-MEEN)
Ich möchte einen Termin für morgen machen.
     appointment

Can you wash and cut my hair?

Können Sie mir die Haare waschen und schneiden?

Don't apply any hairspray.

(HAHR-shpray)

Verwenden Sie kein Haarspray.

hairspray

I would like my hair in bangs. I would like a bun.

(POH-nee)   *(KNOH-ten)*

Ich möchte einen Pony. Ich möchte einen Knoten.

bangs   bun

Here are some German words about hair styling:

legen	to set	**kastanienbraun**	auburn
der Spiegel	mirror	**der Haarschnitt**	haircut
der Pony	bangs	**die Lockenwickel**	curlers
die Maniküre	manicure	**die Locken**	curls
das Haarspray	hairspray	**bürsten**	to brush

Let's try a quick exercise. Fill in the blanks by using the words you have learned in this unit.

1. Morgen gehe ich zum _____.
                          beauty shop

2. Ich muß einen _____ machen.
                       appointment

3. Ich brauche einen _____.
                       haircut

4. Ich habe _____ Haar nicht gern.
                   long

5. Ich möchte auch, daß man mir das Haar wäscht und _____ und
                                               (tönt)   sets

   _____ tönt.
         auburn   tints

6. Ich habe es lieber _____ auf den Seiten und _____ hinten.
                          short   long

7. Vorne trage ich einen _____.
                       bangs

8. Die Friseuse _____ mein Haar und verwendet etwas
                       brushes

   _____.
        hairspray

9. Dann schaue ich mich im _____ an.
                       mirror

ANSWERS

1. Damensalon 2. Termin 3. Haarschnitt 4. langes 5. legt, kastanienbraun 6. kurz, lang 7. Pony 8. bürstet, Haarspray 9. Spiegel

178

(HAHR-pflay-geh)
DIE HAARPFLEGE
hair care

There are plenty of beauty salons throughout Germany to suit every conceivable taste, need and pocket book. Since German hairdressers have to undergo strict exams before being admitted to the profession, they can generally be depended on for competence and cleanliness.

What are known as Unisex Hairdressers in the United States, are more modestly referred to as *Damen- und Herrensalons*. You won't find many of them.

Here are some more terms that might come in handy:

to trim lightly	**nachschneiden**	tint, to tint	*(TÖ-nung)* **die Tönung, tönen**
to blow dry	*(FÖ-nen)* **fönen**	body wave	*(SHTÜTS-wel-eh)* **die Stützwelle**

DER HERRENSALON
Hair Stylist

(SHAY-reh)
die Schere
scissors

(rah-ZEER-mes-eR)
das Rasiermesser
straight razor

(HAHR-shnei-deh-mah-shee-neh)
die Haarschneidemaschine
clippers

der Friseur
barber

(rah-ZOOR)
eine Rasur
shave

(rah-ZEER-kraym)
die Rasierkrem
shaving cream

(rah-ZEER-en)
sich rasieren
to shave oneself

sich das Haar kämmen lassen
to have one's hair combed

(zein) (EI-ge-nes) (hahr) (KE-men)
sein eigenes Haar kämmen
to comb one's own hair

Mann mit
man with
(SHNUR-baRt)
Schnurrbart,
moustache,
(baRt) *(ko-te-LET-en)*
Bart und Koteletten
beard and sideburns

179

(SHTUTS-en)
stutzen
to trim

(HAHR-shnit)
ein Haarschnitt
hair cut

(GLAT-seh)
die Glatze
bald head

Here's a tale about Anton's trip to the hair stylist. Auf Deutsch, natürlich!

Anton geht zum Friseur, weil er einen Haarschnitt braucht. Zuerst rasiert ihn der Friseur mit einem Rasiermesser und stutzt seinen Bart, seinen Schnurrbart und seine Koteletten mit der Haarschneidemaschine. Dann wäscht er ihm die Haare und gibt ihm einen Haarschnitt. Weil Anton sein Haar sehr gern kurz trägt, schneidet der Friseur viel von oben und hinten ab. Anton ist sehr
(MÜD-eh)   (shtool)
müde und schläft im Stuhl ein.

Der Friseur schneidet mehr und mehr.
(ENT-liç)
Endlich sagt er:

„Also, mein Herr." Anton schaut sich im Spiegel an und sieht, daß er ganz kahl ist.

Anton goes to the barber because he needs a haircut. First the barber shaves him with a straight razor and trims his beard, his moustache, and his sideburns with the clippers. Then he gives him a shampoo and a haircut. Because Anton likes to wear his hair short the barber cuts off a lot on top and in back. Anton is very tired and falls asleep in the chair.

The barber cuts more and more. Finally he says, "There you are, sir." Anton looks at himself in the mirror and sees that he is entirely bald.

(SHUL-diç) **„Wieviel bin ich Ihnen schuldig,"** fragt er.	"What do I owe you?" he asks.
Der Friseur sagt: „Sieben Mark. Wissen	The barber says, "Seven marks. You
Sie, ich glaube nicht, daß Sie sehr bald	know something, I don't think you'll be
zurück sind."	back very soon."

(feR-SOO-chen)   *(FOL-gen-den) (FRAH-gen)*
Versuchen Sie, die folgenden Fragen zu beantworten.
try   following   questions

1. Warum geht Anton zum Friseur? _____

    (VOH-mit)
2. Womit stutzt der Friseur seinen Bart? _____
    with what

3. Warum schneidet der Friseur viel ab? _____

4. Wo schaut sich Anton an? _____

5. Was sieht er dann? _____

6. Wieviel muß Anton bezahlen? _____

Here are some expressions that might come in handy:

Wo gibt es einen guten Friseur?	Where is a good barber?
Wer kommt jetzt dran?	Whose turn is it now?
Ich brauche einen Haarschnitt.	I need a haircut.
Ich brauche eine Rasur.	I need a shave.
Hinten lang und vorne kurz.	Long in back, short in front.
Schneiden Sie ein wenig mehr hier.	Cut a little bit more here.
Bitte verwenden Sie nicht die	Please don't use the clippers.
Haarschneidemaschine.	
So ist es gerade richtig.	It's fine that way.
Wieviel bin ich Ihnen schuldig?	How much do I owe you?

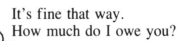

(mayR)
Mehr Fragen.
more

1. Was soll der Friseur nicht verwenden? _____

2. Womit rasiert ihn der Friseur? _____

3. Was stutzt er mit der Haarschneidemaschine?

_____, _____, _____

Can you answer these questions in German?

1. What color is your hair? _____

2. How do you wear your hair? Long, short, or medium length? _____

3. Do you like long or short sideburns? _____

4. What does the barber use to cut hair? _____

5. What does the beautician put on the hair when she sets it? _____

6. What do you need if your hair is dirty? _____

Try putting the following fragments in the proper order so that they make sense:

1. Maniküre, mir, können Sie, geben, eine?

_____

2. Spiegel, mich, möchte, anschauen, gern, ich, im

_____

3. muß, Termin, einen, morgen, machen, für, ich

_____

4. Haar, um, schneiden, Schere, verwendet, Friseur, der, das, zu, die

_____

       (noon)   (RAY-tsel) (ǖ-beR-ZE-tsen)   (BOOCH-stah-beh)

Und nun ein kleines Rätsel. Übersetzen Sie die folgenden Wörter. Der erste Buchstabe ist
            now   puzzle   translate   letter

schon da.

1. bald

2. curls

3. to trim

4. mirror

5. to set

6. permanent

7. bald head

8. hair dryer

9. to brush

10. blond

1. K
2. L
3. S
4. S
5. L
6. D
7. G
8. H
9. B
10. B

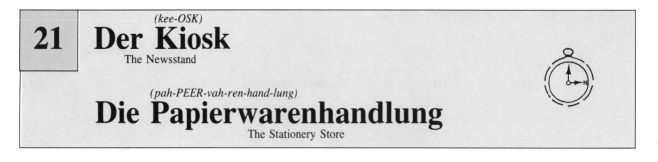

21 Der Kiosk

(kee-OSK)

The Newsstand

Die Papierwarenhandlung

(pah-PEER-vah-ren-hand-lung)

The Stationery Store

AM KIOSK IN WIEN

At the Newsstand in Vienna

(TSEI-tung)
die Zeitung
newspaper

(POST-kar-teh)
die Postkarte
postcard

(AN-ziçts-kar-teh)
die Ansichtskarte
picture postcard

JUNGER MANN **Entschuldigen Sie.**

(TSEI-tung-en)

Haben Sie Zeitungen in

Englisch?

(be-ZITS-eR)

BESITZER DES KIOSKS **Ja, wir**
owner

(OWS-vahl)

haben eine gute Auswahl

von Zeitungen aus England

(oo-es-AH)

und den U.S.A.

JUNGER MANN **Ich möchte auch**

einige Ansichtskarten von

Wien kaufen.

Excuse me. Do you have newspapers

in English?

Yes, we have a nice selection of

newspapers from

England and the U.S.

I would also like to buy a few picture

postcards of Vienna.

184

(BREEF-mar-ken)
Briefmarken
postage stamps

(tsi-ga-RET-en-pah-kung)
die Zigarettenpackung
package of cigarettes

(ma-ga-TSEEN)
das Magazin
magazine

BESITZER **Hier ist eine gute**

Auswahl von Bildern der
(HOWPT-stat)
Hauptstadt Österreichs.

JUNGER MANN **Verkaufen**

Sie Briefmarken?

BESITZER **Ja, aber heute habe ich**

keine Luftpostmarken.

(pointing) **Die können Sie in**
(tra-FIK)
der Trafik* kaufen.

(TAH-bak)
JUNGER MANN **Und Tabak? Ich**

möchte gern eine Packung

amerikanischer Zigaretten

kaufen.

BESITZER **Die können Sie auch in**

der Trafik kaufen.

(FÜ-ren)
JUNGER MANN **Führen Sie auch**

(ma-ga-TSEE-neh)
Magazine mit Fotos? Playboy,

(BEI-shpeel)
zum Beispiel? Es ist nicht für

mich, es ist für meinen

Großvater.

BESITZER (with eyebrows raised) **Ja,**

natürlich.

Here is a good selection of

picture postcards of the capital

of Austria.

Do you sell postage stamps?

Yes, but I don't have any air mail

stamps today. You can buy them

in the *Trafik*.

And tobacco? I would like to

buy a pack of American

cigarettes.

You can buy them in the

Trafik, too.

Do you carry illustrated

magazines, too? *Playboy*, for

example? It isn't for me; it's

for my grandfather.

Yes, of course.

---

*NOTE: In Austria, tobacco products are a government monopoly and can be sold in a *Trafik* or *Tabak-Trafik* only; in West Germany, they can be sold in a *Tabakladen* (tobacco shop) or at a kiosk where postage stamps are also available.

JUNGER MANN	**Ich nehme die**	I'll take the
	Zeitung, die Ansichtskarten	newspaper, the picture postcards,
	und das Magazin. Wieviel	and the magazine. What do
	bin ich Ihnen schuldig?	I owe you?

Try reading aloud several times the conversation between the youth and the owner of the kiosk. When you feel confident of its meaning, see if you can fill in the missing words below:

1. *Junger Mann:* Entschuldigen Sie. Haben Sie _____ in Englisch?

2. *Besitzer:* Ja, wir haben eine Auswahl von Zeitungen aus _____.

3. *Junger Mann:* Ich möchte auch gern _____ von Wien kaufen.

4. Haben Sie _____?

5. *Besitzer:* Sie können sie in der _____ kaufen. Die haben auch

_____, wenn Sie eine Packung _____ brauchen.

6. *Junger Mann:* _____ (I'll take) die Ansichtskarten, eine Zeitung und

dieses _____ mit Fotos. Wieviel bin ich Ihnen _____?

Try answering the following questions in German.

1. What types of reading material can you buy at a kiosk?

_____, _____

2. Besides at the post office, where else can you buy postage stamps?

_____, _____

3. What handy phrase can you use to beg someone's pardon or excuse yourself?

_____

4. If you want your friends back home to know you're abroad, what might you send them?

_____

5. What must you put on your postcards if you want them to arrive back home? _____

6. If you want postcards to arrive quickly in the U.S., what should you put on them? _____

7. When you are ready to pay for an item, what do you say?

_____

IN DER PAPIERWARENHANDLUNG
At the Stationery Store

Here are some items you can purchase at a stationery store. Be sure that you write the new words in the blanks under the pictures and say them aloud several times:

(BLEI-shtift)
der Bleistift
pencil

(BREEF-um-shlak)
der Briefumschlag
envelope

(KOO-gel-shrei-beR)
der Kugelschreiber
ballpoint pen

_____

_____

_____

(DURÇ-ziç-tig-eh)
der durchsichtige
(KLAY-beh-shtrei-fen)
Klebestreifen
cellophane tape

(BINT-fah-den)
der Bindfaden
string

(noh-TEETS-buch)
das Notizbuch
notebook

_____

_____

_____

(SHREIP-blok)
der Schreibblock
writing pad

(BREEF-pah-peer)
das Briefpapier
stationery

_____

_____

Words you have just learned are contained in the following paragraph.

Wenn ich einen Kugelschreiber oder einen Bleistift brauche, gehe ich in die Papierwarenhandlung. Wenn ich

If I need a ball-point pen or a pencil, I go to the stationery store. When I einen Brief schreiben will,

benutze ich Briefpapier und
(SHTE-keh)
ich stecke den Brief in einen Briefumschlag.

In der Papierwarenhandlung verkauft man
(noh-TEETS-bü-çeR)
auch Notizbücher. Ich kann Notizen in

einem Notizbuch oder auf einem

Schreibblock machen. Wenn ich ein Paket

machen will, brauche ich Klebestreifen.

Um etwas zu verlangen sage ich: „Ich

möchte ————————— **kaufen."**

want to write a letter,

I use letter paper, and I stick the letter

in an envelope. Notebooks are sold in the

stationery store, too. I can make notes in a

notebook or on a pad. If I want to prepare a

package, I need tape. To ask for

something, I say: "I would like to buy ————

————————————————

————. "

Please answer in German:

1. What two instruments can you use for writing?

————————————————————, ——————————————

2. If you write a letter, what do you write on? ——————————————

3. What three things can you use to prepare a package? ————————————,

————————————————, ——————————————

4. What do you put a letter in before you mail it? ——————————————

5. What two things can you write notes on? ——————————————

————————————————————

6. Where can you buy a ball-point pen? ——————————————

————————————————————

You've learned a lot about items sold at a newsstand and a stationery store. Can you list ten items they carry that are made of paper?

1. _____   6. _____

2. _____   7. _____

3. _____   8. _____

4. _____   9. _____

5. _____   10. _____

EVA **Wo, um Gottes willen, bekomme ich Zigaretten?**

Where, for heaven's sake, do I get cigarettes?

OTTO (overhearing her) **In der Tabak-Trafik. Geradeaus, bis zum Damenbekleidungsgeschäft, dann nach rechts an der Papierhandlung vorbei, wo Sie nach links abbiegen.**

In the Tabak-Trafik. Straight ahead to the women's clothing store, then to the right, past the stationery store where you make a left turn.

EVA	**Danke schön.** Sie haben mir das Leben gerettet.	Thanks a lot. You saved my life.
OTTO	**Brauchen Sie noch etwas?**	Do you need anything else?
EVA	**Ja. Ein Brot.**	Yes. A loaf of bread.
OTTO	**Aha. Also auf dem Weg zurück biegen Sie links ab, gehen Sie ein** *(BIS-çen)* **bißchen geradeaus, und dann nach** *(zoh-FORT)* **rechts. Sie sehen sofort die Bäckerei.**	Aha. Well, on the way back you make a left, go a little straight ahead, and then right. You'll see the bakery right away.
EVA	**Herzlichen Dank.**	Thanks a lot.

190

DER JUWELIER

Let's look at a dialogue in a jewelry store. There are a number of new words, but some are very similar to English. Remember to read the dialogue out loud.

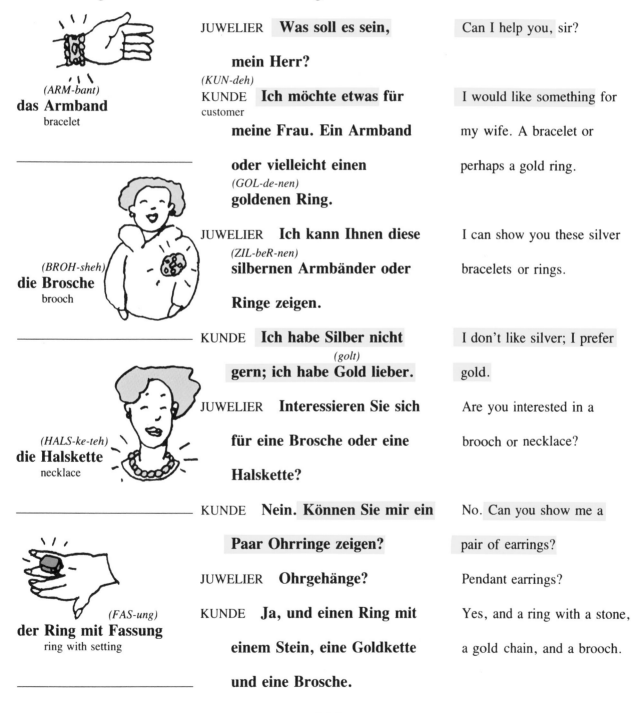

(ARM-bant)
das Armband
bracelet

(BROH-sheh)
die Brosche
brooch

(HALS-ke-teh)
die Halskette
necklace

(FAS-ung)
der Ring mit Fassung
ring with setting

JUWELIER	**Was soll es sein, mein Herr?**	Can I help you, sir?
KUNDE (KUN-deh) customer	**Ich möchte etwas für meine Frau. Ein Armband oder vielleicht einen** (GOL-de-nen) **goldenen Ring.**	I would like something for my wife. A bracelet or perhaps a gold ring.
JUWELIER	**Ich kann Ihnen diese** (ZIL-beR-nen) **silbernen Armbänder oder Ringe zeigen.**	I can show you these silver bracelets or rings.
KUNDE	**Ich habe Silber nicht** (golt) **gern; ich habe Gold lieber.**	I don't like silver; I prefer gold.
JUWELIER	**Interessieren Sie sich für eine Brosche oder eine Halskette?**	Are you interested in a brooch or necklace?
KUNDE	**Nein. Können Sie mir ein Paar Ohrringe zeigen?**	No. Can you show me a pair of earrings?
JUWELIER	**Ohrgehänge?**	Pendant earrings?
KUNDE	**Ja, und einen Ring mit einem Stein, eine Goldkette und eine Brosche.**	Yes, and a ring with a stone, a gold chain, and a brooch.

(OHR-ge-heng-eh)
die Ohrgehänge
pendant earrings

JUWELIER	**Diese Ohrgehänge,**	These pendant earrings,

JUWELIER   **Diese Ohrgehänge,**   These pendant earrings,

dieser Ring und diese   this ring, and this gold chain

Goldkette passen sehr gut   go very well together.
(tsu-ein-AN-deR)
zueinander.

KUNDE   **Gut. Wieviel kosten sie?**   Good. What do they cost?

JUWELIER   **4000 Mark.**   4000 marks.

KUNDE   **Die kosten sehr viel. Na ja,**   They cost a lot. Oh well,

ich möchte meiner Frau   I want to please my wife.
(FROY-deh)
eine Freude machen.   I'll take the jewelry.
(shmook)
Ich nehme den Schmuck.   (He takes something out of

(Er nimmt etwas aus der   his pocket.) But I'm not paying!
(TA-sheh)
Tasche.) Aber ich bezahle   Hands up! I have a revolver!

nicht! Hände hoch! Ich habe
(re-VOL-veR)
einen Revolver.

(KE-teh)
die Kette
chain

(ring) *(OH-neh)* *(shtein)*
ein Ring ohne Stein
ring   without   a stone

(OHR-ring-eh)
Ohrringe
earrings

Practice writing the new words on the lines provided under the pictures:

(dee-a-MANT)
der Diamant
diamond

(PER-leh)
die Perle
pearl

(sa-FEER)
der Saphir
sapphire

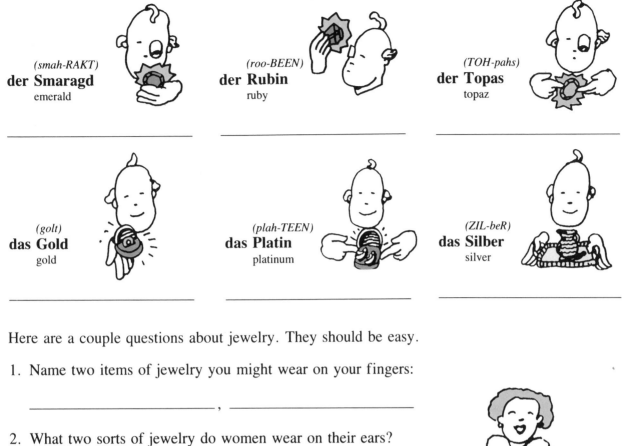

(smah-RAKT)
der Smaragd
emerald

(roo-BEEN)
der Rubin
ruby

(TOH-pahs)
der Topas
topaz

(golt)
das Gold
gold

(plah-TEEN)
das Platin
platinum

(ZIL-beR)
das Silber
silver

Here are a couple questions about jewelry. They should be easy.

1. Name two items of jewelry you might wear on your fingers:

   _____ , _____

2. What two sorts of jewelry do women wear on their ears?

   _____ , _____

3. What items of jewelry are worn around the neck?

   _____ , _____

4. What might a woman pin on her dress? _____

You've been introduced to the names of precious stones. Do you remember them? Try writing the German word next to the English.

1. diamond _____   3. sapphire _____   5. ruby _____

2. pearl _____   4. emerald _____   6. topaz _____

ANSWERS

Questions.
1. Ring mit Stein (mit Fassung), Ring ohne Stein 2. Ohrringe, Ohrgehänge 3. Goldkette, Perlenkette
4. eine Brosche
Precious stones.
1. der Diamant 2. die Perle 3. der Saphir 4. der Smaragd 5. der Rubin 6. der Topas

193

Can you give the German word for the following precious metals?

1. gold _____ 2. silver _____ 3. platinum _____

Can you match the stone with its color? Draw a line from the stone to its corresponding color:

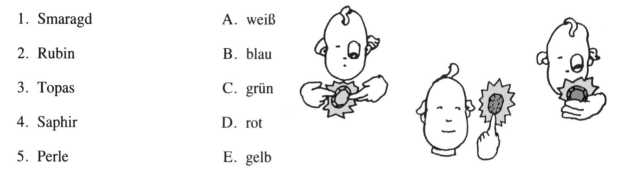

1. Smaragd   A. weiß

2. Rubin   B. blau

3. Topas   C. grün

4. Saphir   D. rot

5. Perle   E. gelb

Here you have some useful phrases you might want to use at the jeweler's. Try saying them aloud, and write them in the space provided.

Haben Sie einen Ring mit einem Diamanten (einem Smaragd, etc.)?

_____

Können Sie mir ein goldenes (silbernes) Armband zeigen?

_____

Ich suche eine silberne (goldene) Halskette.

_____

Ich interessiere mich für ein Paar Ohrringe.

_____

(kah-RAHT)
Wieviel Karat (carats) hat es?

_____

Imagine now that you are looking for something quite specific at the jeweler's. How would you begin your conversation with him? Once you've found what you want, what else do you need to ask?

ANSWERS

Precious metals.
1. das Gold 2. das Silber 3. das Platin
Matching.
1. C 2. D 3. E 4. B 5. A

DER UHRMACHER
The Watchmaker

(VEK-eR)
der Wecker
alarm clock

_____

(ARM-bant-ooR)
die Armbanduhr
wrist watch

_____

der Uhrmacher
watchmaker

_____

(OOR-mach-eR-lah-den)
der Uhrmacherladen
watchmaker's shop

_____

Practice writing the new words by filling in the blanks near the pictures. Once you have done this, read aloud the sentences below. They may help you when you visit the watchmaker's. After you have practiced them aloud, try writing them out in the spaces provided:

Can you fix this watch for me? **Können Sie mir diese Uhr reparieren?**

_____

(REI-ni-gen)
Can you clean it? **Können Sie sie reinigen?**
clean

_____

My watch is fast. **Meine Uhr geht vor.**

_____

(SHTAY-en-ge-blee-ben)
It's stopped. **Sie ist stehengeblieben.**
stopped

_____

It doesn't run well. **Sie geht nicht gut.**

_____

Notice that in German watches and clocks don't run. They take their time and walk. The verb *gehen*, in its literal sense, means "to walk."

(OWF-tsee-en)

I can't wind it. **Ich kann sie nicht aufziehen.**
wind

My alarm clock is slow. **Mein Wecker geht nach.**

(OOR-glas)

I need a crystal. **Ich brauche ein Uhrglas.**
crystal

When will it be ready? **Wann wird sie fertig sein?**

(KVI-tung)

Can you give me a receipt? **Können Sie mir eine Quittung geben?**
receipt

Try reading the following paragraph to see if you understand it. You may want to refer to the previous sentences.

(MANÇ-mal)

Meine Armbanduhr geht nicht gut. Manchmal geht sie vor; manchmal geht sie nach.
sometimes

Heute bleibt sie auch stehen, und ich kann sie nicht aufziehen. Ich bringe sie zum

(dort)

Uhrmacher und der Uhrmacher repariert sie. Er reinigt sie auch. Wenn ich die Uhr dort
(LA-seh)   *(lohs)*   there

lasse, gibt er mir auch eine Quittung. Was ist mit deiner Uhr los, wenn du immer spät
leave   what is the matter with your watch

ankommst?

196

The following German sentences about watches need to be completed. Give them a try.

1. Meine Uhr _____ gut; sie _____ .
   <u>is not running well</u>   <u>is slow</u>

2. When you always seem to be early for appointments, what might be the matter?

   Meine Uhr _____ .
   <u>is fast</u>

3. When the hands of your watch don't move, how do you describe the problem?

   Meine Uhr bleibt _____ .
   <u>is stopped</u>

   Ich muß sie _____ .
   <u>wind</u>

4. Where do you take your watch for repairs?

   Ich nehme meine Uhr zum _____ .
   <u>watchmaker</u>

5. What is the man called who works on your watch?

   Er heißt _____ .
   <u>watchmaker</u>

6. When you leave your watch, what does the watchmaker give you?

   Er gibt mir eine _____ .
   <u>receipt</u>

197

| 23 | **Der Geschenkartikelladen** *(ge-SHENK-ar-tee-kel-lah-den)* |

Der Geschenkartikelladen
(ge-SHENK-ar-tee-kel-lah-den)
Gift Shop

Das Musikgeschäft
(moo-ZEEK-ge-sheft)
Music Store

Das Photogeschäft
(FOH-toh-ge-sheft)
Photo Shop

IM GESCHENKARTIKELLADEN
At the Gift Shop

Here are some words that will come in handy at a gift shop.

das Geschenk *(ge-SHENK)*
gift

die Geldtasche *(GELT-tash-eh)*
or
das Portemonnaie *(PORT-mon-nay)*
wallet (purse)

die Handtasche *(HANT-tash-eh)*
handbag

das Bild *(bilt)*
picture

der Ring *(ring)*
ring

das Parfüm *(par-FÜM)*
perfume

der Schlüsselring *(SHLÜS-el-ring)*
key ring

die Nippsachen *(NIP-sa-chen)*
knick-knacks

der Schal *(shahl)*
scarf

der Parfümzerstäuber *(par-FÜM-tser-shtoy-beR)*
atomizer

der Anhänger *(AN-heng-eR)*
pendant

(TOY-eR)			
teuer	expensive	**die Figurine**	figurine
(PREIS-vayRt)			
preiswert	a good value	**der Schmuck**	jewelry
(TÜ-pish)			
typisch	typical		

VERKÄUFER **Kann ich Ihnen behilflich** *(be-HILF-liç)*

sein?

Can I help you?

TOURISTIN **Ich möchte etwas typisch**
(ÖS-teR-rei-çish-es)
österreichisches.

I would like something typically Austrian.

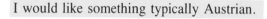

VERKÄUFER **Für einen Herrn oder für**

eine Dame?

For a gentleman or for a lady?

TOURISTIN **Eine Dame.**

A lady.

VERKÄUFER **Vielleicht eine Petit-Point-**
(HANT-ta-sheh) *(me-dal-YONG)*
Handtasche? Oder ein Medaillon? Das

kommt von den österreichischen
(VERK-shte-ten) *(shahl)*
Werkstätten. Oder einen Schal?

Maybe an embroidered evening handbag?

Or a locket? This one comes from the Austrian

jewelry factories. Or a scarf?

TOURISTIN **Wieviel kostet der Schal?**

How much is the scarf?

VERKÄUFER **500 Schilling.**

500 schillings.

TOURISTIN **Zeigen Sie mir diesen.**

Show me that one.

VERKÄUFER **Gern. Der ist sehr hübsch** *(hüpsh)*

und kostet etwas weniger. 450

Schilling.

Gladly. This one is very pretty, and costs

somewhat less. 450 schillings.

TOURISTIN **Sie haben recht. Der Schal ist**

sehr hübsch und preiswert. Ich kaufe ihn.

You are right. The scarf is very pretty

and a good value. I'll buy it.

VERKÄUFER **Wollen sie auch Parfüm** *(OWS-vahl)*

kaufen? Wir haben eine gute Auswahl.

Would you also like to buy perfume?

We have a good selection.

199

TOURISTIN   **Nein, danke. Ich kaufe nie**   *(nee)*

        Parfüm. Mein Mann kauft es für mich.

No thanks. I never buy perfume.

My husband buys it for me.

Did you notice? The tourist in this dialogue is a woman, so we added *-in* to *Tourist* to form *Touristin* (female tourist).

IM MUSIKGESCHÄFT
At the Music Store

Some of the more important words to remember when shopping at a music store:

(SHTAY-ray-oh-an-lah-geh)
die Stereoanlage
stereo system

(TOHN-arm)
der Tonarm
pick-up arm

(RAH-dee-oh)
das Radio
radio

(ka-SET-eh)
die Kassette
cassette

(PLAT-en-shpeel-eR)
der Plattenspieler
record player

(TOHN-bant-shpoo-leh)
die Tonbandspule
tape reel

(mee-kro-FOHN)
das Mikrophon
microphone

(SHAL-plat-eh)
die Schallplatte
record

(KLAS-ish-eh)
die klassische Musik
classical music

(FOLKS-moo-zeek)
die Volksmusik
folk music

(SHAL-diç-teh) *(TSEL-eh)*
schalldichte Zelle   soundproof booth

(TOHN-bant)
das Tonband   tape (recording tape)

(TOHN-bant-ge-rayt)
das Tonbandgerät   tape recorder

(NAH-del)
die Nadel   needle

(POP-moo-zeek)
die Popmusik   pop music

(SHLAH-geR)
der Schlager   hit

(KOPF-hör-eR)
der Kopfhörer   earphones

(an-TEN-neh)
die Antenne   antenna

Let's read a paragraph about listening to records.

Herr Müller hat klassische Musik sehr gern, und er hat nicht viel Geld. Er hat keine Stereoanlage. Jeden Samstag nachmittag nimmt er den Bus oder die U-Bahn und besucht ein Schallplatten- oder Musikgeschäft in einem anderen Stadtteil. Er nimmt drei oder vier Platten, setzt sich in eine schalldichte Zelle und hört seinen (LEEP-lings-kom-poh-nis-ten) **Lieblingskomponisten zwei oder drei Stunden lang zu. Dann geht er glücklich nach Hause und freut sich auf das** (kont-SAYRT) **Konzert nächste Woche.**

Mr. Müller likes classical music very much, and he does not have much money. He doesn't have a stereo system. Every Saturday afternoon he takes the bus or the subway and visits a record- or music store in a different part of town. He takes three or four records, sits down in a booth, and listens to his favorite composers for two or three hours. Then he goes home happily and looks forward to next week's concert.

Now, see if you can answer the following questions. *Auf Deutsch, bitte.*

1. Was tut Herr Müller jeden Samstag? _____

_____

2. Ist Herr Müller reich? _____

_____

3. Wem hört er zwei oder drei Stunden lang zu? _____

_____

4. Warum ist er glücklich, wenn er nach Hause geht? _____

_____

(ROK-moo-zeek)

ROCKMUSIK
Rock Music

VERKÄUFER	**Womit kann ich Ihnen dienen?**	What can I do for you?
TOURISTIN	**Geben Sie mir den größten deutschen Schlager. Für einen jungen Amerikaner.**	Give me the biggest German hit. For a young American.
VERKÄUFER	**Ich habe gerade was Sie brauchen. Hier. Der größte Schlager von Rocky Rock.**	I have just what you need. Here. The biggest hit of Rocky Rock.
TOURISTIN	**Wer ist das?**	Who is that?
VERKÄUFER	**Ein großer Rockstar. Die** *(gah-ran-TEE)* **Platte kommt mit Garantie.**	A great rockstar. The record comes with a warranty.
TOURISTIN	**Was für eine Garantie?**	What kind of warranty?
VERKÄUFER	*(TRO-mel-fel)* *(ka-PUT)* **Ihr Trommelfell kaputt nach zweimal Hören oder Ihr Geld zurück.**	Your eardrums will be split after listening twice, or your money back.

IM PHOTOGESCHÄFT

At the Photo Shop

Let's learn some words about photography.

(foh-toh-grah-FEE)
die Photographie (Fotografie) photography

(foh-toh-GRAHF)
der Photograph (Fotograf) photographer

(GLANTS-pah-peeR)
das Glanzpapier glossy paper

(ma-TEERT)
mattiert matte

(shvarts) *(veis)*
in schwarz und weiß black and white

(FARP-film)
der Farbfilm color film

(OWS-lö-zeR)
der Auslöser shutter release

(be-LIÇ-tung)
die Belichtung exposure

(ZOO-cheR)
der Sucher viewfinder

(ent-FER-nungs-me-seR)
der Entfernungsmesser range finder

(BLITS-liçt)
das Blitzlicht flash

202

Here's a short dialogue that might take place at a photo shop. Don't forget to read it aloud. Your German probably sounds pretty authentic by now.

KUNDE **Möchten Sie diesen Film**
(ent-VIK-eln)
entwickeln?

Would you develop this film?

VERKÄUFER **Diapositive oder Abzüge?**

Slides or prints?

KUNDE **Abzüge.**

Prints

VERKÄUFER **7 mal 11 cm?**

7 by 11 centimeters?

(ge-NOW)
KUNDE **Genau. Wann sind sie fertig?**

Exactly. When will they be ready?

VERKÄUFER **In drei Tagen. Hier ist Ihr**
(shein)
Schein.

In three days. Here is your receipt.

KUNDE **Geben Sie mir auch einen**
(FÜNF-unt-drei-sik) *(mil-lee-MAY-teR)*
fünfunddreißig millimeter (35 mm)
(OWF-nah-men)
Film, 20 Aufnahmen, in schwarz und

weiß.

Give me also a roll of 35 mm film, 20 exposures,

in black and white.

VERKÄUFER **Sehr gut. Noch etwas?**

Very well. Anything else?

KUNDE **Nein, danke. Das wäre es.**

No, thank you. That will be all.

(AP-tsook) *(ko-PEE)*
der Abzug (die Kopie)
print

(KAH-me-ra)
die Kamera
camera

(veR-GRÖ-se-rung)
die Vergrößerung
enlargement

(ba-te-REE)
die Batterie
battery

(dee-ah-poh-zi-TEEF)
das Diapositiv
slide

(film)
der Film
film

Here's a good way to review this unit. Choose gifts for the following people:

1. your mother: _____

2. your grandfather: _____

3. your nephew (teenage boy): _____

4. your niece (teenage girl): _____

5. your uncle who brought you a pink elephant last time (he knows you like German *(shnaps)* Schnaps): _____

Word Hunt. There are seven German words in this puzzle. Can you find them?

C	L	P	F	A	N	D	A
O	T	O	N	B	A	N	D
P	A	P	O	Z	D	E	O
F	L	M	N	U	E	G	R
L	A	U	T	G	L	O	T
R	L	S	T	A	D	T	N
S	I	I	R	G	O	N	E
I	T	K	L	M	K	L	A

Reparaturen: Optiker

(re-pah-rah-TOO-ren) *(OP-ti-keR)*

Repair Services   Optometrist

(SHOO-ma-cheR)

Schuhmacher

Shoemaker

As you travel, you'll want to learn about each new city you visit. Here are some useful tips on getting to know a city.

(OWS-ge-tseich-ne-teh) *(me-TOH-deh)*

Eine ausgezeichnete Methode, eine fremde

An excellent method of getting acquainted

Stadt kennenzulernen, ist es, dort zu Fuß

with a foreign city is by walking. You

(feR-SHVIN-det)

zu gehen. Man verschwindet in der Menge;

disappear in the crowd; you observe the

(be-OH-bach-tet) *(ge-ZIÇ-teR)*

man beobachtet die Gesichter der Leute,

faces of the people, walk into stores, examine

geht in Geschäfte hinein, sieht die

the produce in open-air markets,

Produkte auf den offenen Märkten an,

stop as long as you wish to read

bleibt solange stehen, wie man will, um die

inscriptions on statues. To the American,

(IN-shrif-ten) *(DENK-may-lern)*

Inschriften an den Denkmälern zu lesen.

who is accustomed to taking his car for

Für den Amerikaner, der daran gewöhnt

everything, this can be an

ist, bei Schritt und Tritt sein Auto zu nehmen,

entirely novel experience.

(eR-LAYP-nis)

kann das ein ganz neues Erlebnis sein.

Did you get some good ideas about familiarizing yourself with a new city? Look at the following statements and write in the blank whether each is *richig* *(RIÇ-tik)* (true) or *falsch* *(falsh)* (false).

1. Man kann eine fremde Stadt kennenlernen wenn man dort zu Fuß geht. _____

2. Es ist eine gute Idee, die Gesichter der Leute zu beobachten. _____
   (ee-DAY)
   idea

3. Man soll nicht in Geschäfte hineingehen. _____

4. Denkmäler haben Inschriften. _____

5. Amerikaner fahren lieber als zu Fuß zu gehen. _____

BEIM OPTIKER
At the Optometrist

(ZON-en-bril-eh)
die Sonnenbrille
sun glasses

(OP-ti-keR)
der Optiker
optometrist (optician)

(RAH-men)
der Rahmen
frame

(kon-TAKT-lin-zeh)
die Kontaktlinse
contact lens

If you wear glasses or contact lenses, you probably won't have any trouble with them on your trip. But look at the following dialogue closely just in case you need to visit an optometrist.

TOURISTIN	*(RAH-men)* **Der Rahmen und ein Glas** *(BRIL-eh)* **von meiner Brille sind kaputt. Sehen Sie?**	The frame and a lens of my glasses are broken. You see?
OPTIKER	**Wie ist das passiert?**	How did it happen?

	(VAY-rent)
TOURISTIN	**In der U-Bahn während der**
	(HOWPT-feR-kehrs-tseit) *(drenkt)*
	Hauptverkehrszeit. Jemand drängt
	(ZOY-leh)
	mich und ich stoße gegen eine Säule
	an. Ich weiß nicht, was ich tun soll.
	(überR-HOWPT)
	Ich sehe überhaupt nichts ohne Brille.
	(eR-ZATS-bril-eh)
OPTIKER	**Haben Sie eine Ersatzbrille?**
	(LEI-deR)
TOURISTIN	**Leider nicht.**

In the subway during the rush hour. Somebody pushes me and I hit a pillar. I don't know what to do. I can't see anything without glasses.

Do you have a spare pair?

Unfortunately not.

OPTIKER	**Also gut. Setzen Sie sich dort**
	(zoh-FORT)
	hin. Ich versuche, das sofort zu
	reparieren. Aber Ihre Brille ist
	(leiçt) *(tseR-BREÇ-liç)*
	leicht zerbrechlich. Sie müssen
	(FOHR-ziç-tiç)
	vorsichtig sein.

Okay. Sit down over there. I'll try to repair this immediately. But your glasses are very fragile. You must be careful.

TOURISTIN	**Vielen Dank. Ich bin Ihnen**
	(VIRK-liç)
	wirklich sehr dankbar.

Thank you. I am really grateful to you.

OPTIKER	**Kann ich Ihnen einen Rat**
	geben?
TOURISTIN	**Ja?**

May I give you some advice?

Yes?

OPTIKER	**Nehmen Sie nächstes Mal**
	während des Hauptverkehrs ein Taxi.

Take a taxi next time during rush hour.

Which entry in Column 2 goes best with each entry in Column 1?

1. Wie lange haben Sie offen?	A. Morgen, wenn möglich.
2. Wann brauchen Sie die Brille?	B. Vielen Dank.
3. Haben Sie eine Ersatzbrille.	C. Der Rahmen und eine Linse.
4. Was ist kaputt?	D. Bis sechs Uhr abends.
5. Hier haben Sie die Brille.	E. Leider nicht.

ANSWERS

Matching. 1. D 2. A 3. E 4. C 5. B

Fill in the correct words:

1. Der Rahmen und ein _____ sind gesprungen.

2. Der Optiker versucht, die Brille zu _____.

3. Die Dame sieht fast nichts ohne _____.

4. Leider hat sie keine _____.

5. Die U-Bahn in dieser Stadt ist immer sehr _____.

BEIM SCHUHMACHER
At the Shoemaker

(SHOO-mach-eR)	*(SHNŪR-zen-kel)*	*(zan-DAH-leh)*	*(pahR) (SHOO-eh)*
der Schuhmacher	**der Schnürsenkel**	**die Sandale**	**ein Paar Schuhe**
shoemaker	shoelace	sandal	a pair of shoes

You are more likely to have trouble with your shoes while traveling than with your eyeglasses. So read the following dialogue for hints on how to speak with a shoemaker.

TOURISTIN *(AP-zats)* **Guten Tag. Der Absatz von meinem Schuh ist kaputt. Können Sie ihn reparieren?**

Hello. My shoe's heel is broken. Can you repair it?

SCHUHMACHER **Lassen Sie mal sehen. Ich** *(PLAS-tik)* **glaube nicht. Das ist Plastik. Wann brauchen Sie Ihre Schuhe?**

Let's see. I don't think so. It's plastic. When do you need your shoes?

TOURISTIN **Morgen, wenn möglich. Ich bleibe nur ein paar Tage hier. Ich bin** *(too-RIS-tin)* **Touristin.**

Tomorrow if possible. I am staying only for a few days. I am a tourist.

SCHUHMACHER **Ich kann versuchen, ihn** *(proh-vee-ZOH-rish) (AN-tsoo-lei-men)* **provisorisch anzuleimen.**	I can try to glue it temporarily.
TOURISTIN **Das ist alles, was ich brauche. Wie lange haben Sie offen?**	That's all I need. How long are you open?
SCHUHMACHER **Bis 19 Uhr.**	Till 7 P.M.
TOURISTIN **Wunderbar! Dann komme ich später zurück.**	Perfect. I'll come back later.
SCHUHMACHER **Gut.**	Good.
TOURISTIN **Können Sie auch Schuhe schnell** *(be-ZOH-len)* **neu besohlen?**	Can you also quickly put new soles on shoes?
SCHUHMACHER **Aber natürlich.**	Of course.
TOURISTIN **Dann bringe ich Ihnen die Schuhe meines Mannes.**	Then I'll bring you my husband's shoes.

Which expression or word does not belong?

1. Absatz, Schuhe, Brille, Sandalen

2. sofort, gleich, diesen Moment, ich bin Ihnen dankbar

3. ersetzen, reparieren, anleimen, stoßen

4. Optiker, Schuhmacher, Tourist, offen

ANSWERS
1. Brille 2. ich bin Ihnen dankbar 3. stoßen 4. offen

ESSENTIAL SERVICES

(DEENST-leis-tun-gen)

Wichtige Dienstleistungen

25	*(BANK-vay-zen)* **das Bankwesen** Banking	⏱

(BANK-noh-ten)   *(unt)*   *(MÜN-tsen)*

BANKNOTEN UND MÜNZEN

Bills and Coins

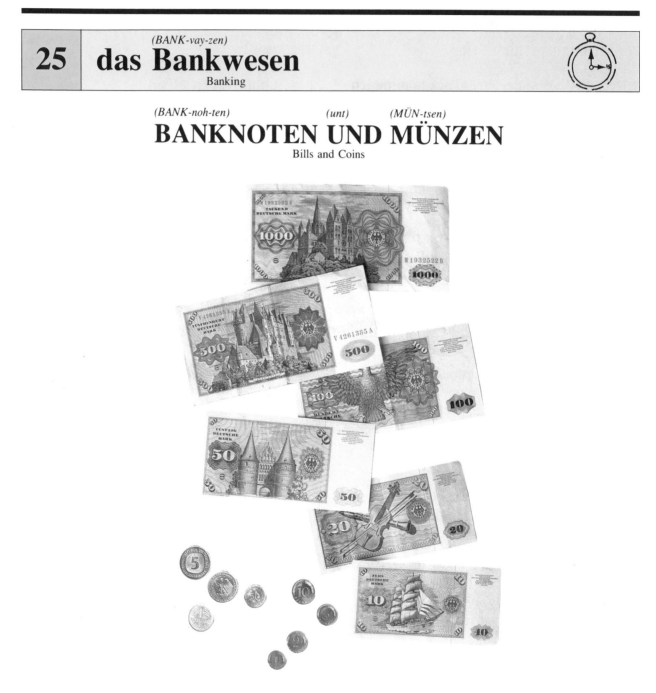

(courtesy of Ernst Klett Verlag, Stuttgart)

The basic unit of currency in West Germany is the Mark, known as the Deutsche Mark or DM. It is divided into 100 Pfennigs.

(pa-PEER-gelt)

DAS PAPIERGELD
bills

(BANK-noh-ten)   *(FOL-gen-den)* *(NEN-veR-teh)*

Deutsche Banknoten haben die folgenden Nennwerte.
bank notes   following   denominations

5 Mark	100 Mark
10 Mark	500 Mark
20 Mark	1 000 Mark
50 Mark	

(KLEIN-gelt)

DAS KLEINGELD
change

(MÜN-tsen)   *(UM-lowf)*

Die folgenden Münzen sind im Umlauf.
coins   circulation

Pfennig:	Mark:
(PFE-niç)	*(mark)*
1 Pfennig	1 Mark
2 Pfennig	2 Mark
5 Pfennig	5 Mark
10 Pfennig	
50 Pfennig	

(BAN-ken)   *(GELT-vek-sel)*

BANKEN, GELDWECHSEL
Banks, Exchanging Money

(REI-zeh-sheks)

UND REISESCHECKS
and Traveler's Checks

(DOY-tcheh) *(BUN-des-bank)*

The central bank of West Germany is the **Deutsche Bundesbank**, headquartered in Frankfurt.
German Federal Bank

The country has many banks that deal with the public, and most offer a wide range of services. The largest banks are the *Deutsche Bank, Dresdner Bank,* and *Commerzbank.* In addition, many foreign banks, including U.S. banks, have offices in West Germany. You can exchange currency at banks and also at smaller exchange offices. Credit cards are accepted by major establishments and by many other businesses. But Germans use credit cards much less than Americans, so be prepared to pay in cash during your daily excursions. Banking and money conditions are similar in Austria and Switzerland.

Menschen und Dinge
People and Things

das Geld
money

(BANK-be-am-teh)   *(BANK-be-am-tin)*
der Bankbeamte, die Bankbeamtin
bank employee

die Bank
bank

die Reiseschecks
traveler's checks

(dee-REK-tohR)
der Direktor
manager

(AN-lei-eh)   *(DAR-layn)*
die Anleihe, das Darlehn
loan

(EIN-tsah-lungs-be-layk)
der Einzahlungsbeleg
deposit slip

(KA-sen-shal-teR)
der Kassenschalter
teller's window

(Ka-SEE-reR)   *(ka-SEE-reR-in)*
der Kassierer, die Kassiererin
teller (cashier)

(AP-hay-bungs-be-layk)
der Abhebungsbeleg
withdrawal slip

(BANK-noh-teh)   *(GELT-shein)*
die Banknote, der Geldschein
bill

(BAHR-gelt)
das Bargeld
cash

(SHEK-booch)
das Scheckbuch
checkbook

212

Wie man . . .

How to . . .

(VEK-seln)   *(TOW-shen)*
wechseln, tauschen
to exchange

(VEK-sel-koors)
der Wechselkurs
rate of exchange

(TSAH-len)
zahlen
to pay

(eR-ÖF-nen)
ein Konto eröffnen
to open an account

(EIN-tsah-lung)
die Einzahlung
deposit

(day-poh-NEE-ren)
einzahlen, deponieren
to deposit

(AP-hay-ben)
abheben
to withdraw

(un-teR-SHREI-ben)
unterschreiben
to sign

(EIN-lö-zen)
einen Scheck einlösen
to cash a check

You've been introduced to a number of useful words. See if you remember them by circling the term that correctly describes each of the following pictures.

1.
das Geld
der Kassenschalter

2.
das Scheckbuch
das Bargeld

3.
der Direktor
die Banknote

4.
die Kassiererin
der Direktor

213

5.

der Einzahlungsbeleg
der Abhebungsbeleg

6.

die Reiseschecks
das Bargeld

Now, try to complete the following:

1. Ich möchte zehn U.S. Dollars ———————————.
   exchange

2. Ich möchte 100 Mark ———————————.
   withdraw

3. Ich möchte einen Reisescheck ———————————.
   cash

4. Ich möchte 300 Mark ———————————.
   deposit

GELDWECHSELN

JULIE   (to teller at a bank in Munich)

Können Sie mir diesen Reisescheck	Can you change this traveler's check for $100
für 100 Dollar in Mark umwechseln?	into marks?
KASSIERER **Ich brauche Ihren Paß.**	I need your passport.
JULIE **Warum?**	Why?
KASSIERER *(OWS-veis)* **Persönlicher Ausweis.**	Personal identification.
JULIE **Was meinen Sie?**	What do you mean?

214

KASSIERER	*(ee-den-tee-TAYT)* **Ihre Identität.**	Your identity.
JULIE	**Ah.—Ich habe ihn vergessen. Im Hotel.**	Ah.—I forgot it. At the hotel.
KASSIERER	**Es tut mir leid. Haben Sie** *(ee-den-ti-fi-TSEE-rung)* **etwas anderes zur Identifizierung?**	I am sorry. Do you have something else to identify yourself with?
JULIE	*(MUT-eR-mahl)* **Ich hab' ein Muttermal** *(SHUL-teR)* **an der rechten Schulter.**	I have a mole on the right shoulder.

der Paß
passport

Try to fill in the missing dialogue parts without looking them up:

1. „Können Sie mir diesen _____ für 100 Dollar in Mark _____?"

2. „Ich brauche Ihren _____."

3. „Ich habe ihn _____."

4. „Ich hab' ein Muttermal an der rechten _____."

(vits) EIN KLEINER WITZ
joke

(day-fi-nit-see-OHN) **Definition einer Bank**	Definition of a bank
(in-sti-toot-see-OHN) **Eine Bank ist eine Institution, wo man** *(be-VEI-zen)* **Geld borgen kann, wenn man beweisen kann, daß man es nicht braucht.**	A bank is an institution where one can borrow money if one can prove that one does not need it.

Are the following statements about the dialogue true or false?

1. Julie möchte einen Reisescheck in Mark umwechseln. _____

2. Der Kassierer sagt, er braucht ihren Paß. _____

3. Julie versteht den Mann sofort. _____

4. Sie hat ihren Paß bei sich. _____

5. Sie holt den Paß vom Hotel. _____

6. Der Beamte gibt ihr das Geld ohne Paß. _____

7. Julie hat ein Muttermal an der linken Schulter. _____

8. Der Beamte sagt, „Es tut mir leid." _____

Pick the right word:

9. In den meisten Ländern braucht man als persönlichen Ausweis

   a. eine Flugkarte   b. eine Postkarte   c. einen Paß

10. Wie heißt der Mann in der Bank, der Ihnen das Geld wechselt?

   a. der Kassierer   b. der Direktor   c. der Kellner

11. Was bekommt man zurück, wenn man Geld bei der Bank deponiert hat?

   a. einen Abhebungsbeleg   b. einen Einzahlungsbeleg   c. Bargeld

12. Was bekommt man, wenn man einen Scheck einlöst?

   a. einen neuen Scheck   b. Bargeld   c. nichts

216

Here's a short story about banking.

(eR-TSAYLT) **Mein Freund in München erzählt mir die** *(ge-SHIÇ-teh)* **folgende Geschichte:**	My friend in Munich tells me the following story:
(FOH-ri-geh) **Vorige Woche eröffnet mein junger Sohn** **zum ersten Mal in seinem Leben ein Konto** *(OWF-ge-raykt)* **bei der Bank. Heute fragt er mich, ganz aufgeregt:**	Last week my young son opens an account at the bank for the first time in his life. Today he asks me, all excited:
„Vati, warum sagst du mir, ich soll mein **Geld bei so einer Bank einzahlen?"**	"Dad, why did you tell me to deposit my money with such a bank?"
„Was meinst du?" frage ich ihn.	"What do you mean?" I ask him.
(bank-ROT) **„Die Bank ist doch bankrott," sagt er.**	"The bank is bankrupt," he says.
(SHTERK-steh) **„Wieso? Das ist doch die stärkste Bank** **in Deutschland."**	"How come? That is the strongest bank in Germany."
„Hier. Schau dir diesen Scheck an," **antwortet er.**	"Here. Look at this check," he replies.
„Mein Scheck für 30 Mark. Die Bank **schickt ihn mir zurück und schau, Vati: mit** *(OWF-druk)* **Aufdruck *keine Deckung*."**	"My check for 30 marks. The bank sends it back to me, and look, dad: Printed on it is *no funds*."

Please fill in the missing words:

1. Vorige Woche _____ mein Sohn ein Konto.

2. Warum soll ich das Geld bei so einer Bank _____?

3. Das ist doch die stärkste _____ in Deutschland.

4. Die Bank schickt mir den Scheck _____.

5. Der Scheck hat einen Aufdruck: _____.

(FRAH-gen)

Bitte beantworten Sie die folgenden Fragen.
questions

1. Wer erzählt die Geschichte? _____

2. Wo eröffnet der Junge das Konto? _____

3. Wann eröffnet er das Konto? _____

4. Warum ist der Junge ganz aufgeregt? _____

5. Was tut die Bank mit dem Scheck? _____

6. Was steht auf dem Scheck? _____

Match each word in Column 1 with the proper English translation in Column 2.

1. **der Wechselkurs**   A. teller's window

2. **der Reisescheck**   B. to withdraw

3. **der Kassenschalter**   C. exchange rate

4. **abheben**   D. traveler's check

5. **unterschreiben**   E. deposit

6. **die Einzahlung**   F. no funds

7. **keine Deckung**   G. to sign

8. **das Darlehn**   H. cashier

9. **der Kassierer**   I. manager

10. **der Direktor**   J. loan

218

And here is a puzzle you'll enjoy. Just enter the German translation of each English term. We've supplied the first letter of each German word.

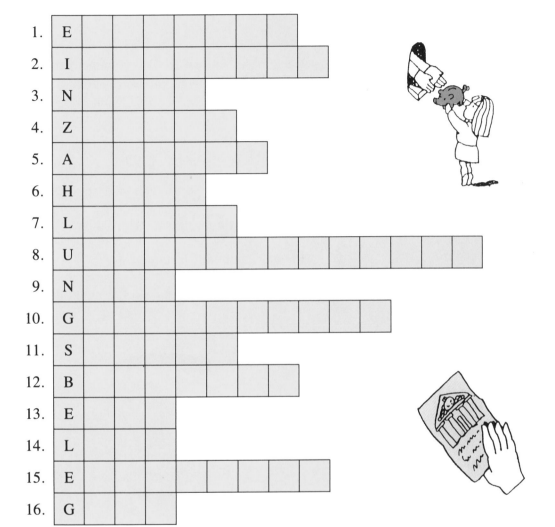

1. E
2. I
3. N
4. Z
5. A
6. H
7. L
8. U
9. N
10. G
11. S
12. B
13. E
14. L
15. E
16. G

1. to open (an account)
2. identity
3. not
4. to pay
5. loan
6. hotel
7. unfortunately
8. to sign

9. no
10. money exchange
11. check
12. bill (bank note)
13. corner
14. long
15. to deposit
16. money

(BUN-des-post)
The federal postal service (die Bundespost) in West Germany is known for its efficiency. It also operates telephone and telex systems and provides passenger-bus service. Large numbers of telephones are usually located at the main post office in major cities.

The following story is about an amateur letter carrier.

(root) (sprict)   *(U-lee)*
Ruth spricht mit ihrem Sohn Uli, fünf Jahre alt.   Ruth talks to her son Uli, five years old.

(frü)
„Was machst du so früh, Uli?"   "What are you doing so early, Uli?"

(BREEF-tray-geR)(MA-mee)
„Ich spiele Briefträger, Mami."   "Playing mailman, Mommy."

„Briefträger? Wie kannst du das ohne   "Mailman? How can you do that without

Briefe machen?"   letters?"

„Aber ich habe ja Briefe."   "But I do have letters."

„Was für Briefe?"   "What kind of letters?"

(KAS-ten)
„Die in dem Kasten in deinem   "The ones in the big box in your room,

Zimmer, ein ganzes Paket, mit einem   whole package, with a beautiful pink ribbon

schönen rosa Band um sie herum . . ."   around them . . ."

„Und mit denen spielst du Briefträger?"   "And with those you play mailman?"

(MU-tee)
„Ja, Mutti. Ich steck' einen Brief nach dem   "Yes, Mommy. I put one letter after another

anderen auf der Straße unter jede Haustür."   under each front door on the street."

(pa-KAYT)
das Paket
package

(BREEF-tray-geR)
der Briefträger
letter carrier

(BREEF-kas-ten)
der Briefkasten
mailbox

John wants to mail a package to the U.S.A., and Alois takes him to the post office.

(AH-loh-is)

ALOIS	**Wissen Sie, daß die Bundespost**	Do you know that the federal postal service

(be-FÖR-deRt)
täglich Millionen Briefe befördert? — forwards millions of letters a day?

(fan-TAS-tish)
JOHN **Fantastisch!** — Fantastic!

ALOIS **Die Bundespost ist einer der größten** — The federal postal service is one of the

(DEENST-leis-tungs-be-tree-beh) (oy-ROH-pa)
Dienstleistungsbetriebe in Europa. — biggest service establishments in Europe.

JOHN **Großartig!** — Great.

ALOIS **Der Telefondienst gehört** — The telephone service belongs to it, of course.

natürlich dazu.

JOHN **Und wenn ich ein** — And if I want to send

(SHIK-en)
Telegramm schicken möchte? — a telegram?

(GLEIÇ-fals)
ALOIS **Dann gehen Sie gleichfalls** — Then you also go to the

aufs Postamt. — post office.

(They arrive at the post office.)

(pah-KAYT-an-nah-meh)
Also hier haben Sie die Paketannahme. — Here you have the parcel post window.

(POST-be-am-teR)
POSTBEAMTER **Wollen Sie bitte diese** — Would you please complete this parcel form?
postal employee (OWS-fül-en)
Paketkarte ausfüllen?

JOHN **Sehr gut. Haben Sie auch Briefmarken?** Very good. Do you also have stamps?

POSTBEAMTER **Die bekommen Sie beim** — Those you get at the stamp window over there.

Briefmarkenschalter dort

drüben.

JOHN **Auch Postkarten?**	Postal cards also?
POSTBEAMTER **Ja, natürlich.**	Yes, of course.
(TCHOK-oh-lay-deh) JOHN **Großartig! Und auch Schokolade?**	Great! And also chocolate?
POSTBEAMTER **Leider nicht.**	Unfortunately not.

Bitte nicht vergessen
Please don't forget

das Postfach
post office box

der Beamte
employee

das Telegramm
telegram

die Briefe
letters

(POST-vert-tsei-çen)
die Briefmarke *or* **das Postwertzeichen**
postage stamp

(mil-YOHN) **eine Million**	one million
Millionen	millions
(BREEF-kas-ten-lay-rung) **die Briefkastenleerung**	mail collection
(POR-toh) **das Porto**	postage
Die Post kommt zweimal täglich.	Mail is delivered twice daily.
Der Postbeamte leert den Briefkasten.	The postal worker empties the mailbox.

222

(NUTS-li-çeh) (OWS-drü-keh)

Nützliche Ausdrücke

Useful expressions

Bitte gehen Sie doch.
The *doch* in this sentence is very hard to translate. It often expresses interest or impatience:
Please *do* go. There are other little words like this, sometimes called flavoring or intensifying
particles, e.g., *denn* in *Gehst du denn nicht*? Aren't you going? Replying to this, one might say
(expressing annoyance): *Ich gehe ja*. I *am* going!

Haben Sie etwas dagegen?   Do you mind?

Ich habe nichts dagegen.   I don't mind;
                                           I have no objection to it.

Here's a quick quiz about the German postal service.

Fill in the correct German words:

1. Die Bundespost befördert
   Millionen

   _____ täglich.

2. Sie ist einer der größten
   Dienstleistungsbetriebe in

   _____ .

3. John will auch _____ kaufen.

4. Die Bundespost ist ein _____ .
                          service establishment

5. Mit dem Paket geht man zur _____ .
                              parcel post window

6. Leute, die fürs Postamt arbeiten, heißen _____ .
                                            postal employees

Draw lines between the matching English and German:

1. Bundespost   A. to forward
2. Dienstleistungsbetrieb B. post office box
3. Paketannahme   C. postal card
4. Postbeamter   D. service establishment
5. Briefmarke   E. federal postal service
6. befördern   F. postal employee
7. Postfach   G. postage
8. Porto   H. parcel post window
9. Postkarte   I. postage stamp

ANSWERS

Matching. 1. E 2. D 3. H 4. F 5. I 6. A 7. B 8. G 9. C

Fill-in. 1. Briefe 2. Europa 3. Briefmarken 4. Dienstleistungsbetrieb 5. Paketannahme 6. Postbeamte

223

(MA-chen)

Machen
To Make

Machen is one of the most useful words in the German language. It can have a number of meanings.

Geschäfte machen mit	to do business with
(da-ROWS) *Mach' dir nichts daraus!*	Don't worry about it.
Das macht nichts!	It doesn't matter.
Mach's gut!	Take care of yourself.
Da kann man nichts machen.	It can't be helped.
Laß mich nur machen!	Leave it to me!
Wie geht's? Es macht sich.	How are things? Pretty good. So-so.
Gemacht!	Agreed! Okay!

224

(te-le-FOHN-deenst)

Der Telefondienst

Telephone Service

(HA-loh)   *(HA-loh)*

HALLO...HALLO?

Hello . . . Hello?

anrufen	
telefonieren	to make a telephone call
Bleiben Sie am Apparat.	Stay on the line; don't hang up.
(fer-MIT-lung)	
Hallo, Vermittlung. ⎱	Hello, operator?
Hallo, Fräulein. ⎰	
(ORTS-ge-shprayç) *(FERN-ge-shprayç)*	
das Ortsgespräch, Ferngespräch	local call; long distance call
(ER-ge-shprayç)	
das R-Gespräch	collect call, reverse charges
Hören Sie mich jetzt besser?	Can you hear me better now?
(FOHR-an-mel-dung)	
mit Voranmeldung	person-to-person
(a-pa-RAHT) *(be-ZETST)*	
Der Apparat ist besetzt.	The line is busy.
(VAY-len)	
eine Nummer wählen	to dial a number

(tsvoh)

On the telephone, it is customary to say *zwo* instead of *zwei* if you use the number 2. The reason is that *zwei* and *drei* sound alike on the phone. *Zwo* prevents confusion.

John and Mary would like to pay a visit to their relatives in Munich, but John has to call them first.

JOHN   (to a passerby in the street)

Können Sie mir bitte sagen,   Could you please tell me

wo ich einen öffentlichen   where I find a public
(FERN-shpre-çeR)
Fernsprecher finde?   telephone?

VORBEIGEHENDER   **Dort drüben**   Over there at the street

an der Straßenecke ist eine   corner there is a telephone
(tay-lay-FOHN-tse-leh)
Telefonzelle.   booth.

JOHN   **Dort?**   There?

VORBEIGEHENDER   **Ja, die gelb**   Yes, the one that is painted
(AN-ge-shtri-çe-neh)
angestrichene. Kann ich   yellow.
(be-HILF-liç)
Ihnen behilflich sein?   May I help you?
(LEE-bens-vür-diç)
JOHN   **Danke, nein. Sehr liebenswürdig.**   No, thank you. You're very kind. I'll find it.

Ich find' sie schon. Komm, Mary.   Come, Mary.

(at the booth)

MARY   **Hast du Münzen?**   Do you have coins?

JOHN   **Ja—also willst du**   Yes—do you want to wait

draußen warten? Für zwei   outside? For two it is a bit small.

ist es ein bißchen eng.

(he takes off the receiver, inserts the money and dials)

Franz? Kann ich bitte mit   Franz? Can I speak with

Franz sprechen?   Franz, please?

Franz—Grüß dich! Ja, wir   Franz—Hi!

sind in München. Um 17 Uhr? . . .   Yes, we are in Munich. At 17 hours (5 P.M.)? . . .

Wunderbar. Bis später.   Great. Until later.

Fill in the correct German word:

1. Die Telefonzelle ist _____ angestrichen.

2. Mary fragt John: ,,Hast du genug _____?''

3. Man findet die Nummer im _____.

4. Wann werden sie die Verwandten besuchen? Um _____.

5. Beim Telefonieren sagt man _____ anstatt zwei.

6. Wie sagt man 1½ auf Deutsch? _____.

7. Wie sagt man ½? _____

8. Und wie sagt man ⅓? _____

ORTSGESPRÄCH ODER FERNGESPRÄCH?
Local or Long Distance?

John and Mary are back at the hotel at 21 hours. There is still time to place a call to his cousin Lotte in Stuttgart.

JOHN **Hallo, Fräulein.**   Hello, operator.

FRÄULEIN **Ortsgespräch oder**   Local call or long distance?

    Ferngespräch?

JOHN **Ferngespräch.**   Long distance.

ANSWERS

Fill-in.
1. gelb 2. Münzen 3. Telefonbuch 4. 17 Uhr 5. zwo 6. anderthalb 7. ein halb 8. ein Drittel

227

FRÄULEIN	**Mit Voranmeldung?**	Person-to-person?
JOHN	**Ja, bitte.**	Yes, please.
FRÄULEIN	- **Ein R-Gespräch?**	Collect?
JOHN	**Nein, das geht auf meine Hotelrechnung.**	No; that goes on my hotel bill.

FRÄULEIN	**Namen und Nummer, bitte.**	Name and number, please.
JOHN	**Lotte Müller, 84-56-13. Meine Nummer ist 63-47-82. Wie lange muß ich warten?**	Lotte Müller, 84-56-13. My number is 63-47-82. How long do I have to wait?
FRÄULEIN	**Einen Moment, bitte. Bleiben Sie am Apparat. Ich verbinde Sie. . . . Keine Antwort.**	One moment, please. Stay on the line. I'll connect you . . . . No answer.
JOHN	**Danke. Ich versuche später nochmals.**	Thank you. I'll try again later.

Circle the correct answer for the following questions.

1. Mit welcher Farbe ist der öffentliche Fernsprecher angestrichen?
   a. blau   b. gelb   c. rot

2. Von wo telefoniert er Franz?
   a. vom Hotel   b. vom Kino   c. von einer Telefonzelle

3. Wann sollen sie bei den Verwandten sein?
   a. um 13 Uhr   b. um 7 Uhr   c. um 17 Uhr

4. Wem telefoniert er um 9 Uhr abends?
   a. seiner Kusine Lotte   b. seinem Bruder Paul   c. seiner Tante Lilly

5. Wie schreiben Sie die Zahl 33 aus?
   a. dreißig-drei   b. dreiunddreißig   c. dreißigunddrei

   (fer-GLEI-çen)
6. Vergleichen Sie (compare) ein Ortsgespräch mit einem Ferngespräch:
   a. Ein Ortsgespräch ist billiger. b. Ein Ferngespräch ist billiger. c. Sie kosten dasselbe.

228

Bitte nicht vergessen . . .

Please don't forget . . .

die Adresse   address

der Apparat   apparatus, telephone receiver

der Moment   moment

die Auskunft   information

Wie spät ist es?
or
Wieviel Uhr ist es?

die Nummer   number

das Telefon   telephone

das Telefonbuch   telephone book

die gelb angestrichene Telefonzelle

the yellow telephone booth

Draw lines between the matching words or expressions.

1. der Fernsprecher

2. eine Nummer wählen

3. die Auskunft

4. das Ortsgespräch

5. die Münzen

6. die Straßenecke

7. öffentlich

8. liebenswürdig

A. local call

B. street corner

C. telephone

D. to dial

E. public

F. information

G. kind

H. coins

229

Frau Hauser tries to call a grocery store.

Hallo? Frau Hauser hier, Schillerstraße

115. Schicken Sie mir bitte ein kleines
(GRIL-en)
Huhn zum Grillen. Haben Sie nicht. Das
(SHAH-deh)
ist schade. Also vielleicht ein Pfund
(ge-KOCH-ten)　(dün)　(ge-SHNIT-en)
gekochten Schinken, dünn geschnitten—

Haben Sie auch nicht. Wieso? Das ist doch

unmöglich. Also dann eventuell ein Pfund
(MAH-ger-es) (HAK-fleish)
mageres Hackfleisch—auch kein

Hackfleisch?? Es ist nicht zu glauben! Ist

denn das nicht Herr Blunz, der Metzger?
(BLOOM-en-hend-leR)
Sie sind Blunz, der Blumenhändler? Ach,
(feR-TSEI-en)
bitte verzeihen Sie mir. Aber warum sagen

Sie nicht sofort, daß Sie nicht Fleisch

verkaufen? . . . Weil ich so viel rede! Sie
(freç)
sind ja frech!

Hello? This is Frau Hauser, 115 Schillerstraße. Send me, please, a small chicken for grilling. You don't have it. That's too bad. Well, maybe a pound of boiled ham, sliced thin—you don't have that either. How come? That's impossible. Maybe a pound of lean hamburger—no hamburger?? That's incredible! Isn't this Herr Blunz, the butcher? You are Blunz, the florist? Oh, please excuse me. But why didn't you say right away that you don't sell meat? . . . Because I talk so much! You are really fresh!

Ein Rätsel

Here's an interesting change of pace—a word-search puzzle. Find the nouns with or without their articles. Circle them. The nouns are not capitalized in this puzzle.

1. the street corner
2. number
3. the information
4. moment
5. the address
6. the man
7. one quarter

a	e	z	m	b	o	r	n	l	p	r	b	o	n
d	i	e	a	u	s	k	u	n	f	t	z	i	u
s	n	l	n	m	i	k	l	s	c	o	n	r	m
a	v	b	n	o	n	a	z	r	s	t	m	u	m
d	i	e	s	t	r	a	ß	e	n	e	c	k	e
a	e	c	k	l	m	o	p	r	s	t	v	u	r
n	r	g	i	a	m	o	i	s	t	n	m	l	z
s	t	a	g	h	u	n	m	s	p	r	a	l	t
d	e	r	m	a	n	n	p	o	r	s	g	g	n
e	l	n	m	o	m	e	n	t	p	l	a	e	i
d	i	e	a	d	r	e	s	s	e	g	s	o	p

(ah-nah-toh-MEE-ü-bung)

EINE KURZE ANATOMIEÜBUNG
A Short Lesson in Anatomy

Kurt und Trude are testing each other on the parts of the human body.

KURT	**Also wer fängt an, du oder ich?**	Well, who'll start, you or I?
TRUDE	**Du fragst mich zuerst.**	You ask me first.
KURT	**Gut. Also was hast du da?**	Good. What do you have here?
TRUDE	*(HAH-reh)* **Die Haare.**	The hair.

KURT	**Zwischen den Haaren und** *(OW-gen)* **den Augen?**	Between the hair and the eyes?

TRUDE	*(shtirn)* **Die Stirn.**	The forehead.
KURT	**Über den Augen. . .?**	Over the eyes . . .?

TRUDE	*(OW-gen-brow-en)* **Die Augenbrauen.**		The eyebrows.
KURT	**Und was macht man zu,**		And what does one
	wenn man schläft?		close when sleeping?
TRUDE	*(OW-gen-lee-deR)* **Die Augenlider.**		The eyelids.
KURT	**Und auf den Augenlidern**		And on the eyelids
	haben wir . . .		we have . . .
TRUDE	*(VIM-pern)* **Wimpern.**		lashes.
KURT	**Und zwischen**		And between
	den Augen ist . . .		the eyes is . . .
TRUDE	*(NAH-zeh)* **die Nase.**		the nose.
KURT	**Und zwischen der Nase**		And between the nose
	(munt) **und dem Mund**		and the mouth
	tragen viele Männer . . .		many men wear . . .
TRUDE	*(SHNUR-bart)* **einen Schnurrbart.**		a moustache.
KURT	**Du hast zwei**		You have two
TRUDE	*(OH-ren)* **Ohren**		ears
KURT	**und zwei**		and two
TRUDE	*(VAN-gen)* *(BA-ken)* **Wangen (oder Backen).**		cheeks.
KURT	**Aber du hast nur ein**		But you have only one
TRUDE	*(ge-ZIÇT)* **Gesicht**		face
KURT	**und nur einen**		and only one
TRUDE	*(kopf)* **Kopf.**		head.
KURT	**Wenn du lachst,**		When you laugh, one sees the
	sieht man die		

233

	(TSAY-neh)	
TRUDE	**Zähne.**	teeth.

KURT	**Wenn du zum**	When you go to
	Doktor gehst, zeigst du ihm die	the doctor, you

	(TSUNG-eh)	
TRUDE	**Zunge, aaah. . . .**	show him your tongue, aaah . . . .

KURT	**Das ist das**	This is the
	(kin)	
TRUDE	**Kinn,**	chin,

KURT	**und das ist der**	and that is the
	(hals)	
TRUDE	**Hals.**	neck.

KURT	**Hier sind zwei**	Here are two
	(SHUL-teRn)	
TRUDE	**Schultern,**	shoulders,
KURT	**vier**	four

	(AR-meh)	
TRUDE	**Arme**	arms,
KURT	**und zwei**	and two

	(EL-boh-gen)	
TRUDE	**Ellbogen.**	elbows.

KURT	**Hier sind zwei**	Here are two
	(HEN-deh)	
TRUDE	**Hände**	hands
KURT	**und zehn**	and ten
	(FING-eR)	
TRUDE	**Finger.**	fingers.

KURT	**Jetzt komm' *ich* dran.**	Now it's *my* turn.
TRUDE	**Also das ist der**	This is the

KURT *(RÜK-en)* **Rücken,**   back,

TRUDE *(FOR-neh)* **und da vorne ist die**   and here in front is the

KURT *(brust)* **Brust.**   chest.

TRUDE **Etwas tut dir weh, wenn**   Something hurts you, when

du zuviel Kuchen ißt: you eat too much cake:

KURT *(MAH-gen)* **Der Magen.**   the stomach.

TRUDE **Und etwas tiefer ist der**   and a little lower is the

KURT *(bowch)* **Bauch.**   belly.

TRUDE **Und da hinten hast du den**   And there in the back you have the

KURT *(poh-POH)* **Popo.**   fanny.

TRUDE **Und von hier bis hier**   And from here to here you

hast du zwei   have two

KURT *(SHEN-kel)* **Schenkel.**   thighs.

TRUDE **Dann hast du zwei**   Then you have two

KURT *(KNEE-eh)* **Knie.**   knees.

TRUDE **Und weiter unten sind**   And farther down are the

KURT *(VAH-den)* **die zwei Waden.**   two calves.

TRUDE **Dann kommen die zwei**   Then come the two

KURT *(KNÖ-çel)* **Knöchel.**   ankles.

TRUDE **Und darunter sind die**   And under them are the

großen   big

KURT *(FÜS-eh)* **Füße**   feet

TRUDE **mit den zehn**   with the ten

KURT *(TSAY-en)* **Zehen.**   toes.

Draw lines between
the matching words:

1. **die Stirn**

2. **die Zehen**

3. **der Mund**

4. **die Knöchel**

5. **die Zunge**

6. **die Augenlider**

7. **der Magen**

8. **das Gesicht**

9. **der Schnurrbart**

10. **die Zähne**

A. tongue

B. face

C. eyelids

D. forehead

E. ankles

F. toes

G. stomach

H. mouth

I. teeth

J. moustache

(MUS-kel)
der Muskel
muscle

(ar-TAYR-ee-eh)
die Arterie
artery

(VAY-neh)
die Vene
vein

(MAH-gen)
der Magen
stomach

(darm)
der Darm
intestine

(ge-DER-meh)
die Gedärme
intestines

(LUN-geh)
die Lunge
lung

(herts)
das Herz
heart

(NEE-reh)
die Niere
kidney

(LAY-beR)
die Leber
liver

(BLAH-zeh)
die Blase
bladder

A very comprehensive system of mandatory health insurance guarantees free medical and dental care, the cost of medication, laboratory tests, and unlimited hospitalization to the insured and his or her family, which means to every citizen of the Federal Republic.

ANSWERS

Matching.
1. D 2. F 3. H 4. E 5. A 6. C 7. G 8. B 9. J 10. I

The procedures for getting medical care are relatively simple. Most Germans go to their *(KRAN-ken-kas-en-artst)* *Krankenkassenarzt* (health insurance doctor) for their medical or dental needs. A *Krankenschein* *(KRAN-ken-shein)* (medical certificate) is prepared by the physician for prescriptions, and, if necessary, a stay in the hospital. The patient is free to choose his or her own doctor from a sizable number of general practitioners or specialists.

While traveling in Germany, Austria, or Switzerland, you should have no difficulty receiving adequate medical care. Noncitizens are not covered by the German health-insurance system. Medical fees vary greatly and are set by the physician or dentist you consult. Your best bet would be to ask a German friend for a recommendation. By the way, German doctors still make house calls, though reluctantly.

DER ZAHNARZT: MUND AUFMACHEN!
(munt) *(OWF-ma-chen)*
Open Wide!

John has a toothache. His cousin recommends a dentist with whom she is most satisfied. John's appointment is today at 14 hours.

JOHN   (to receptionist)
(AN-ge-mel-det)
Ich bin angemeldet.   I have an appointment.

(SHPREÇ-shtun-den-hil-feh)   *(emp-FANGS-dah-meh)*
SPRECHSTUNDENHILFE or EMPFANGSDAME
receptionist
Mit Dr. Scherer?   With Dr. Scherer?

JOHN   **Ja, für 14 Uhr.**   Yes, for 14 hours (2 P.M.).

SPRECHSTUNDENHILFE   **Ihr Name, bitte?**   Your name, please?

JOHN   **John Wagner.**   John Wagner.

237

SPRECHSTUNDENHILFE **Lassen Sie mich im**
(tayr-MEEN-kah-len-deR)
Terminkalender nachsehen. 14 Uhr,

stimmt. Wir haben heute eine Menge
(pah-tsee-EN-ten)
Patienten. Bitte nehmen Sie Platz.

Sind Sie zum erstenmal hier?

JOHN **Ja.**

SPRECHSTUNDENHILFE **Wollen Sie bitte**

diese Karte ausfüllen?

(after one hour)
(TSAHN-artst-helf-eR-in)
ZAHNARZTHELFERIN **Herr Wagner?**
Dental Assistant

JOHN **Ja?**

ZAHNARZTHELFERIN **In diesen Stuhl, bitte.**

Der Arzt ist gleich hier.

(after fifteen minutes)
(TSAHN-artst)
ZAHNARZT **Herr Wagner?**
Dentist

Also wo tut es weh? Hier? Lassen Sie
(shmertst)
mich sehen. Schmerzt das? Und das?
(VA-kelt)
Ja—also, das wackelt auch ein
(FÜL-ung)
bißchen. Sie haben die Füllung
(feR-LOH-ren)
verloren. Ich gebe Ihnen eine
(SHPRI-tseh) *(ÖRT-li-çeh)* *(be-TOY-bung)*
Spritze für örtliche Betäubung.

Jetzt warten wir ein bißchen, und
(BRÜ-keh)
dann füllen wir den Zahn. Die Brücke
(KROH-neh)
sitzt nicht recht und die Krone hier
(DURÇ-ge-bis-en)
ist halb durchgebissen.

Let me look in the appointment book. 14 hours,

right. We have a lot of patients today. Please

take a seat. Is this your first visit?

Yes.

Please fill out this card.

Mr. Wagner?

Yes?

In this chair, please.

The doctor will be here soon.

Mr. Wagner?

Well, where does it hurt? Here? Let me look.

Does this hurt? And that? Yes—well, This

wobbles a bit. You have lost the filling. I'll give

give you an injection for local anaesthesia. Now

we'll wait a little, and then we'll fill the tooth.

The bridge doesn't sit right, and the crown here

is half bitten through.

In zwei bis drei Jahren brauchen Sie	In two to three years you'll probably
(TSAHN-proh-tay-zeh)	
wahrscheinlich eine Zahnprothese.	need dentures.
JOHN **Da freu' ich mich schon.**	I'm looking forward to it.
ZAHNARZT **Auf Wiedersehen, Herr**	So long, Mr. Wagner.
Wagner. Und schöne Ferien!	And have a nice vacation.

BITTE „AAAH" SAGEN!
Say "Aaaah," Please.

Mary has developed a sore throat. While waiting at the doctor's office, she speaks with another patient.

PATIENT **'Ja, Dr. List ist eine sehr gute**	Yes, Dr. List is a very good physician.
Ärztin.	
MARY **Ist sie Spezialistin?**	Is she a specialist?
PATIENT **Nein, sie ist**	No, she is in general practice.
praktische Ärztin.	

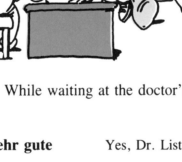

EMPFANGSDAME **Frau Wagner? Frau**	Mrs. Wagner? The doctor will be here soon.
Doktor wird gleich da sein.	
DR. LIST **Frau Wagner? Ich bin Dr. List.**	Mrs. Wagner? I am Dr. List. Nice to meet you.
(KEN-en-tsu-ler-nen)	
Schön, Sie kennenzulernen.	How can I help you?
Wie kann ich Ihnen helfen?	

MARY	**Ich kann kaum reden.**	I can hardly talk.
DR. LIST	**Öffnen Sie, bitte, den Mund.**	Open your mouth, please. Say "Aaaah." Good.
	Sagen Sie „Aaaah." Gut. Ja, das ist *(ge-RÖ-tet)* **ein wenig gerötet. Wie fühlen Sie sich** **sonst?**	Yes, this is a little red. How do you feel otherwise?
MARY	*(SHOYS-liç)* *(fer-SHTOPF-teh)* **Scheußlich. Eine verstopfte Nase** *(KOPF-vay)* **und Kopfweh.**	Rotten. A stuffed-up nose and a headache.
DR. LIST	**Fieber?**	Fever?

MARY	**Nein. Die Temperatur ist ganz** **normal.**	No. The temperature is quite normal.
DR. LIST	**Na ja. Hier ist ein Rezept.** *(me-di-TSEEN)* **Nehmen Sie die Medizin dreimal** *(TAYG-liç)* **täglich.**	Okay. Here is a prescription. Take the medicine three times a day.
MARY	**Danke schön!**	Thank you.

Let's try a few questions about the dialogues in this unit.

True or False?

1. John ist um 16 Uhr angemeldet. _____

2. Er hat eine Füllung verloren. _____

3. Er bekommt Spritze. _____

4. Dr. List ist eine Spezialistin. _____

5. Mary hat Zahnschmerzen. _____

ANSWERS

1. F 2. T 3. T 4. F 5. F

240

Bitte nicht vergessen . . .
Please don't forget . . .

(artst)
der Arzt   doctor (man)

(ERTS-tin)
die Ärztin   doctor (woman)

(pah-tsi-ENT)
der Patient   patient

(PRAK-sis)
die Praxis   practice

(roo-TEE-neh)
die Routine   routine

(shpets-ee-a-LIST)   *(FAÇ-artst)*
der Spezialist *or* **der Facharztt**   specialist

(tem-peR-ah-TOOR)
die Temperatur   temperature

(ÇI-rurk)
der Chirurg   surgeon

(HARN-proh-beh)
die Harnprobe   urine specimen

(ge-VIÇT)
das Gewicht   weight

(ray-TSEPT)
das Rezept   prescription

(un-teR-ZOO-chung)
die Untersuchung   (medical) examination

(me-di-TSEEN)
die Medizin   medicine

(RÖNT-gen-owf-nah-meh)
der Röntgenaufnahme   Xray

(KAR-teh)
die Karte
card

(FEE-beR)
das Fieber
fever

(BLOOT-druk)
der Blutdruck
blood pressure

(KRAN-ken-hows-heeR-ahR-çee)
DIE KRANKENHAUSHIERARCHIE
Hospital Hierarchy

(SHEF-artst)
der Chefarzt
medical director

(OH-beR-artst)
der Oberarzt
assistant medical director

(artst)
der Arzt
physician on the hospital staff

(ze-kun-DAHR-artst)
der Sekundararzt
hospital physician (in Austria)
without his own ward

(a-sis-TENTS-artst)   *(HILFS-artst)*
der Assistenzarzt, der Hilfsarzt
assistant physician on the hospital staff

(PFLIÇT-a-sis-ten-ten)
die Pflichtassistenten
interns

(OH-beR-shves-ter)
die Oberschwester
head nurse

(KRAN-ken-shves-teR)   *(SHVES-teR)*
die Krankenschwester, die Schwester
nurse

(OHN-maçt)
die Ohnmacht
fainting spell

(HERTS-an-fal)
der Herzanfall
heart attack

Andreas, Aunt Sophie's husband, has a fainting spell. The ambulance takes him to the hospital; Sophie and Mary are in the waiting room.

SOPHIE *(HERTS-krank)*
Nein, er ist nicht herzkrank. Ich   No, he doesn't have heart trouble. I

(ROOF-eh) (zoh-FORT)
rufe   sofort den Doktor an, bestelle   call the doctor right away, send for

einen Krankenwagen, und zehn   an ambulance, and ten minutes later

(an-DRAY-as)
Minuten später ist Andreas im   Andreas is in the hospital.

Krankenhaus.

MARY **Wo ist er jetzt?**   Where is he now?

(in-ten-ZEEF-shtah-tsee-ohn)
SOPHIE **In der Intensivstation.**   In the intensive care unit.

MARY **Sprichst du mit dem Arzt?**   Do you speak with the doctor?

SOPHIE **Nur ganz kurz. Ich glaube, man**   Only quite briefly. I think they are examining
(un-ter-ZUCHT)
untersucht ihn jetzt.   him now.

MARY **Hier kommt die Krankenschwester.**   The nurse is coming.

KRANKENSCHWESTER **Sie können jetzt in**   You may go into his room now.

sein Zimmer gehen.

SOPHIE **Danke, Schwester. Wie geht's**   Thank you, nurse.

meinem Mann?   How is my husband?

KRANKENSCHWESTER **Gut, Frau Kleist.**   Fine, Mrs. Kleist. The doctor is very satisfied.
(tsoo-FREED-en)
Der Doktor ist sehr zufrieden.

(in the room)

SOPHIE (to Andreas) **Wie fühlst du dich,**   How do you feel, darling?

Liebster?

ANDREAS **Nicht schlecht.**	Not bad.	

DR. SCHMITT **Machen Sie sich keine große**
(ZOHRG-en)
Sorgen, Frau Kleist. Ihr Mann ist
(eR-SHÖPFT)
erschöpft. Er braucht vor allem
(BET-roo-eh)
Bettruhe. Und mit dem Rauchen muß

Schluß sein. Also—Frau Kleist,

gehen Sie nach Hause und ruhen

Sie sich aus.

There is no need to worry too much, Mrs. Kleist.

Your husband is exhausted.

He needs bed rest above all.

And there must be an end to his

smoking. OK—Frau Kleist,

you go home and

get some rest.

Here are some questions about the dialogues in this unit.

1. Was hat John verloren?
   a. ein Buch b. Geld c. eine Füllung

2. Was ist mit Johns Brücke los?
   a. Sie sitzt nicht recht. b. Sie ist in Ordnung. c. Er braucht keine.

3. Was braucht er in zwei bis drei Jahren?
   a. eine Goldkrone b. eine Zahnprothese c. nichts

4. Wer ist in Dr. Scherers Wartezimmer?
   a. nur John b. nur drei Patienten c. eine Menge Patienten

5. Warum geht Mary zum Arzt? Sie hat
   a. Bauchschmerzen b. Halsschmerzen c. Ohrenschmerzen

6. Wer hat einen Herzanfall?
   a. Andreas b. John c. Sophie

7. Später braucht Andreas vielleicht
   a. Schokolade jeden Tag b. einen Herzschrittmacher c. eine gute Zigarre

Eine komische Geschichte

(KOH-mi-sheh) *(ge-SHIÇ-teh)*

A Strange Story

Ein junger Mann kommt in das
(be-RÜMT-en)
Wartezimmer eines berühmten
(KNOCH-en-shpe-tsee-a-LIST-en)
Knochenspezialisten. Er sagt der

Sprechstundenhilfe, er möchte den
(pree-VAHT)
Arzt privat sprechen.

„Gehen Sie in dieses Zimmer hier,

ziehen Sie sich aus und warten Sie."

„Aber—"

„Was ist los mit Ihnen?" fragt

ihn der Doktor.

„Ich bin hier," antwortet der

junge Mann, „weil ich Ihr
(a-bo-ne-MANG)
Abonnement für den *Stern*
(eR-NOY-ern)
erneuern möchte."

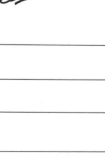

A young man comes into the

waiting room of a famous bone

specialist. He says to the

receptionist that he wants to talk

to the doctor in private.

Go into this room here, get

undressed, and wait.''

''But—''

''What's the matter with you?''

the doctor asks him.

''I am here,'' replies the young

man, ''because I would like to

renew your subscription to

Stern magazine.''

Können sie diese Fragen beanworten?

1. Wer kommt ins Wartezimmer?_____

2. Was sagt er der Sprechstundenhilfe? _____

3. Wen möchte er gern privat sprechen?_____

4. Wo zieht der junge Mann sich aus? _____

5. Was antwortet er dem Arzt? _____

ANSWERS

5. Ich bin hier, weil ich Ihr Abonnement für den *Stern* erneuern möchte.

1. ein junger Mann   2. Er möchte den Arzt privat sprechen.   3. den Arzt   4. in einem Zimmer

BEFORE YOU LEAVE

(fohR)   *(AP-reiz-eh)*
Vor der Abreise

You've learned a lot of German by now—probably much more than you realize. This section is a very important final step in the learning process—a step in which you review and solidify your understanding of your new language.

We've organized the section around basic situations tourists encounter. For each situation there are a number of questions about appropriate German expressions. If you have difficulty remembering what to say in a particular situation, review the relevant unit in this book.

Good luck!

Und gute Reise!

(zi-tu-at-si-OHN)
SITUATION 1: Leute kennenlernen

Getting to know people

1. It is afternoon, and you meet someone.
   What do you say in order to start a conversation?
   A. Guten Tag. ☐
   B. Auf Wiedersehen. ☐
   C. Bitte. ☐

2. You meet someone you'd like to get to know better. You might say:
   A. Ich bin müde. ☐
   B. Möchten Sie mit mir essen? ☐
   C. Die Katze ist groß. ☐

3. Someone asks you how you are. Which of the following is *not* possible as an answer?
   A. Danke, nicht schlecht. ☐
   B. Danke, sehr gut. ☐
   C. Danke, guten Tag. ☐

4. And how do you say good-bye?
   A. Danke ☐
   B. Auf Wiedersehen ☐

ANSWERS

Situation 1. 1. A 2. B 3. C 4. B

245

SITUATION 2: Ankunft
Arrival

1. You do not have a reservation at the hotel. What do you say?
   A. Wie geht's, mein Herr? ☐
   B. Entschuldigen Sie, bitte. Ich habe keine Reservierung. ☐
   C. Guten Tag, mein Herr. Wie heißen Sie? ☐

2. You want to say that you really need a room. You say:
   A. Ich brauche dringend ein Zimmer, bitte. ☐
   B. Bitte, ich brauche kein Badezimmer. ☐

3. You want to inquire about price. So you say:
   A. Ihr Name, bitte? ☐
   B. Wo ist das Badezimmer? ☐
   C. Können Sie mir sagen, wieviel das Zimmer kostet? ☐

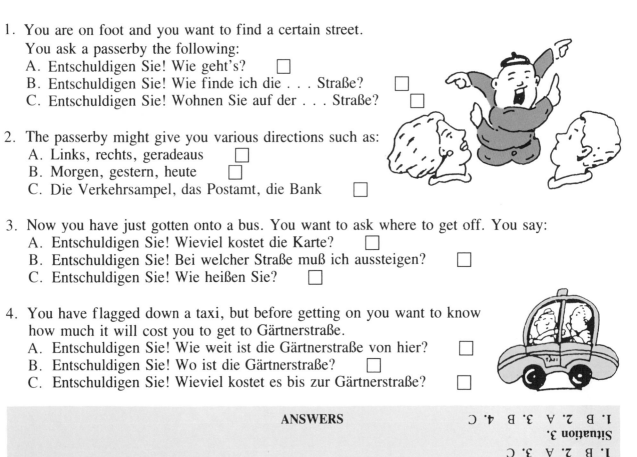

SITUATION 3: Sehenswürdigkeiten besichtigen
Seeing the Sights

1. You are on foot and you want to find a certain street.
   You ask a passerby the following:
   A. Entschuldigen Sie! Wie geht's? ☐
   B. Entschuldigen Sie! Wie finde ich die . . . Straße? ☐
   C. Entschuldigen Sie! Wohnen Sie auf der . . . Straße? ☐

2. The passerby might give you various directions such as:
   A. Links, rechts, geradeaus ☐
   B. Morgen, gestern, heute ☐
   C. Die Verkehrsampel, das Postamt, die Bank ☐

3. Now you have just gotten onto a bus. You want to ask where to get off. You say:
   A. Entschuldigen Sie! Wieviel kostet die Karte? ☐
   B. Entschuldigen Sie! Bei welcher Straße muß ich aussteigen? ☐
   C. Entschuldigen Sie! Wie heißen Sie? ☐

4. You have flagged down a taxi, but before getting on you want to know
   how much it will cost you to get to Gärtnerstraße.
   A. Entschuldigen Sie! Wie weit ist die Gärtnerstraße von hier? ☐
   B. Entschuldigen Sie! Wo ist die Gärtnerstraße? ☐
   C. Entschuldigen Sie! Wieviel kostet es bis zur Gärtnerstraße? ☐

ANSWERS

Situation 3.
1. B   2. A   3. B   4. C

Situation 2.
1. B   2. A   3. C

246

5. You have forgotten your watch. You stop a passerby to ask what time it is. You say:
   A. Entschuldigen Sie! Können Sie mir sagen, wieviel Uhr es ist? ☐
   B. Entschuldigen Sie! Haben Sie eine Uhr? ☐
   C. Entschuldigen Sie! Haben Sie Zeit? ☐

6. The passerby would *not* answer:
   A. Es ist zwei Uhr fünfundzwanzig. ☐
   B Es ist Mittwoch. ☐
   C. Es ist halb zwei. ☐

7. You are at the train station and want to buy a ticket. You might say:
   A. Entschuldigen Sie! Wieviel kostet eine Fahrkarte nach Wien? ☐
   B. Entschuldigen Sie! Wo ist Wien? ☐
   C. Entschuldigen Sie! Wo bin ich hier? ☐

8. The clerk answers that there is no seat left on the train. He might say something like:
   A. Es tut mir leid, aber Sie sind verrückt. ☐
   B. Es tut mir leid, aber Sie sprechen nicht Deutsch. ☐
   C. Es tut mir leid, aber wir haben keinen Platz. ☐

9. You want to say to someone that you are American
   and speak only a little German. You might say:
   A. Ich bin Amerikaner (Amerikanerin) und spreche nur ein bißchen Deutsch. ☐
   B. Ich spreche Englisch und bin kein Italiener. ☐
   C. Ich bin kein Italiener, ich bin Amerikaner. ☐

10. If someone were to ask you what nationality you are, he/she would *not* say:
    A. Sind Sie Kanadier? ☐
    B. Sind Sie Deutscher? ☐
    C. Sind Sie intelligent? ☐
    D. Sind Sie Spanier? ☐
    E. Sind Sie Franzose? ☐

11. You want to rent a car at a good rate. You might ask the clerk:
    A. Ich möchte einen sehr teuren Wagen mieten. ☐
    B. Ich möchte einen sehr preiswerten Wagen mieten. ☐
    C. Ich möchte einen neuen Wagen mieten. ☐

12. You want to fill up your car. You might say:
    A. Ein neues Auto, bitte. ☐
    B. Auffüllen, bitte! ☐
    C. Bitte, das kostet zu viel. ☐

247

13. You have just been in a car accident and wish to ask how the other motorist is. You might say:
    A. Guten Tag, wie geht's ☐
    B. Sind Sie verletzt? ☐
    C. Wie heißen Sie? ☐

14. A service station attendant might tell you that your car needs repairs. He would *not* say:
    A. Ihr Auto ist schön. ☐
    B. Ihr Auto braucht eine neue Bremse. ☐
    C. Ihr Auto braucht einen neuen Motor. ☐

15. You ask a "camping employee" if there are essential services. You would not say:
    A. Gibt es hier Wasser? ☐
    B. Gibt es hier Toiletten? ☐
    C. Gibt es hier ein Kino? ☐
    D. Gibt es hier einen Spielplatz für Kinder? ☐

16. As an answer to "How much do you charge?"
    (Wieviel kostet das?), the clerk might respond:
    A. Hundert Mark ☐
    B. Fünfzig Dollar ☐
    C. Vierzehn Uhr ☐

17. If someone were to ask you about the weather back home, you would *not* say:
    A. Es kann nicht sprechen. ☐
    B. Es ist schönes Wetter. ☐
    C. Es ist schlechtes Wetter. ☐
    D. Es regnet immer. ☐
    E. Es schneit immer. ☐

18. As an answer to „Was ist das Datum heute?" (What's today's date?), you would not hear:
    A. Es ist der dreißigste März. ☐
    B. Es ist der zweite Tag. ☐
    C. Es ist der dritte Mai. ☐

19. At the airport, you might hear this over the loudspeaker:
    A. Der Flug 303 nach New York ist interessant. ☐
    B. Der Flug 303 nach New York kommt nicht an. ☐
    C. Der Flug 303 nach New York startet um 3.30. ☐

20. To ask an airline employee at what time your flight leaves, you would say:
    A. Entschuldigen Sie! Um wieviel Uhr fliegt meine Maschine ab? ☐
    B. Entschuldigen Sie! Wann kommt mein Flug an? ☐
    C. Entschuldigen Sie! Fliegen Sie oft? ☐

ANSWERS
13. B 14. A 15. C 16. A 17. A 18. B 19. C 20. A

Situation 3.

SITUATION 4: Unterhaltung
Entertainment

1. You are at a ticket agency. The clerk would *not* ask you:
   - A. Wollen Sie eine Karte für die Oper? ☐
   - B. Wollen Sie eine Karte fürs Kino? ☐
   - C. Wollen Sie eine Karte fürs Frühstück? ☐
   - D. Wollen Sie eine Karte fürs Theater? ☐

2. If someone were to ask you what your favorite sport was („Was ist Ihr Lieblingssport?"), you would *not* say:
   - A. Ich spiele gern Tennis. ☐
   - B. Ich schwimme gern. ☐
   - C. Ich spiele gern Fußball. ☐
   - D. Ich spiele gern italienisch. ☐
   - E. Ich wandere gern. ☐
   - F. Ich fahre gern Rad. ☐

SITUATION 5: Essen bestellen
Ordering Food

1. You want to ask what kind of restaurants are available? You might ask:
   - A. Ißt man in Deutschland gut? ☐
   - B. Was für Restaurants gibt es hier? ☐
   - C. Wo sind die Badezimmer? ☐

2. As a possible answer, you would *not* hear:
   - A. Hier sind die besten Restaurants. ☐
   - B. Hier sind die Bars. ☐
   - C. Hier sind die Gasthäuser. ☐

3. When a waiter asks you to order, he might say:
   - A. Möchten Sie schwimmen? ☐
   - B. Was soll es sein? ☐
   - C. Möchten Sie zahlen? ☐

4. To see the menu, you would say:
   - A. Kann ich die Küche sehen? ☐
   - B. Kann ich die Speisekarte sehen? ☐
   - C. Kann ich den Direktor sehen? ☐

5. One of the following is not connected with eating:
   - A. Frühstück ☐
   - B. Mittagessen ☐
   - C. Benzin ☐
   - D. Abendessen ☐

249

SITUATION 6: Im Geschäft

At the Store
At the Store

1. Which of the following would you *not* say in a clothing store:
   A. Entschuldigen Sie! Wieviel kostet dieses Hemd? ☐
   B. Entschuldigen Sie! Wieviel kostet dieser Wagen? ☐
   C. Ich möchte die Schuhe, die Socken und die Krawatte. ☐

2. One of the following lists has nothing to do with clothing:
   A. blauer Anzug, rote Jacke, weißes Hemd ☐
   B. Wollanzug, Baumwolljacke, Seidenhemd ☐
   C. italienisch, deutsch, spanisch ☐

3. You would *not* hear which of the following in a supermarket:
   A. Wieviel kostet das Obst? ☐
   B. Wo sind die Erdbeeren? ☐
   C. Wieviel kostet das Kleid? ☐
   D. Das Fleisch kostet 13 Mark pro Kilo. ☐
   E. Der Fisch ist frisch. ☐
   F. Wir haben keinen Kuchen mehr. ☐

4. You want to order a drug at the pharmacy. You might say:
   A. Dieses Gemüse, bitte. ☐
   B. Diese Medizin, bitte. ☐
   C. Dieses Obst, bitte. ☐

5. A pharmacist would *not* ask you one of the following:
   A. Möchten Sie ein Glas Wein? ☐
   B. Brauchen Sie Aspirin? ☐
   C. Haben Sie ein Rezept für die Medizin? ☐

6. You are at the laundry. You would *not* ask one of the following:
   A. Wo ist der Trockenapparat? ☐
   B. Wieviel kostet es, diesen Anzug zu reinigen? ☐
   C. Wieviel kostet die Schokolade? ☐

7. You are at the barber's and want a haircut. You might say:
   A. Geben Sie mir bitte eine Packung Zigaretten. ☐
   B. Schneiden Sie mir bitte die Haare kurz. ☐
   C. Geben Sie mir bitte eine Karte. ☐

8. The hairdresser might ask you (choose three things):
   A. Soll ich Ihr Haar waschen? ☐
   B. Wollen Sie ein Stück Kuchen? ☐
   C. Soll ich das Haar tönen? ☐
   D. Soll ich das Haar schneiden? ☐

ANSWERS

1. B 2. C 3. C 4. B 5. A 6. C 7. B 8. A, C, D

Situation 6.

Choose the store for each question: (Match them up.)

1. Können Sie diese Schuhe reparieren?
2. Wieviel kostet dieses Armband?
3. Ich brauche Briefpapier.
4. Ich nehme zwei Magazine und eine Zeitung.
5. Ich möchte eine rote Handtasche kaufen.
6. Geben Sie mir ein Kilo Äpfel.
7. Ich brauche einen Tisch und vier Stühle.
8. Ich nehme zwei Hemden und eine Krawatte.

A. Obsthandlung
B. Kiosk
C. Lederwaren
D. Schuhmacher
E. Möbelhandlung
F. Herrenmode
G. Papierwarenhandlung
H. Juwelier

SITUATION 7: Wichtige Dienstleistungen
Essential services

1. You are at a bank and want to exchange a traveler's check.
   A. Entschuldigen Sie! Wieviel Uhr ist es? ☐
   B. Entschuldigen Sie! Können Sie mir diesen Reisescheck wechseln? ☐
   C. Entschuldigen Sie! Verkaufen Sie Briefmarken? ☐

2. Now you want to deposit some money.
   A. Ich möchte Geld einzahlen. ☐
   B. Ich möchte eine Rechnung bezahlen. ☐
   C. Ich brauche etwas Geld. ☐

3. A bank employee would *not* ask you:
   A. Bitte unterschreiben Sie auf diesem Formular. ☐
   B. Bitte essen Sie den Kuchen. ☐
   C. Bitte füllen Sie dieses Formular aus. ☐

4. You want to buy stamps at a post office.
   A. Ich möche Erdbeeren kaufen. ☐
   B. Ich möchte Zeitungen kaufen. ☐
   C. Ich möchte Briefmarken kaufen. ☐

5. Which of the following would you *not* say in a post office?
   A. Bitte schicken Sie den Brief per Luftpost. ☐
   B. Einschreiben, bitte. ☐
   C. Können Sie den Brief jetzt schreiben? ☐

6. When you answer the telephone, you might say:
   A. Hallo, Miller hier. ☐
   B. Auf Wiedersehen. ☐
   C. Tschüß. ☐

7. You want to make a long distance phone call. You would say:
   A. Ich möchte meine Telefonrechnung bezahlen. ☐
   B. Ich möchte ein Ferngespräch machen. ☐
   C. Ich möchte Ihre Telephonnummer haben. ☐

8. You want to ask someone how to dial a number. You would say:
   A. Entschuldigen Sie bitte! Wie wähle ich die Nummer? ☐
   B. Entschuldigen Sie bitte! Wann kann ich telefonieren? ☐
   C. Entschuldigen Sie bitte! Wo ist das Telefon? ☐

9. Which of the following would *not* be used to seek help in an emergency?
   A. Bitte bestellen Sie einen Krankenwagen. ☐
   B. Bitte rufen Sie die Polizei an. ☐
   C. Bitte rufen Sie die Feuerwehr an. ☐
   D. Sagen Sie mir bitte, wo ich erste Hilfe bekommen kann? ☐
   E. Sagen Sie mir bitte, wo Sie wohnen? ☐

10. Which of the following would you *not* say to a doctor?
    A. Herr Doktor, ich habe Kopfweh. ☐
    B. Herr Doktor, Sie sind verrückt. ☐
    C. Herr Doktor, ich habe Magenschmerzen. ☐
    D. Herr Doktor, ich habe Fieber. ☐

ANSWERS

2. A 3. B 4. C 5. C 6. A 7. B 8. A 9. E 10. B

Situation 7.

252

mögen

Warum ißt Franz kein Gemüse?

stehen
1. Was tut Kurt?

sitzen
2. Was tut der Patient?

schneiden

Was tut der Friseur?

helfen

Was tut der Gepäckträger?

essen - fressen

1. Was tut Fritz?   2. Was will der Hund?

schlafen

Was tut Lise?

haben

Was hat Kurt auf dem Kopf?

trinken

Was tut Hans?

fragen

1. Was tut der Mann rechts?   2. Was tut der Besitzer des Kiosks?

mögen Weil er es nicht **mag.**	**stehen** 1. Kurt **steht** vor dem Fenster. **sitzen** 2. der Patient **sitzt** auf dem Tisch.	**schneiden** Er **schneidet** die Haare. der Friseur (-s, -e)
helfen Der Gepäckträger **hilft** dem Fahrgast.	**essen** **fressen** 1. Fritz **ißt.** 2. Der Hund will **fressen.** der Hund (-es, -e)	**schlafen** Lise **schläft.**
haben Kurt **hat** eine Mütze auf dem Kopf. der Kopf (-es, ̈-e)	**trinken** Hans **trinkt** Wein. der Wein (-es, -e)	**fragen** 1. Der Mann **fragt** nach Auskunft. **antworten** 2. Der Besitzer des Kiosks **antwortet** dem Mann.

bringen

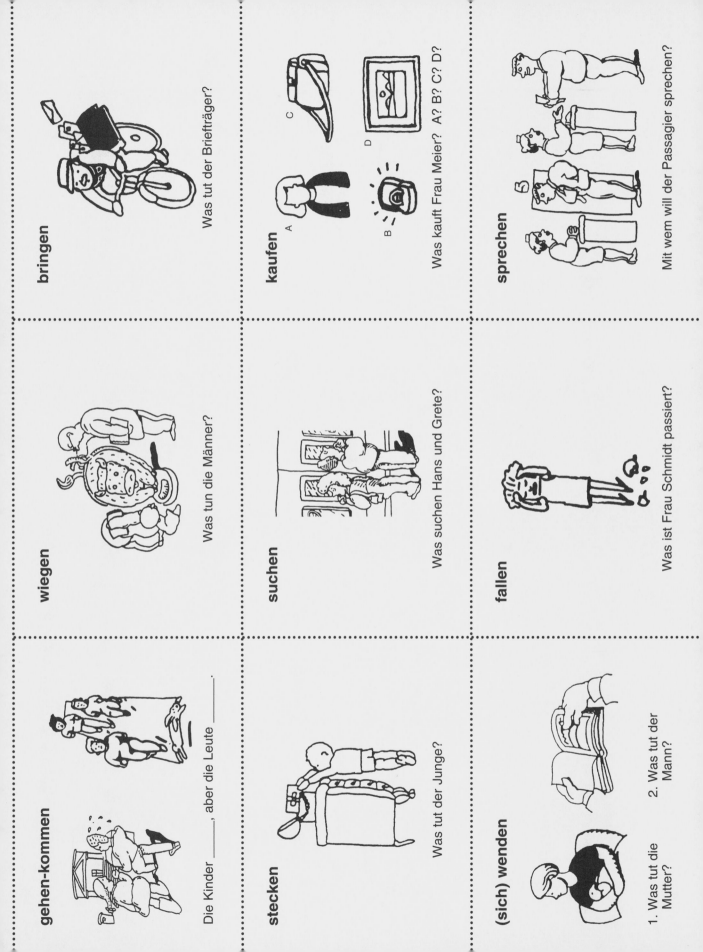

Was tut der Briefträger?

kaufen

A   C

B   D

Was kauft Frau Meier? A? B? C? D?

sprechen

Mit wem will der Passagier sprechen?

wiegen

Was tun die Männer?

suchen

Was suchen Hans und Grete?

fallen

Was ist Frau Schmidt passiert?

gehen-kommen

Die Kinder _____, aber die Leute _____.

stecken

Was tut der Junge?

(sich) wenden

1. Was tut die Mutter?

2. Was tut der Mann?

bringen

Er **bringt** die Post.

der Briefträger (-s, -)

wiegen

Die Männer **wiegen** das Tier.

gehen-kommen

Die Kinder **gehen**, aber die Leute **Kommen**.

kaufen

A. Frau Meier kauft **einen Schal.**
der Schal (-es, -s)

B. Frau Meier kauft **einen Ring.**
der Ring (-es, -e)

C. Frau Meier kauft **eine Handtasche.**
die Handtasche (-, -n)

D. Frau Meier kauft **ein Bild.**
das Bild (-es, -er)

suchen

Hans und Grete **suchen** das Lebensmittelgeschäft.

das Lebensmittelgeschäft (-es, -e)

stecken

Der Junge **steckt** die Briefe in den Kasten.

sprechen

Der Passagier will mit der Flugbegleiterin **sprechen.**

fallen

Frau Schmidt hat die Vase **fallen** lassen.

die Vase (-, -n)

(sich) wenden

1. Die Mutter **wendet sich.**
2. Der Mann **wendet** die Seiten im Buch.

der Mann (-es, -̈er)

schwimmen

Was tut Hans?

für

Für wen kauft Frau Meier den Schal?

mit

Womit schreibt Herr Smith?

(sich) waschen

1. Was tut Olga?

2. Was tut die Frau?

auf

Wo sitzt die Familie?

in

Wohin geht Paul?

tragen

1. Was tut Fritz?

2. Was tut Lise?

anrufen

Was tut Erika?

vor

Wo stehen die Leute?

schwimmen

Er **schwimmt** im Wasser.

(sich) waschen

1. Olga **wäscht sich** die Haare.
2. Die Frau **wäscht** die Wasche.

---

tragen

1. Fritz **trägt** die Koffer.
2. Lise **trägt** eine Brosche.

der Koffer (-s, -)
die Brosche (-, -n)

---

für + *accusative*

Sie kauft ihn **für** ihre Tochter.

---

auf + *dative*

Die Familie sitzt **auf** dem Sofa.

---

anrufen

Sie **ruft** ihre Freundin **an.**

---

mit + *dative*

Herr Smith schreibt **mit** dem Kugelschreiber.

der Kugelschreiber (-s, -)

---

in + *accusative*

Paul geht **in** den Bus.

der Bus (-ses, -se)

---

vor + *dative*

Die Leute stehen **vor** dem Schalter.

um

Wohin legt die Mutter ihren Arm?

hübsch

Das Mädchen ist **hübsch**, aber der Mann ist _____ .

zornig

Die Frau ist **zornig**, aber das Kind ist _____ .

nur

Trägt Karin 6 Bücher?

offen (auf)

Der Kofferraum ist **offen (auf)**, aber die Motorhaube ist _____ .

der Bahnsteig

Wo wartet Lise auf den Eilzug?

neben

Wo steht das Mädchen?

unter

Wo sitzt Frau Schmidt?

spielen

1. Was tun die Jungen?   2. Was tut Bertha?

um + *accusative*

Die Mutter legt ihren Arm **um** das Kind.

das Kind (-es, -er)

---

nur

Nein, sie trägt **nur** 5 Bücher.

---

neben + *dative*

Das Mädchen steht **neben** dem Vater.

---

häßlich

Der Mann ist **häßlich**, aber das Mädchen ist ____.

---

zu (geschlossen)

Die Motorhaube ist **zu (geschlossen)**, aber die Tür ist ____.

---

unter + *dative*

Frau Schmidt sitzt **unter** dem Haartrockner.

---

zufrieden

Das Kind ist **zufrieden**, aber die Frau ist ____.

---

der Bahnsteig (-es, -e)

Sie wartet auf **dem Bahnsteig**.

---

spielen

1. Die Jungen **spielen** zusammen.
2. Bertha **spielt** mit dem Ball.

hoch-tief
1. Wie ist der Kontrollturm?
2. Wie ist das Wasser?

schnell-langsam
1. Wie fährt das Auto?
2. Wie fährt der Bus?

der Name

Klein-groß
1. Wie ist Brigitte?
2. Wie ist Herr Schmidt?

scharf-stumpf
1. Wie ist das Rasiermesser?
2. Wie ist die Schere?

hart-weich
1. Wie ist der Stuhl?
2. Wie ist die Luftmatratze?

schwer
Der Koffer ist **schwer**, aber der Korb ist _____.

lustig-traurig
1. Ist dieser Mann lustig?
2. Ist dieser Mann traurig?

oben-unten
1. Wo liegt das Gepäck?
2. Wo sitzen die Fahrgäste?

hoch-tief

1. Der Kontrollturm ist **hoch**.
2. Das Wasser ist **tief**.

klein-groß

1. Brigitte ist **klein**.
2. Herr Schmidt ist **groß**.

leicht

Der Korb ist **leicht**, aber der Koffer ist

_____

der Mann (-es, ̈-er)

schnell-langsam

1. Das Auto fährt **schnell**.
2. Der Bus fährt **langsam**.

scharf-stumpf

1. Das Rasiermesser ist **scharf**.
2. Die Schere ist **stumpf**.

lustig-traurig

1. Ja, dieser Mann ist **lustig**.
2. Ja, dieser Mann ist **traurig**.

der Name, (-ns, -n)

Mein **Name** ist _____ .

your name

hart-weich

1. Der Stuhl ist **hart**.
2. Die Luftmatratze ist **weich**.

oben-unten

1. Das Gepäck liegt **oben**.
2. Die Fahrgäste sitzen **unten**.

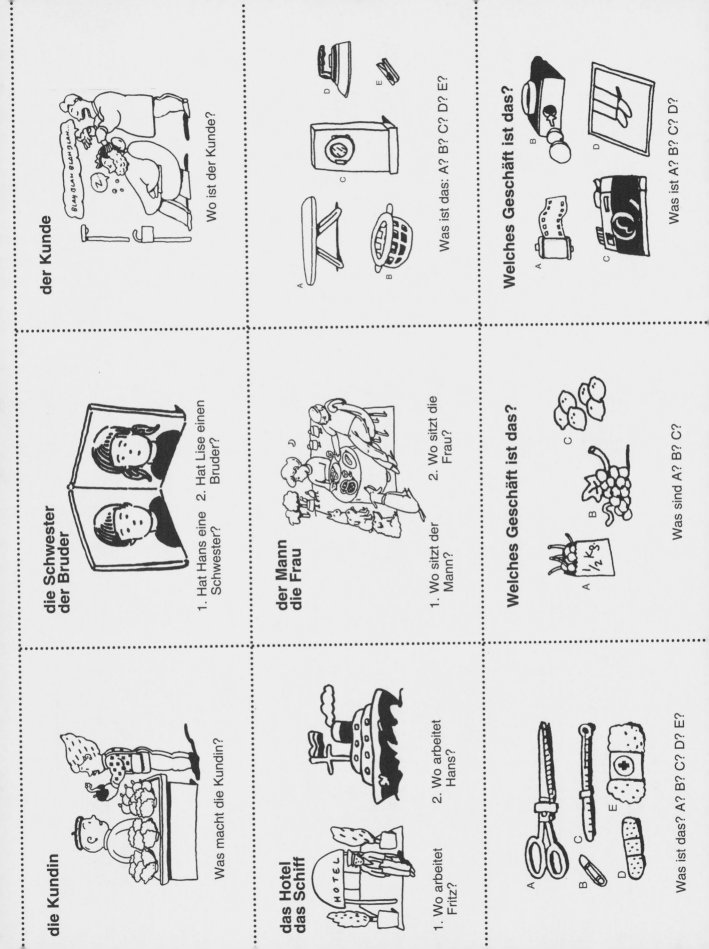

der Kunde

Wo ist der Kunde?

Was ist das: A? B? C? D? E?

Welches Geschäft ist das?

Was ist A? B? C? D?

die Schwester
der Bruder

1. Hat Hans eine   2. Hat Lise einen
   Schwester?   Bruder?

der Mann
die Frau

1. Wo sitzt der   2. Wo sitzt die
   Mann?   Frau?

Welches Geschäft ist das?

Was sind A? B? C?

die Kundin

Was macht die Kundin?

das Hotel
das Schiff

1. Wo arbeitet   2. Wo arbeitet
   Fritz?   Hans?

Was ist das? A? B? C? D? E?

der Kunde (-n, -n)

Der Kunde ist im Herrensalon.

---

die Schwester, (-, -n)
der Bruder, (-s, -̈)

1. Ja, Hans hat eine Schwester.
2. Ja, Lise hat einen Bruder.

A. Das ist ein Bügelbrett.
   das Bügelbrett (-es, -er)

B. Das ist ein Waschkorb.
   der Waschkorb (-es, -er)

C. Das ist eine Waschmaschine.
   die Waschmaschine (-, -n)

D. Das ist ein Bügeleisen.
   das Bügeleisen (-s, -)

E. Das ist eine Wäscheklammer.
   die Wäscheklammer (-, -n)

---

der Mann, (-es, -̈er)
die Frau, (-, -en)

1. Der Mann sitzt vorm (vor + dem) Tisch.
2. Die Frau sitzt hinter dem Tisch.

---

die Kundin, (-, -nen)

Die Kundin kauft einen Apfel.

---

das Hotel (-s, -s)
das Schiff (-es, -e)

1. Fritz arbeitet in einem Hotel.
2. Hans arbeitet auf dem Schiff.

Das ist das Photogeschäft.

A ist der Film. (-es, -e)
B ist die Batterie. (-, -n)
C ist die Kamera. (-, -s)
D ist der Abzug. (-es, -̈e)

Das ist die Obsthandlung. (-, -n)

A sind Kirschen.
B sind Weintrauben.
C sind Zitronen.

A. Das ist eine Schere.
   die Schere (-, -n)

B. Das ist eine Sicherheitsnadel.
   die Sicherheitsnadel (-, -n)

C. Das ist ein Thermometer.
   das Thermometer (-s, -)

D. Das ist ein Heftpflaster.
   das Heftpflaster (-s, -)

E. Das ist ein Paket Watte.
   die Watte (-, -)

Welches Geschäft ist das?

Was ist A? B? C? D? E?

Welches Geschäft ist das?

Was ist A? B? C? D?

Welches Geschäft ist das?

Was ist A? B? C? D?

das Frühstück

Was ist das? A? B? C? D?

Was ist A? B? C? D? E?

der Geldschein
der Reisescheck

Womit zahlt Herr Meier?

das Getränk

Was für Getränke sind das? A? B? C? D? E?

Was ist A? B? C? D?

1. Was ist A? B? C? 2. Was ist A? B? C?

Das ist der Damensalon.

A ist **ein Shampoo.**
(das Shampoo, -s, -s)

B ist **ein Haartrockner.**
(der Haartrockner, -s, -s)

C ist **eine Haarbürste.**
(die Haarbürste, -, -n)

D ist **ein Lockenwickel.**
(der Lockenwickel -s, -)

E ist **ein Spiegel.**
(der Spiegel, -s, -)

das Frühstück (-s, -)

A. Es ist **Toast.**

B. Es ist **Marmelade.**

C. Es ist **Butter.**

D. Es ist **Orangensaft.**

das Getränk, (-s, -e)

A ist **Mineralwasser.**
das Mineralwasser (-s, -)

B ist **Milch.**
die Milch (-, -)

C ist **Tomatensaft.**
der Tomatensaft (-es, ̈e)

D ist **Rheinwein.**
der Rheinwein (-es, -e)

E ist **Kaffee.**
der Kaffee (-s, -)

Das ist der Geschenkartikelladen.

A ist **ein Anhänger.**
(der Anhänger, -s, -)

B ist **ein Parfümzerstäuber.**
(der Parfümzerstäuber, -s, -)

C ist **ein Schlüsselring.**
(der Schlüsselring, -s, -e)

D ist **eine Geldtasche.**
(die Geldtasche, -, -n)

A ist **ein Brot.** (das Brot, -es, -e)

B ist **ein Salat.** (der Salat, -es, -e)

C ist **ein Bier.** (das Bier, -es, -e)

D ist **ein Schweinebraten.**
(der Schweinebraten, -s, -)

E ist **ein Fisch.** (der Fisch, -es, -e)

A ist **ein Armband.**
das Armband (-es, ̈er)

B ist **eine Kette.**
die Kette (-, -n)

C ist **ein Ohrring.**
der Ohrring (-es, -e)

D ist **eine Perle.**
die Perle (-, -n)

Das ist das Musikgeschäft.

A ist **ein Mikrophon.**
(das Mikrophon, -es, -e)

B ist **ein Plattenspieler.**
(der Plattenspieler, -s, -)

C ist **eine Schallplatte.**
(die Schallplatte, -, -n)

D ist **eine Stereoanlage.**
(die Stereoanlage, -, -n)

der Geldschein (-es, -e)
der Reisescheck (-s, -s)

Herr Meier zahlt mit einem Geldschein
oder mit **einem Reisescheck.**

1. A ist **ein Bleistift.**
der Bleistift (-es, -e)

B ist **ein Briefumschlag.**
der Briefumschlag, (-es, ̈e)

C ist **ein Kugelschreiber.**
der Kugelschreiber (-s, -)

2. A ist **ein Schreibblock.**
der Schreibblock (-es, ̈e)

B ist **ein Bindfaden.**
der Bindfaden (-s, ̈)

C ist **ein Notizbuch.**
das Notizbuch (-es, ̈er)

Was ist das?

das Fieber

Was hat Michael?

die Waage

Was liegt auf der Waage?

---

der Sommer-der Herbst

1. **Im Sommer** macht man Ferien.
2. **Im Herbst** regnet es.

gut-schlecht

1. Dem Patienten geht es **gut**.
2. Der Apfel ist **schlecht**.

der Monat, (-es, -e)

Die zwölf Monate heißen:

Januar — Juli
Februar — August
März — September
April — Oktober
Mai — November
Juni — Dezember

---

die inneren Körperteile

Nennen Sie die inneren Körperteile!
A? B? C? D? E? F?

die Idee

Was hat Herbert?

Was ist A? B? C? D?

---

der Bahnsteig

A. Lotte sieht **einen Fahrgast.**
   der Fahrgast (-es, "-e)
B. Lotte sieht **einen Eisenbahnwagen.**
   der Eisenbahnwagen (-s, -)
C. Lotte sieht **einen Gepäckträger.**
   der Gepäckträger (-s, -)
D. Lotte sieht **einen Koffer-Kuli.**
   der Koffer-Kuli (-s, -s)

kühl-warm

1. Im Wasser ist es **kühl**.
2. Im Bett ist es **warm**.

das Bett (-es, -en)

der Wochentag, (-es, -e)

Die Wochentage heißen:

Sonntag
Montag
Dienstag
Mittwoch
Donnerstag
Freitag
Samstag (oder: Sonnabend)

Was ist das?

Nennen Sie die Teile des Gesichtes!

leicht-reichlich

1. Wie ist das Abendessen?   2. Wie ist das Mittagessen?

das Schwarzbrot

Was liegt auf dem Teller?

---

die Krankenhaushierarchie

A. der Chefarzt (-es, "-e)
B. die Oberärztin (-, -nen)
C. der Pflichtassistent (-en, -en)
D. die Krankenschwester (-, -n)

der Winter-der Frühling

1. Weihnachten ist **im Winter**.
2. Ostern ist **im Frühling**.

blitzen-neblig

1. Ja, es **blitzt**.
2. Ja, es ist **neblig**.

der Blitz

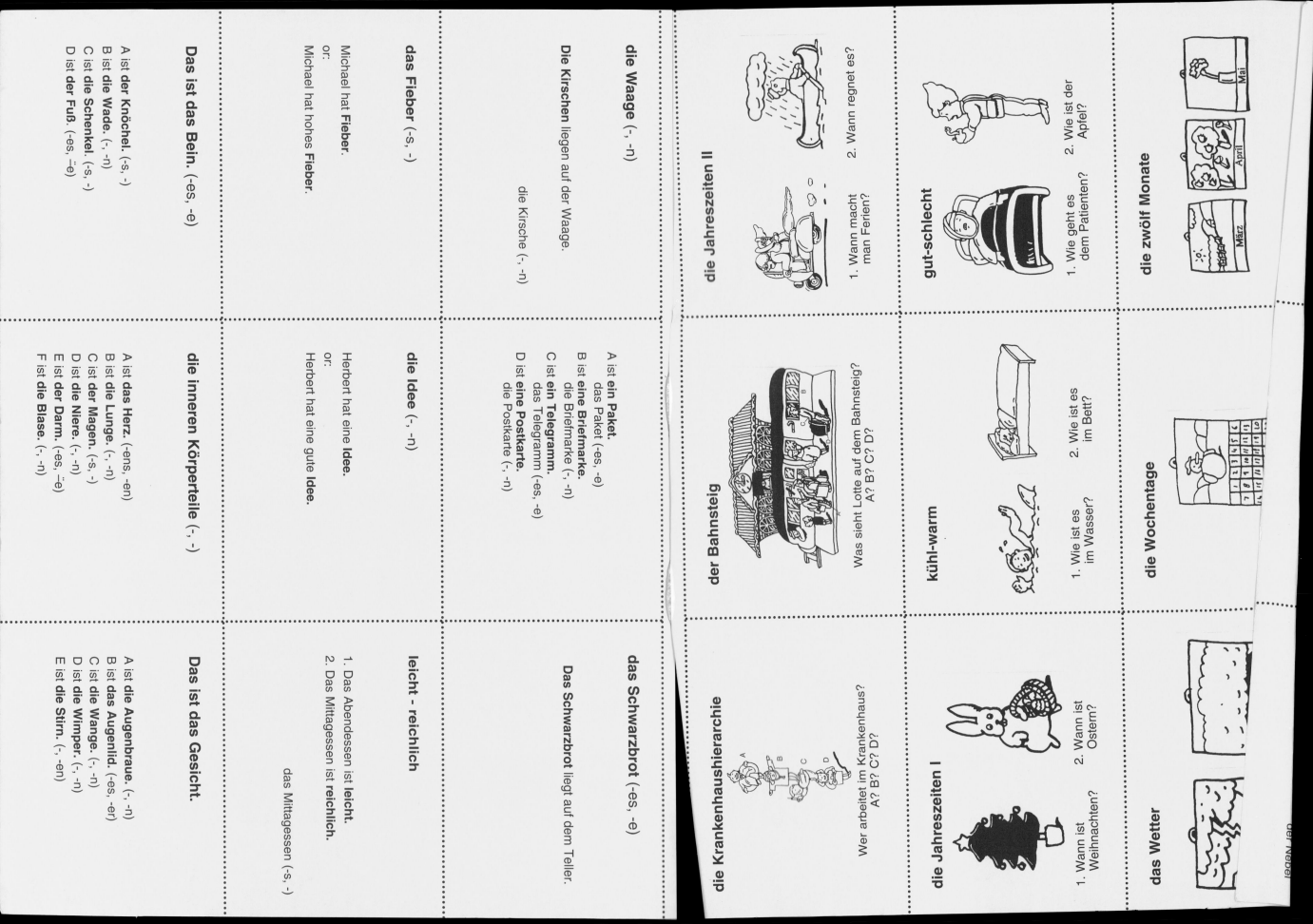

die Waage (-, -n)

Die Kirschen liegen auf der Waage.

die Kirsche (-, -n)

---

das Fieber (-s, -)

Michael hat **Fieber**.
or:
Michael hat hohes **Fieber**.

---

die Idee (-, -n)

Herbert hat eine **Idee**.
or:
Herbert hat eine gute **Idee**.

Das ist das Bein. (-es, -e)

A ist der **Knöchel**. (-s, -)
B ist die **Wade**. (-, -n)
C ist der **Schenkel**. (-s, -)
D ist der **Fuß**. (-es, ¨-e)

A ist **ein Paket**.
   das **Paket** (-es, -e)
B ist **eine Briefmarke**.
   die **Briefmarke** (-, -n)
C ist **ein Telegramm**.
   das **Telegramm** (-es, -e)
D ist **eine Postkarte**.
   die **Postkarte** (-, -n)

die inneren Körperteile (-, -)

A ist das **Herz**. (-ens, -en)
B ist die **Lunge**. (-, -n)
C ist der **Magen**. (-s, -)
D ist die **Niere**. (-, -n)
E ist der **Darm**. (-es, ¨-e)
F ist die **Blase**. (-, -n)

---

leicht - reichlich

1. Das Abendessen ist **leicht**.
2. Das Mittagessen ist **reichlich**.

Das Schwarzbrot liegt auf dem Teller.

das Schwarzbrot (-es, -e)

das Mittagessen (-s, -)

Das ist das Gesicht.

A ist die **Augenbraue**. (-, -n)
B ist das **Augenlid**. (-es, -er)
C ist die **Wange**. (-, -n)
D ist die **Wimper**. (-, -n)
E ist die **Stirn**. (-, -en)

---

die Jahreszeiten II

1. Wann macht man Ferien?
2. Wann regnet es?

gut-schlecht

1. Wie geht es dem Patienten?
2. Wie ist der Apfel?

die zwölf Monate

der Bahnsteig

Was sieht Lotte auf dem Bahnsteig? A? B? C? D?

kühl-warm

1. Wie ist es im Wasser?
2. Wie ist es im Bett?

die Wochentage

die Krankenhaushierarchie

Wer arbeitet im Krankenhaus? A? B? C? D?

die Jahreszeiten I

1. Wann ist Weihnachten?
2. Wann ist Ostern?

das Wetter

der Nebel